THE STATE AND CARING

Also edited by Paul Close and published by Macmillan

FAMILY DIVISIONS AND INEQUALITIES IN MODERN SOCIETY
FAMILY AND ECONOMY IN MODERN SOCIETY (*with Rosemary Collins*)

The State and Caring

Edited by

Paul Close
Senior Lecturer in Social Sciences
Derbyshire College of Higher Education

First published 1992 by
MACMILLAN ACADEMIC AND PROFESSIONAL LTD
Houndmills, Basingstoke, Hampshire RG21 2XS
and London
Companies and representatives
throughout the world

ISBN 0–333–56667–X

A catalogue record for this book is available
from the British Library

Printed in Great Britain by
Billing and Sons Ltd
Worcester

To Mee Yin Lai

Contents

List of Figures and Tables

Acknowledgements

The editor wishes to express his thanks for the help and support received during the preparation of this book from Barrie Seaton, David Drummond, David Pugh, John Brennan, Joyce Seaton, Keith Wright, Mike Houston, Nancy Houston, Paul Stirling, Sheila Wright, and Wilhelmina Drummond.

Notes on the Contributors

Paul Close is a Senior Lecturer in Social Sciences at the Derbyshire College of Higher Education and an Honorary Research Fellow at the University of Kent. He has been a Lecturer in Sociology at Teesside Polytechnic, a Lecturer in Social Policy at Massey University in New Zealand and a Lecturer in Sociology at the University of Western Sydney, Australia. He is co-editor with Rosemary Collins of *Family and Economy in Modern Society* (1985), and editor of *Family Divisions and Inequalities in Modern Society* (1989). He is conducting a research project on 'the state, citizenship and social change' with special reference to the implications of the development of the European Community.

Rosemary Collins has been for several years associated with a research group based in the University of Bristol's Socio-Legal Centre for Family Studies. Her research involvement has included participating in team projects on the overlapping family jurisdiction of magistrates' and county courts; and on a judicial review of adoption. As a research associate during 1988 to 1990, she co-directed with Alison Macleod an Economic and Social Research Council funded project on 'The End of Illegitimacy'. During the early 1980s, she was involved in research on domestic labour which resulted in a book co-edited with Paul Close on *Family and Economy in Modern Society* (1985). She is a post-foundation Course Tutor with the Open University.

Don Edgar is the Director of the Australian Institute of Family Studies in Melbourne, Victoria. Formerly, he was a Reader in Sociology at La Trobe University, Melbourne. He is the author of numerous reports, book contributions, journal articles and other publications, including *Sociology of Australian Education* (1975); *Introduction to Australian Society: a Sociological Perspective* (1980); and (ed.) *Child Poverty* (1989).

Elizabeth Hatton teaches in the Department of Social, Cultural and Curriculum Studies at the University of New England, New South Wales, Australia. Her research interests are in the areas of the sociology of teaching and teacher education. She has published articles in several scholarly journals, including *School Organisation; Discourse; Journal of Education and Teaching; Teaching and Teacher Education; Journal of Curriculum Studies;* and *Anthropology and Education Quarterly*.

Sonia Jackson is a Senior Lecturer in the School of Applied Social Studies at the University of Bristol. Her research interests lie in the areas of day care for young children and its implications for equal opportunities, child protection and child development; the state as substitute parent, its outcomes and possible improvement; and the life experiences of those who have been in state care. Her publications include (with B. Jackson) *Childminder: a Study in Action Research* (1979 and 1981); 'Fathers in Great Britain' in M. Lamb (ed.) *The Father's Role: a Cross-Cultural Perspective* (1986); 'The State as Parent: Assessing Outcomes in Child Care', in J. Hudson and B. Galawy (eds), *The State as Parent: International Perspectives on Interventions with Young Persons* (1989); 'Education of Children in Care', in B. Kahan (ed.), *Child Care Research, Policy and Practice* (1989).

Katsuya Kodama was born in Hiroshima in 1959. He studied peace movements for his PhD – awarded in 1990 – at Lund University in Sweden. Currently, he is a Lecturer in Sociology at Mie University, Japan. He is the editor of the newsletter of the International Peace Research Association. He has several publications on the aftermath of Hiroshima and on peace movements, including: *Life Histories of Atomic Bomb Orphans* (1987); *Peace on the Move* (1990); (ed.) *The Future of Peace Movements* (1989); and (co-ed.) *Towards a Comparative Analysis of Peace Movements* (1990).

Ryuji Komatsu is a Professor of Economics in the Faculty of Economics at Keio University in Tokyo, Japan. His research has been largely in the areas of social policy and welfare in historical and comparative perspective, leading to publications on *The Development of Enterprise-Wide Unionism* (1971); *Social Policy* (1973); *Child Welfare in New Zealand* (1983); *Refugee's Era* (1986); and *Child Welfare in England* (1989).

Julie Leibrich is a Centennial Fellow with the Department of Justice in Wellington, New Zealand. Her areas of research cover mental health, criminal justice, family courts and alternative medicine. She is the author of several published articles relating to her research, including one on 'The Measurement of Efficacy: a Case for Holistic Research', in *British Complementary Medicine*, 1990.

Alison Macleod qualified as a solicitor and subsequently practised family law. In 1979, she joined a team of researchers at the University of Bristol working in the area of divorce. Since, she has worked in the University of Bristol's Socio-Legal Centre for Family Studies on projects concerned with divorce, parental access, non-married parents and the law, childcare and wardship proceedings. During 1988 to 1990, she co-directed, with Rosemary Collins, an Economic and Social Research Council funded project on 'The End of Illegitimacy'. Currently, she is engaged in research on the implementation of the Children Act 1989.

Kaori Okano teaches in Asian Languages in the School of Humanities at La Trobe University, Victoria, Australia. Formerly, she was a research student in the Department of Education at Massey University, New Zealand. Her PhD project on the social process by which high school students in Japan make the transition from school into paid employment, has resulted in various scholarly papers.

Introduction
Paul Close

This collection of essays has been written by an international team of scholars on a range of issues around the theme of the state and caring. Each of the contributors focuses on an aspect of state care which is to be found in all modern societies – that is, in all those societies of the advanced industrial, liberal democratic type. It is in such societies that the state ostensibly plays a leading and major caring role, promoting people's welfare through a wide range of social activities, arrangements and devices, including social policy, social services, education, housing provision, health facilities, income maintenance and the legal framework. A prominent thread running through the essays is composed of the following questions: How well does the state 'care'? Does the state through its caring activities and devices simply add to – or does it also subtract from – people's welfare? How might the answers to the previous questions be accounted for? Why does the state care in the way it does? Is there an associated or hidden agenda behind the state's caring role? In particular, to what extent does state care also entail state *control* – and to what extent can state care be accounted for in terms of state control?

The essays pay most (but not exclusive) attention to evidence on state care in just five modern societies: Britain, Japan, Australia, New Zealand and the United States. Several of the essays concentrate on just one aspect of state care in only one society – such as Katsuya Kodama's, which singles out for scrutiny the Japanese state's caring activities in relation to the victims of the atomic bomb dropped on Hiroshima at the end of the Second World War. Nonetheless, each essay draws on information and develops ideas which help illuminate state care in modern societies in general, and which thus feed into general theory concerning the state and caring. Certain essays focus on the issue of general theory, and so are specifically concerned with state care across the broad sweep of modern societies. For instance, Paul Close's lead essay makes a contribution to the development of general theory by clarifying the contradictory character of state care of whatever kind in whichever advanced industrial, liberal democracy.

While the contributors come from different scholarly traditions, all assume an approach to their topics which lies firmly within the 'critical school' of social science. Thus, in the first place, the writers tend to take a sceptical stance in relation to state care on the grounds that the state not only

1

inadequately but also *detrimentally* affects people's welfare. Of course, this approach has applied implications for the future development of the state's 'caring role', and some of the writers firm these up by making explicit social policy recommendations. However, the primary purpose of the essays overall is to assist with the sociological task of elucidating and accounting for the current content, form and significance of the relationships between caring, the state and other major features and processes of modern society, such as those of the economic variety. Accordingly, there is an emphasis on looking behind (what Elizabeth Hatton in the title of Chapter 8 refers to as 'the facade of care') at the accompanying or underlying social control features of state care, which can then be viewed as an inherently 'critical' source of social experience, social action and social change. All the essays are sensitive to the patterns and processes of power and control which underpin, help account for and in turn are supported by state care. An overall argument which emerges is that state care is doubled-edged in a dual sense: (a) it entails – and is even largely about – state *control*; and (b) due to the latter, state care is a source of everyday criticism, resentment, resistance and perhaps rebellion in favour of progressive change within modern society.

In a sense, this argument represents the principal message of the book, and as such is developed in some detail at the theoretical level by Paul Close in Chapter 1 in order to set the scene for the subsequent essays. Close's chapter is about clarifying the relationship between the state, caring and control by locating it within the context of the broader features and developments of modern society (such as those associated with the economy); by examining details of certain prominent arenas within which state care and state control operate – concentrating especially on the education system; by emphasizing the contradictory character of state care-control within and through such arenas; and by drawing out the implications of this contradictory character for resistance to state care-control and thereby for social change and progress.

Close argues that a master key for unlocking the links between care, control, resistance and change is the social mechanism of contradiction, interpreted and defined in a precise and strictly distinctive manner. A central issue of the chapter is that of the *meaning* of contradiction, or more precisely of the 'best' (or most useful) conceptualization of 'contradiction'. Close tackles the problem of defining the term 'contradiction' with the aim of enhancing its value as a sociological tool in the pursuit of social analysis and theorizing. Accordingly, he is interested in defining 'contradiction' in a way which avoids making the notion superfluous by merely equating it with social phenomena that are already adequately covered by alternative terms – such as 'conflict', 'tension', 'inconsistency', 'anomaly' and 'dilemma'. It is important to emphasize that for Close, while the concept of 'contradiction' has considerable theoretical value (being a key element of general theory), by itself the notion has little or no explanatory value. In other words, contradictions are social processes or mechanisms which – in a similar way to, for instance, socialization and Foucault's discourses (as discussed by Close) – act as channels or vehicles through which patterns of power and control (located within the state, the economy, the sex-gender system, and so on) become translated into resentment, resistance, opposition and challenge, and which in turn (dialectically) shape and transform patterns of power and control.

While Close elucidates the contradictory character of state care largely with reference to the operation of the educational system in modern society, the next four chapters touch on this character by examining various mixtures of family relationships, parent-child relationships and gender relationships. These chapters indicate how the state both (a) loads weighty expectations, demands and pressures on family, parent-child and gender relationships purportedly in order to assist, consolidate and strengthen them – especially along traditional, independent and self-reliant lines – while at the same time, (b) providing only limited practical (especially financial) support to enable its expectations to be realized. The result is considerable stress and strains for the people, relationships and institutions involved, thereby if anything constraining, threatening and weakening them.

Chapters 2 and 3 explore the theme of the state and caring by focusing on the state's social policy towards unmarried parents. In Chapter 2, Rosemary Collins shows how the incidence of births outside marriage rose sharply during the 1980s in England, Australia and the USA. By the end of the decade, children born outside marriage accounted for over a quarter of all the births in England as well as two-thirds of all the births to black women in the USA. Many of the resulting non-marital families received state support, and Collins' discussion centres on how state policy concerning social benefits was both informed by economic liberalism and guided by an emphasis on personal responsibility. As welfare provision was cut back in all three countries during the 1980s, new schemes and legislation emerged in an attempt to get liable fathers to shoulder a greater share of the financial cost of their children. Collins outlines the schemes involved and shows that even where they have been fully implemented – as in Australia and the USA – they fail to come to terms with the poverty of many unmarried parents by failing to do little, if anything, to raise the parents' standard of living.

In Chapter 3, Rosemary Collins and Alison Macleod look more closely at the shift towards higher numbers of births outside marriage by examining the patterns and trends in the context of broader social change in Britain during the 1980s. The chapter discusses how the highest incidence of births outside marriage is among, what might be referred to as, 'the residual dependent' sections of the working class. Collins and Macleod link the increase in births outside marriage to the impoverishment of the working class brought about by Conservative government policies during the Thatcher administrations of the 1980s. Drawing on court-based research on unmarried parents and the law in two English cities, Collins and Macleod trace some of the social dimensions of unmarried parenthood. The account focuses on the impoverished lives of the majority of the families covered by the research, and the authors argue that while state care fails to deal with such poverty, its social benefits and legal systems do serve a useful purpose – that is, they facilitate the process of social control.

In Chapter 4, Sonia Jackson argues that the view in modern society that parents should be able to take responsibility for the care and upbringing of their children with a minimum of state interference is unrealistic. Childrearing practices, children's educational and broader social experiences, the gender division of roles within the family and the incidence of child abuse are all profoundly influenced by state policy. Overtly non-interventionist policies mask an inequitable distribution of financial and other social resources between those people who have children and those who do not. They also lock women into their traditional disadvantaged societal position.

The policies of the British government tend to stand mid-way between those of the United States government on the one hand and those of European governments on the other hand. In Britain, the National Health Service along with vestiges of the welfare state provides a level of basic support to families and a new, comprehensive Children Act lays considerable emphasis on the state's partnership with parents in the area of childcare. However, because day care continues to be left largely to the private sector, it is unaffordable by a large number of poor and single parents. In this regard, the situation in Britain contrasts markedly with that in, for instance, Sweden, France and Italy. Increasingly regressive tax and income support policies bear down especially heavily on families with children, and this helps account for the current levels of family instability, family breakdown, child maltreatment and adolescent homelessness. The families under stress, however, rarely receive the help they require because social workers are overwhelmed by the increase in child protection work. The result is that such families have a high risk of experiencing punitive intervention from the state given that their childrearing standards often fall below what is considered to be minimally acceptable.

Thus, the British and American preoccupation with child abuse is a corollary of the refusal by the state to acknowledge that children are a social asset, and so responsibility, rather than simply a private, parental hobby. Here, Jackson's argument concurs with Close's proposition that, contrary to the state's view and treatment, children in their everyday lives (such as through school work) are engaged in 'productive labour', which in practice is of value to themselves, their parents and society as a whole. Jackson's further suggestion that (while the state could provide more material assistance in support of family life and relationships) 'the state could not fully replace the family with regard to childcare' is echoed in Chapter 5 by Ryuji Komatsu in his discussion of state care in Japan. Komatsu focuses on the case of the provision and organization of foster care in order to illustrate general features of the patterns and developments of social welfare in Japan in comparison with other modern societies, especially Britain, New Zealand and the USA.

Komatsu argues that public, institutionalized childcare cannot substitute for family-based foster care, and that this lies behind a long-term trend away from facility-based care towards foster care in Japan, albeit slowly and somewhat begrudgingly, especially at the level of material support. The Japanese state faces a dilemma as far as foster care is concerned, which is reflected in an ambiguous response and thereby difficulties and confusion for the parents and children involved. In principle the state recognizes the advantages of foster care over institutionalized care in accordance with its acceptance and promotion of the family, or more precisely of traditional family life, relationships and values. Traditional Japanese culture lays an emphasis on personal-linked-to-family independence, self-reliance and responsibility. Therefore, although the Japanese state has come to strongly encourage the foster care of children in 'normal' and 'natural' family settings, it has been dilatory about becoming directly and practically (especially financially) involved because to do so would mean undermining traditional family life and culture.

It is clear from Komatsu's assessment that while the state assumes a somewhat removed stance with regard to foster care in particular and social welfare in general largely on the grounds of its support for traditional family life and culture, the position is also attractive because of its implications for public expenditure. Likewise, Katsuya Kodama discusses how the Japanese state's treatment of the victims of Hiroshima springs not only from its commitment to traditional personal-family self-reliance and responsibility, but also from financial and economic concerns. For Kodama, the state has consistently demonstrated a highly detached approach in relation to the everyday lives and problems of atomic bomb victims, and he argues that this can be largely understood in terms of the combined effects of economic interests and patterns of power and control. That is, the development of the state's policies and practices in relation to atomic bomb victims has been shaped mainly by an interplay between (a) state concerns about financial costs; (b) state judgements about economic returns; and (c) the victims' restricted political power and influence.

The Japanese state's approach to atomic bomb victims may be contrasted with its stance in relation to another category of people, which for the state has major economic importance. As Kaori Okano discusses in Chapter 7, in the case of high school students, the state's commitment to personal-family self-reliance, responsibility and independence is accompanied by considerable attention, intervention and supervision. In particular, the state closely and firmly directs the process by which students make the transition from school into paid employment. Accordingly, in Japan, the state's care and concern about students' 'life-after-school' has been transposed into overt state control, guided by broader social and especially economic interests. Here, state control entails both 'correctly' placing students in the sense of matching their skills to jobs and 'appropriately' preparing students in the sense of socializing them to comply with paid employment requirements, relationships, patterns of power and control, and so on. Okano's research evidence suggests that in Japan the state-controlled 'employment guidance and referral process' tends to run smoothly, efficiently and effectively. However, this is not to ignore those signs whereby students recognize – and to some extent resent – how state control is exercised as a priority over state care, so as to inhibit personal development and fulfilment and so as to contradict the state's emphasis on personal-family self-reliance, responsibility and independence.

Whereas Okano touches on the way the state's ambiguous approach to care is registered by students, Elizabeth Hatton focuses on how state care-control through the education system is experienced by teachers. Hatton explores the consequences of the attempt by the Queensland government in Australia to exercise care-control over the educational system by introducing a new teaching mode – the team teaching, open-plan mode. Hatton employs evidence from her research to show how the changeover has not been completely smooth and successful, and has had certain deleterious effects on the students involved. This reflects a gap which has emerged between the state's guiding 'theory' and the actual operation of the new teaching mode within schools, due to the way in which the mode is in practice filtered and modified through the everyday social fabric and context of schools. Of crucial importance in this regard is the influence of those people located at the cutting edge of the teaching process, namely the teachers. Hatton shows how teachers are engaged not only in caring for students, but also in caring for and protecting themselves. The result is a degree of what is in effect teacher 'resistance' and 'spoiling' in relation to the new teaching mode, which is then implemented in a somewhat partial, diluted and untidy manner, with some features of the old teaching mode being not only retained but also exacerbated. In a sense, the Queensland government's public intentions to 'improve' the care it provides for school students has been upset by (not taking adequate account of) the private interests of those who are crucial to the everyday operation and possible success of state care policies and programmes.

Chapter 9 by Don Edgar also focuses on state care in Australia and on the gap and tensions between social care and private concerns. Edgar's topic is the overall pattern and balance of state welfare policies and measures in relation to non-state, family-centred care and motives. He begins with the assumption that care is not just naturally occurring: that instead it is socially constructed under the influence of, for instance, the state and the family. He then argues that in Australia, as in all modern societies, there is a disjunction between the demands and drives in favour of 'public care' and the emphasis on arrangements and values favouring private care centred on and sustained by the family. The private family life style and family-centred values and morality in modern society are in competition with and undermine social care based on a more inclusive sense of morality. Edgar argues that the way forward is for the state to formulate and implement social policy and programmes based on a 'recognition of interdependency within modern society' – on 'the need to avoid the anomie associated with atomization and to emphasize the mutuality and reciprocity of the various social spheres of care and responsibility'. Edgar is convinced that the answer to the dilemma over care faced by the state lies in 're-surrounding' the private family to enable children to have social experiences which link them with the wider community along with older generations – experiences which in many family settings are lacking at present. This approach will require much greater attention being paid to the quality of childcare in the developmental sense, and an acceptance that children represent a social good not just a private, parental concern.

Edgar recommends the mobilization of people, families and communities to participate fully in the reciprocal enjoyment and provision of social care. That is

Local effort, local networks, local neighbourhoods, local schools, local
decision-making, and local accountability are essential to enable children to have those experiences through which they learn that they and
their families are tied inextricably to others to whom they owe and from
whom they deserve a sense of moral obligation.

Edgar claims that the 'early lessons learned by children, within [for in-
stance] the family, will carry over into a wider sense of moral obligation to
strangers, and thereby into a more 'caring' society.' However, in the final
chapter, Julie Leibrich argues that this latter prospect not only remains a
long way off, but in recent years has been if anything receding. For Leibrich,
this development is amply demonstrated in the 'systematic failure of two
countries' – Britain and New Zealand – 'to provide good care for people
with psychiatric disabilities'. She examines how for several years Britain
and New Zealand have been engaged in a process of reducing the amount
of public institutional care available to those with such disabilities, and
details how this has occurred without the state fully facilitating alternative
sources of care. While the process of 'deinstitutionalization' is otherwise
referred to as the transition to 'community care', the state has been unwilling to provide the resources to enable the community to care properly:
'neither Britain nor New Zealand has yet given community care a secure
and adequate financial backing. In the meantime, the process of
deinstitutionalization continues with somewhat devastating consequences
for the individuals involved'.

Leibrich's conclusion about the trends in state care in relation to the
psychiatrically disabled in Britain and New Zealand neatly represents the
overall lessons of this volume of essays. Perhaps the trend towards what is
variously labelled as the *deinstitutionalization, decentralization, devolution
and democratization* of care is merely the latest expression and phase in the
perennial attempt by the state to achieve an appropriate level of state care –
appropriate in the sense of maintaining people's welfare within the parameters of what is required to retain social control in support of social order.
At the same time, this particular trend may have the unintended, unanti-
cipated and unwanted effect of loosening the process of social control and
threatening social order by virtue of the way it amplifies the disjunction
between (a) the expectations, demands and pressures on people, families
and the community with regard to care and (b) the possibilities available for
the realization of such expectations – especially given the absence of
adequate material resources. Such a disjunction may encourage an increase
in popular disquiet and even unrest, to some extent targeted on but certainly
picked up by the state. In turn, we might predict the state's response to be

another change of strategy, hailing a further phase in its approach to the provision of care combined with the retention of control. This implies not so much that the state will be inevitably successful in its selection and implementation of alternative care-control packages, but rather that (optimistically) the priority given to considerations of social control in shaping state care will be inevitably – at least in the long term – replaced by an interest in people's welfare. This argument is developed by Paul Close in Chapter 1.

1 State Care, Control and Contradictions:
Theorizing Resistance, Change and Progress in Modern Society
Paul Close

The following is about the way the state plays a part in the provision of *care* while at the same time contributing to the process of *control* within modern society; about the character of the conceptual and practical relationship between state care and state control; and about the implications and consequences of this relationship for human and social potential, development and progress. An argument is presented supporting a modified version of the dispersal of discipline thesis, and hinging upon a carefully specified notion of 'contradiction'.

In an attempt to clarify the concept of 'caring', Gillian Dalley makes a distinction between 'caring for' and 'caring about': the 'first is to do with the tasks of tending to another person; the second is to do with feelings for another person' (Dalley, 1988, p. 8). Whereas caring *about* entails feelings of interest and concern towards people, caring *for* covers the activities of 'taking care of', 'looking after', 'waiting on', 'providing for' and 'taking charge' of people and their needs. Dalley argues (ibid., p. 20) that according to popular ideology, the two types or dimensions of caring occur together as part of 'woman's identity' and 'woman's nature', as distinct from 'man's identity' and 'man's nature' (ibid., p. 8). In particular, familial ideology includes the assumption that the integration between caring about and caring for is realized most prominently in motherhood. That is, for Dalley, it is 'in the function of motherhood that the two processes most commonly coalesce' (ibid., p. 8); whereas in the case of men, 'the entanglement of caring for and caring about does not, broadly speaking, exist [. . .] Men, it is recognized, can care about, without being expected to care for' (ibid., p. 12).

This gender dichotomy has implications not only for the private sphere with its division of domestic labour (largely centred on childcare), but also for the public sphere and social care: 'In the public sphere, the same forces are at work; women go into the caring occupations [such as nursing] because their natures and their intertwined capacities for caring for and caring about are thought to suit them well for those types of jobs' (ibid., p. 10).

In Australia, for instance, as reported by Marilyn Poole:

> the majority of women still have limited choices in terms of vocational and life options. Women remain in a narrow band of three main occupational areas: clerical, sales and service, which tend to offer lower status, lower pay and less security than do those occupations more typically held by males. (Poole, 1986, p. 105)

Moreover, although a very similar pattern of gender-differentiated paid labour force participation occurs in all modern Western societies, the Australian 'work-force is the most occupationally segregated by sex of all OECD nations' (Neals, 1990a), with over 60 per cent of employed females working in just three occupational sectors: clerical, sales and tourism (Neales, 1990b). Women's preponderance in service and caring occupations is accompanied by a further concentration whereby women tend to be found in the less remunerative and more subordinate positions. That is, even in 'feminized occupations' men occupy the senior positions 'in a disproportionate way' (Waters and Crook, 1990, p. 201). For instance, as reported by Marilyn Poole, the position of women teachers in the educational hierarchy 'remains abysmally low' within the Australian state of Victoria:

> A 1984 report by the Victorian Education Department indicates that of all the Education Department personnel, 57 per cent were female. Women made up 72 per cent of the primary teaching service. Principals of grade A and grade B band schools totalled 878 positions of which 728 positions were held by males. Women make up 52 per cent of high school teachers yet only 12 per cent are principals and 12 per cent deputy principals; in technical schools women make up 29 per cent of the total and 6 per cent of the principals are female. (Poole, 1986, p. 119)

One consequence of this gender imbalance is that if the state adopts the policy of reducing its provision of and expenditure on social services, women compared with men will be disproportionately affected in two main ways. First, they will be the most susceptible to redundancy, perhaps as reflected in recent Australian figures, according to which in September 1987 the male unemployment rate was 7.5 per cent while the female rate was over 8 per cent.[1] But second, women outside the paid labour force suffer further by virtue of the continuing prevalence of the way, in which following Dalley, caring *about* and caring *for* ideologically cohere in a

woman's identity, especially in motherhood, and in particular with regard to
the division of labour along one of two distinct dimensions of participation
within the unpaid domestic labour force. As the findings and conclusions
of a study with which I was involved over a period of several years during
the 1980s indicate:

> Any increase in men's participation in domestic labour has been largely
> confined to that dimension which may be simply [. . .] labelled 'merely
> doing' domestic labour. This dimension can be distinguished from a
> further one, that which covers 'being responsible for' domestic labour.
> In other words, the [. . .] study detected a tightly woven *social nexus*
> involving a distinction between two basic dimensions or levels of do-
> mestic labour upon which is superimposed a further (roughly congruent)
> distinction between 'masculine' and 'feminine'. The result is (the per-
> sistence of) a sharp gender division of domestic labour: a clear sep-
> aration between a 'masculine orientation' and a 'feminine orientation',
> according to which women (as wives and mothers) shoulder the major
> share of the responsibility for domestic labour. (Close, 1989c, p. 17)

The notion of 'responsibility' is clarified as follows:

> The [. . .] study lends itself to defining [. . .] the notion of being
> responsible for domestic labour in a particular way. That is, participation
> along this dimension (or at this level) is essentially about having and
> meeting an obligation to ensure that domestic labour is performed and
> completed in a proper, effective and satisfactory manner. It constitutes,
> therefore, a distinct [. . .] orienation to domestic labour. It tends to be
> [far] more demanding and onerous. (ibid., p. 18)[2]

Over the last couple of decades there has been a tendency on the part of
Western governments (led by the Thatcher and Reagan administrations in
Britain and the United States) to reduce the state's responsibility for – and
so financial outlay on – care on the grounds that it is proper and preferable
for the community and the family to be largely responsible and self-reliant
in this regard (although recently some writers have detected signs of a brake
being applied to this policy: see Saunders, 1990). However, in practice this
has meant that what is jettisoned by the state will have been gathered and
taken care of by women and mothers by virtue of the way in which caring
about and caring for combine ideologically to underpin their responsibility
for domestic labour (ibid., p. 34). That is, in practice, as Malcolm Wicks has
succinctly put it, 'community care = family care = female care' (Wicks,
1987); which in turn entails a 'triple shift' for women: that of 'the care of

their husbands and children, the care of [. . .] elderly dependent relative[s], plus paid work' (Ungerson, 1985, p. 160).

According to Dalley, the ideological conviction that there is a natural unity between caring for and caring about within woman's identity means that any attempt by a mother to ignore, deny or dissect the unity will result in social disapproval and condemnation. For instance, 'if a mother decides to give up her child, even though she cares about it [. . .] by handing over the "caring for" to another person or [a state] agency', then 'she is regarded as unnatural [and] as deviant' (Dalley, 1988, p. 8). We might anticipate that the condemnation will be exacerbated by the mother deciding to relinquish caring for by passing her child into state care, and therefore care characterized by a more tenuous unity between caring for and caring about. Whereas men may be expected and allowed to exhibit a relative absence of caring about, the state (its services and agencies) is expected to exhibit a relative absence of caring for. After all, a prominent and pervasive theme running through state care is that of protection – of protecting the 'cared for' and of protecting society – which in turn implies the further theme of state *control*, and thereby individual control and social control.

The way in which state care by way of protection becomes state control is perhaps most apparent in those cases where children are not passed into state care voluntarily by their parents, but instead are forcibly removed from their parents – either to 'protect' the children (as when actual or suspected child abuse occurs) or to 'protect' society (as when child delinquency – perhaps drug abuse – occurs). One of the best known and most controversial cases of such 'protective custody' occurred on a mass scale in Middlesbrough in the north-east of England towards the end of the 1980s, and is outlined by Sonia Jackson in the present volume. However, the practical association between state care and state control occurs far more broadly than when children are removed from family care and placed in state care (ranging from total institutions – such as in cases of child abuse and child delinquency – to educational organizations). Lois Bryson, for instance, makes a point in this context by comparing the power relationship between men and women with that between the state and the recipients of state care:

> within the home, women may gain benefits from a reduction in the amount of dreary chores and demanding organisational and childcare work they are required to do, but inevitably forfeit some control they previously had and indeed become more subject to control by their spouse. (Bryson, 1985, p. 97)

For Bryson, this situation is similar to what happens as a result of the provision and receipt of state welfare benefits, in that 'the quality of life of the working class has improved through available income support systems and general welfare services, but at the same time the provision by the state of benefits and services inevitably extends its realm of control over individuals' (ibid., p. 97). This argument is supported by, for instance, K. Saville-Smith in her discussion of 'women and the state' in New Zealand. She begins with the claim:

> the fundamental characteristic of the state is that it operates in a contradictory institutional position. These contradictions condition state policies and create both inconsistencies in the policies themselves and in the effects of those policies on gender relations. (Saville-Smith, 1987, p. 197)

What Saville-Smith seems to have in mind here is the way the state is caught between – faces the dilemma of – both (a) supporting conventional family life and gender relationships and (b) undermining, weakening and threatening the very same social arrangements. She illustrates this with reference to the Domestic Purposes Benefit (DPB), introduced by the New Zealand government in 1974 (following the Royal Commission on Social Security, 1972). The DPB is a statutory benefit for people, such as sole parents, who are responsible for the care of dependants living at home. A large proportion of the benefits are paid to women as sole mothers with dependent children, which has resulted in the popular view of the DPB as a 'woman's benefit'. Saville-Smith argues that state policies and benefits reflect the common, conventional assumption that women (and their children) are normally and preferably attached to and dependent upon men, who in turn are *normally* and preferably in paid employment and so in receipt of a family wage. When this chain is broken, so that women and their children are left to fend and care for themselves, the state steps in with help and support – to 'compensate' women for the absence or loss of a breadwinner – through the DPB (and the Widows Benefit) (ibid., p. 201). In this way, Saville-Smith asserts, a woman's dependency relationship is transferred from a man to the state. The irony is that the DPB provision, while reflecting and confirming women's view that security lies with a man and in marriage, nonetheless undermines and threatens conventional family and marital relationships by offering women the financial means of (even a financial inducement to) escape from such arrangements. The state is then faced with having encouraged conventional family and marital breakdown, with its subsequent personal and social problems, and with having created a large financial bill to be covered out of taxation.

The state's DPB bill is the cost it has to bear for the purpose of ensuring that the financial and social circumstances associated with sole motherhood do not undermine social control and threaten social order. The DPB provisions represent a mechanism which, for instance, allows sole mothers to maintain parental control, while at the same time allowing the state to maintain centralized social control. That is, in return for receiving DPB, sole mothers relinquish a degree of personal control over their lives and relationships by transferring control to the state. The DPB provisions serve the purpose of helping the state retain its central part in the process of social control in the interests of social order by virtue of the way sole mothers are dependent upon these provisions. This dependency enables the state (on the grounds of minimizing the cost of sole parenthood) to closely scrutinize and monitor, and thereby exercise everyday control over, the personal and intimate lives of sole mothers (ibid., p. 204). In this way not only the dependency of, but also the control over, women is transferred from men to the state.

The price paid by women in receipt of the DPB is the loss of privacy and personal control. For instance, the state and its agents assume the right to investigate financial circumstances, restrict paid employment participation, visit and examine homes, and even restrict sexual activity. According to Saville-Smith, the state demands that the women to whom it gives financial support should refrain from having *de facto* husbands or regular, steady sexual relationships with men given that such personal arrangements would be grounds for expecting the men to provide the support. Saville-Smith reports how to a large extent the state's immediate, everyday scrutiny over and intervention in the lives and relationships of sole mothers falls to the personal social services and so social workers; this having been acknowledged and excused by the state itself through the New Zealand government's Domestic Purposes Benefit Review Committee (1977). That social workers perform the task of social control on behalf of the state not only in New Zealand but elsewhere has been assessed by John Rodger, for whom 'both education and social work are concerned with qualifying and requalifying people for membership in society: for socializing or re-socializing them for harmonious social intercourse; and for exercising social control against those who would deviate from established cultural and/or political patterns' (Rodger, 1988, p. 569). In this context, Rodger refers to

an interpretation of the social worker's role not as caring helper, but as gatekeeper for problem populations or, as Davies (1983) would have it, the social worker has to persuade the poor, the feckless and the deviant 'to accept the terms currently offered to them by the state' (Davies 1983: 155). Joel Handler has identified the social worker's role as that of the 'coercive social worker' fulfilling an inevitable social control function of the modern state. (ibid., p. 568)[3]

The possibility arises that whenever individuals are brought into state care (which may mean simply into receipt of any social service, including what are officially referred to in Britain as 'social security benefits'[4]), they will pay the price of relinquishing a degree of individual control to (of becoming controlled by or through) the state: of coming under or extending state control. In my view, the state control involved will be an expression of three principal, immediate features of the relationship between the state and its welfare recipients in Western societies: (a) the state has the power to set the limits on the care and services provided and received; (b) the state has the power to impose the rules and conditions under which the care and services are received – as exemplified by the rules and conditions surrounding benefits going to the unemployed (which in recent years have become much tighter in Britain, the USA and Australia – see the chapters in this volume by Collins and Collins & Macleod), along with those going to sole parents; and (c) the circumstances of the recipients of state care and services, and in particular the dependency of such recipients. As far as some writers are concerned, in recent years there has been a considerable – not to say worrying and regrettable – increase in the degree of 'welfare dependency'.

For instance, Peter Swann and Mikhail Bernstam tell us that in Australia there is 'an alarming and rapidly growing social problem of welfare dependency from puberty to the grave', due especially to easy 'access to [state] benefits for single parents' (Swann and Bernstam, 1987, p. 22). As a result, according to Swann and Bernstam, there 'can be no doubt that Australians have taken to welfare like junkies to a fix' (ibid., p. 24). As a solution, Swann and Bernstam recommend that 'the participation of sole parents in the work force could be greatly improved [. . .] with the supporting parent required to work a minimum number of hours per week in return for the pension' (ibid., p. 25). Swann and Bernstam acknowledge how their proposal is in line with trends in the United States, where in some states 'workfare rather than welfare is now the rule' (ibid., p. 25).

The concerns of Swann and Bernstam have been echoed elsewhere, such as by Simon Upton in relation to New Zealand (Upton, 1988). Upton argues that the development of 'welfarism' has entailed a 'benefit bonanza [covering] everything from child benefit to superannuation', and has resulted in 'an attitudinal climate of dependency in which individuals are separated from responsibility for themselves and those dependent on them'. For Upton, New Zealand society is characterized by a 'cult of dependency', which in turn has brought about 'social and economic sclerosis'. For instance, there are

> some single young New Zealanders [who] see child-bearing as the key
> to a better income than they can earn elsewhere [and] fathers [who]
> just walk away from children they have fathered and leave the state to
> pick up the tabs. People [who] run up bills they have no way of meeting, safe in the knowledge that discretionary supplementary assistance
> will square off the creditors. (ibid.)

Upton asserts that these categories of people are 'passive recipients of welfare', and as such are distinguishable from 'deserving cases', the 'truly needy': from the 'people whose need of assistance is borne of circumstances beyond their control', such as 'those who are struck down by debilitating, chronic illness; who become the parents of a disabled child or are the victims of domestic violence or abuse.'[5]

The claims made by Swann and Bernstam in relation to Australia and by Upton in relation to New Zealand have implications for the issue of the way the provision and receipt of social services turn state care into state control, although in these particular accounts there are somewhat ambiguous messages with regard to the resulting balance between *state* control and *individual* control along with *social* control. Whereas individual control covers the process by which individual actions are directed and constrained ('held in check') perhaps to some extent through the exercise of state power and state control, social control, according to Paul Rock, refers to 'all constraints and patterns which generate discipline and social order' (Rock, 1983, p. 360).[6]

Social control is the process covering and circumscribed by all the activities and arrangements which produce and reproduce social order: the process by which social interaction, relationships, institutions, organizations and structure operate in an orderly, cohesive and stable manner. The state may make a contribution to this process by virtue of its state care activities, arrangements and agencies, and thereby through the exercise of state control over individuals in receipt of (or prospectively in receipt of) social services. The issues of the conceptual and practical relationships and problematics between 'state care', 'state control', 'individual control' and 'social control' are indicated by Paul Spicker. After pointing out that social control is about 'the maintenance of social order', Spicker refers to 'several different models of control' (Spicker, 1988, p. 101).[7]

First, the maintenance of social order is assisted by 'norms and values' in a manner which has been described as 'social control by "self-determination" ' (ibid., p. 101).[8] Second, there is social control by virtue of 'pressures for conformity, paternalistic policies, and "integration" – the adjustment of the individual to the [social] environment' (ibid., p. 101).[9] Third, there is social control through '"co-optation", the diffusing of protest by involving people in decision-making' (ibid., p. 102).[10] Fourth, there are 'more extreme forms of social control': those entailing coercion or force. One possibility here is that of the state manipulating 'welfare [to] deliberately [. . .] discourage people from dependence' – through stigmatization and degradation' – and instead to encourage people to acquire (often low-) paid employment in 'the interests of employers' (ibid., p. 102).[11]

Of course, the issue arises of the adequacy and exhaustiveness of the modes of control[12] listed by Spicker; not to mention the further issue of the relationship between this list and those presented by other writers with social control and social order in mind: including (a) the ground breaking example devised by Robert K. Merton; and (b) those intended to assist with the analysis of youth cultures and sub-cultures.[13] This aside, the four modes of control listed by Spicker might be alternatively labelled: first – 'conformity' through normative or ideological commitment[14] (entailing an affective orientation to social welfare); second – 'co-operation' through normative complicity (entailing an instrumental orientation to social welfare); third – 'co-option' through incorporation into the exercise of power, and thereby the acquisition of a stake in society (entailing an interest in social welfare); fourth – 'coercion' through the forceful exercise of state power.

Spicker indicates a possible example of the fourth mode of control in operation when he refers to the rules and conditions set by the state with regard to the provision of unemployment benefits:

> There are certainly measures associated with social services which directly involve control. For example, Unemployment Benefit [sic] may be suspended for a period if a person is considered to be unemployed 'voluntarily' without 'just cause' or through 'misconduct' (a term mainly applied to people who have been sacked). However, this is a long way from saying that the social welfare services are about control; welfare provisions may pull in contradictory directions. The issue is not that social services generally control people, but that welfare provision can be spoiled by the use of power in a way which works against the interests of the recipients. (ibid., p. 102)

Spicker fails to clearly and consistently distinguish between the concepts of 'individual control' and 'social control'; and thereby fails to elucidate adequately the practical relationship between state control, individual control and social control by way of *state care*. However, he is aware of the important point that the provision of state care and services can operate to help meet the welfare needs of people, while also contributing to the process of social control in the interests of (not so much welfare recipients but) the most privileged and powerful members and sections of society. That is, the part played by the state through social care within the process of social control leading to social stability may be 'seen as working in the interests of the dominant class, removing any threat to their pre-eminence' (ibid., p. 101), and thereby 'against the interests of' the 'dominated' class(es). As Spicker goes on to discuss, this view is adopted in various guises in 'Marxist analyses' of the state provision of care and social services (ibid., pp. 104–11).

I will argue that the importance of this point lies mainly in spotlighting what Spicker refers to as the 'contradictory directions' in which the less privileged and less powerful members and sections of society are pushed or led by state care: contradictory directions due to the way state care means that individuals have welfare needs satisfied, while at the same time experiencing (increased) control; the way state care means that the status quo receives support, while at the same time individual development and social progress are promoted; and the way state care means that social control, stability and order are enhanced, while social awareness, resentment and resistance in favour of fundamental social change is encouraged.

The state's dual care-control character has been widely recognized and extensively discussed,[15] and may be thought to be self-evident in that apart from anything else the state tries to promote welfare through social policy and social services, while at the same time trying to control, for instance, crime and criminals through penal policy and penal services (or 'corrective services' as they are sometimes labelled). However, the idea that the state plays a part in care through the social services while playing a part in control through the penal services reflects just one representation or form of the state's dual care-control activities. My proposal is that there are (at least) three representations or forms of the state's dual care-control involvement. The state, by virtue of the parts it plays in both care and control, may be portrayed, figuratively, wholly or partly as (a) two-bodied; or (b) two-headed; or (c) two-faced. In the case of (a), care and control are (viewed as being) conducted separately – within a division of labour between specialized organizations – where, for instance, care is performed by the social services and control is performed by the penal services. Hence, the *specialist* form or view of state care-control. In the case of (b) care and control are conducted together in an integrated fashion within the same organization(s) – such as within schools. Hence, the *integrated* form or view. In the case of (c) care and control are again conducted together, but in an amalgamated fashion – perhaps within the whole range of caring organizations (simply by virtue of the characteristics of an organization as a distinct social phenomenon) – in so far as care inherently entails control. Hence, the *amalgamated* form or view.

The integrated view is assumed by John Rodger in his argument about the dispersal of discipline thesis (Rodger, 1988). Rodger summarizes this thesis as proposed with respect to the development of social policy and penal policy in general, but with reference to its applicability to social work practice, care and control in particular (ibid., p. 563).[16] Essentially, the thesis is that the development of modern society has been accompanied by a trend whereby 'social discipline' is maintained not just through 'institutions explicitly concerned with punishment', but also through 'institutions of welfare', such as 'those of social work' (ibid., p. 563). Thus, the process of modernization has been characterized by the dispersal or division of 'social control' within an increasingly complex range of institutions, involving in particular the creation or generation and regeneration or usurpation of institutions of welfare to share in the process of social control.

According to the thesis, the evolution of social policy with regard to social control (and with particular reference to the control of deviance) has meant a decline in the use of, first, physical (bodily) punishment and, second, physical incarceration; and an increase in the use of non-custodial and non-punitive approaches, solutions and mechanisms. Initially, this entailed a process of 'institutional differentiation' between the penal (mainly prison) and the welfare sectors or wings, resulting in different (specialized) tasks (ibid., p. 563).[17] However, the evolutionary developments have proceeded even further: the penal sector has been 'decentred', so that whereas it was once the central mainstay of social policy and practice in relation to social (deviance) control, it has become 'one institution of social control among many, all seeking to perform different tasks within an elaborate penal/welfare division of labour'. At the same time, the two sectors of 'deviance control' are 'inextricably bound together', so much so that there has been a 'blurring of the boundaries' between them. In other words, there has been a trend towards a more 'inclusivist'[18] social policy approach to 'deviance control': a more pervasive and invasive approach 'involving dispersed centres of supervision and social control throughout the community' (ibid., p. 563).[19]

While John Rodger subscribes to the dispersal of discipline thesis, it seems to me to attract several queries and doubts. First of all, there is the possibility of misrepresenting or misinterpreting (perhaps exaggerating) the changes which have taken place; of not recognizing that welfare institutions have always been to some extent about discipline and control, either in accordance with Rodger's integrated view or the alternative amalgamated view. The possibility arises that a more accurate interpretation of what has happened is that amalgamated care-control through welfare institutions has simply been increasingly transformed into integrated care-control, so that the control side of welfare institutions has become more upfront, obvious and acute. If so, this may account for Rodger's misrepresentation or misinterpretation, and brings to mind the issue of the consequences of this paradigm shift for people's experiences, perceptions and conceptions of welfare institutions, and thereby for people's everyday practices in relation to social welfare and the state. The possibility arises that as state control becomes more evident and less shrouded behind state care – and perhaps more to the point, the clearer it becomes that state care is really about (really entails or facilitates) state *control* – the more state control will feed into a mechanism whereby welfare recipients and potential welfare recipients resent and resist state control, demanding and initiating change.

Second, there is the possibility of the dispersal of discipline thesis being applied in a too-inclusive manner. For instance, while (some version of) it may be applicable to the transformation of social (especially penal) policy and institutions concerned with the care-control of adults, it may not be strictly or completely applicable in the case of the care-control of children. In fact, a contrary trend may have been occurring, in such a way as to emphasize and strengthen any line of demarcation (or, more accurately, period of transition) between 'the world of adulthood' and 'the world of childhood'. Contrary to the general application of the dispersal of discipline thesis to recent patterns and trends with regard to social control in modern society, I wish to argue that in the particular case of children there has been something of a shift in the opposite direction. Although there may have been a trend towards the decentralization and de-institutionalization of control in the case of *deviance* and *deviants*, there has been a somewhat competing trend towards state-centred and institutionalized social control over and through children, especially by way of the expansion of the system of formal education. The increase in compulsory education (and perhaps non-compulsory education) lends itself to – and therefore may be accounted for in terms of – an increase in state control, especially by virtue of the way this trend has enhanced the distance and separation of 'children' from paid labour, as well as from (in a sense to be examined) 'labour' in general.

The possibility arises of care-control in relation to children having become less dispersed, given the way in which it has in particular become more centralized and concentrated within and through the education system (especially the school), at the expense of for instance the family and parents.[20] This development (redistribution) of care-control in favour of education, combined with the evolutionary process whereby state care-control in relation to children (through education) has been assuming less of an *amalgamated* and more of an *integrated* form, may help account for any increase (even upsurge) in resistance (perhaps rebellion) among children – in relation not only to school and education, but also to adults and adult society across the board (see Musgrave, 1987).

The process of control in relation to and over children has become more apparent as it has been prised away from its masking, and thereby mitigating, amalgamation with care. It has become more centred on and concentrated within the education system; has become more concentrated in a social location within which (following Dalley) there is less unity (compared with that which occurs within the family by virtue of motherhood) of caring *about* and caring *for*; and has become more concentrated in a social location in which caring for is given priority over caring about, in which the predominant orientation is the *instrumental* rather than the *affective*, emotional and sentimental and in which 'the objective' has priority over 'the subjective' (Foucault, 1982).

In the daily lives of children, education and control have come to predominate; and control has become increasingly stark and raw (having been stripped of its mantle of care); and moreover this has happened (and continues to happen) in a manner which is a denial of certain underlying realities of being a child (and so of becoming an adult) in modern society. Education has become more and more engrossing with regard to children's time and attention by increasingly competing with, challenging and displacing the family's (the mother's) predominance in the process of care-control. Moreover, this has occurred as education has expanded along the life-span. For instance, in Britain, for 'almost a dozen years during a formative period of their development children spend almost as much of their waking life at school as at home. Altogether this works out at some *15,000 hours* (from the age of five until school leaving) during which schools and teachers may have an impact on the development of the children in their care' (Rutter, 1980, p. 1).

A similar expansion has been underway in all Western societies. Commenting on the trends which have been occurring in social services, Ramesh Mishra notes:

> A notable feature here is the policy variation between the major services, namely education, health, income maintenance and housing. Thus education seems to be the one service that is provided along 'institutional' lines everywhere. Countries such as Japan and the United States which have tended to lag behind European countries in respect of state respons-

ibility for income maintenance, health and housing [. . .], have long instituted free and compulsory schooling for all. Schooling of about eight to ten years' duration is free and compulsory throughout the advanced capitalist world. (Mishra, 1977, p. 103)

Reference to government expenditure figures confirms a long-term, general expansion of state (public) education throughout advanced Western societies, even though in recent years (since in particular the early 1970s and the 'oil crisis') the same figures indicate if anything a less consistent and more complicated picture. Such figures are supplied by the Organization for Economic Co-operation and Development under the heading of 'social expenditure', which the OECD defines as 'direct public expenditure on education, health services, pensions, unemployment compensation and other income maintenance programmes and welfare services' (OECD, 1985, p. 18). Within OECD countries overall,[21] between the early 1960s and the 1980s there was a marked pattern of social expenditure growth (ibid., p. 21). At the same time, there was also considerable diversity within this pattern: a 'substantial variation in the proportion of GDP allocated to social expenditure' (ibid., p. 21). Thus:

In 1981 five countries – Germany, Belgium, Denmark, the Netherlands and Sweden – spent over 30 per cent of GDP on social programmes. Of these, only Denmark was not among the big spenders in 1960. At the same time, in two countries – Greece and Switzerland – the expenditure share was less than 15 per cent. These countries, along with Japan (where the expenditure share remains low by international standards) were also at the bottom of the league in 1960. There has been some variation in the pattern of social expenditure growth. Amongst the seven major countries Japan is at the upper end of the range of social expenditure growth rates and the United Kingdom [along with] New Zealand [is] at the lower end of the range. (ibid., p. 22)

Between 1980 and 1985/6 the changes in the shares (percentages) of GDP being spent by governments in selected OECD countries on (a) total social expenditure compared with (b) education were as in Table 1.1.[22]

Such expenditure patterns indicate that the state in all advanced Western societies attributes considerable importance and value to education as a social service, even though there is the further common tendency for governments to trim back their educational budgets in response to general economic pressure and downturn. At the same time, the figures given are narrow data in that they under-represent the full amounts (the full proportions of GDP) spent on education because they do not cover non-public

Table 1.1 Social expenditure and education: comparative data[23]

| | Total social expenditure | | Education | |
	1980	*1985/6*	*1980*	*1985/6*
Australia	17.3	18.4 (1985)	5.9	5.7 (1986)
Japan	16.1	16.0 (1986)	4.9	4.2 (1985)
New Zealand	22.4	21.0 (1985)	5.8	4.1 (1985)
United Kingdom	20.0	20.6 (1986)	5.5	5.1 (1986)
United States	18.0	18.2 (1985)	5.5	5.3 (1985)

Source: OECD, 'OECD in Figures: Statistics on the Member Countries', *Supplement to the OECD Observer*, 158, June/July 1989, pp.16–17.

expenditure: 'In many countries there are large private sectors in social provision – [including] private schools and universities' (OECD, 1985, p. 18). This probably applies most of all to Japan and the United States, although complete and conclusive information in this regard is not available (ibid., p. 18).[24]

Also, of course, quantitative data relating to the long-term expansion of public (and private) education, and reflecting in particular the extension of the period within the life-span occupied by compulsory (primary and secondary) schooling – but alongside a similar trend in non-compulsory (tertiary) education – does not by itself tell us anything directly about patterns and trends with respect to the *quality* of education. Educationists often express the view that the increased quantity of education has not necessarily meant improved quality, but that if anything there has been an accompanying drop in quality. Such educationists include some who occupy commanding positions within the system itself. Thus:

A leading educationist has criticised the education system as being too concerned with students' career prospects and thus failing to foster a thirst for learning. The headmaster of Sydney Grammar School, Dr Ralph Townsend, said last week that the education industry had suffocated the culture of learning for its own sake and students were feeling alienated from the learning process. 'The result is that we are now producing efficient technocrats who lack the qualities of discernment, civility and judgement essential if technical knowledge is to build up a society . . . in which some kind of durable happiness beyond the pragmatic is available to the majority,' he said [. . .] Dr Townsend said the rights to education, both secondary and tertiary, established in the 1960s reduced the need for students to make a personal commitment to their education. 'Many of the present generation are aware chiefly of the tyranny of learning . . . Students speak gloomily of themselves as passive packages of the conveyor belt, often with little enthusiasm for learning.' [. . .] 'Something important was lost when education became synonymous with schooling, and more particularly, when that schooling was modelled almost wholly on the book learning of the elite,' Dr Townsend said. (Ferrari, 1990)

Essentially, for Dr Townsend, students are becoming more alienated from educational processes in response to the increasingly 'narrow approach to education, where the relevance of learning [is] tied to its usefulness for career' (ibid.). Students are responding to the instrumental approach to education, whereby educational processes are guided by the ' "desire to use" [rather than] the explorer's instinct" ' (ibid.), which would drive students 'to know' (ibid.) for its own sake: for its more immediate and intrinsic satisfactions and rewards. Modern educational processes are (increasingly, as far as Dr Townsend is concerned) out of touch with, estranged and alienated from, these deeper personal and human qualities, possibilities and motives.

While student alienation may be a response to the way in which modern educational processes are guided by instrumental purposes, such alienation may then help account for any student reaction in the form of student resistance, even to the point of student rebellion. In turn, the occurrence of student resistance may well evoke instrumentally orientated and rationalized calls for greater student 'discipline and control'.[25] Signs along the lines of student alienation and resistance are to be found in recent incidents in Sydney and elsewhere in Australia. For instance:

An inner-city high school teacher who had his clothes set alight on a bus after a group of students lit a box of matches and placed it in his coat pocket [. . .] A head teacher who was thrown to the ground and punched by a child [. . .] A gang of teenagers who had left their inner-city school, returned and assaulted a teacher [. . .] A teacher in the south-west of Sydney who was kick-boxed by a student. He [. . .] was kicked in the head and chest [. . .] Two teachers who were injured during a fight in the playground. [. . .] One teacher is still off work with back problems; the other is suffering psychological problems [. . .] A number of incidents, including one recently in Sydney's west, during which a female teacher was threatened by a student with sexual assault and damage to her home and property [. . .] A deputy principal of an inner-city school who was punched and jostled [. . .] A female teacher in Sydney's south-west who returned from maternity leave and was verbally abused and threatened by a female pupil. (Totaro, 1990)

Apparently, these 'violent incidents' were revealed to the *Sydney Morning Herald* during interviews with teachers, who 'agreed to speak on the basis that they not be named to protect their schools' identity' (ibid.). However, there is increasing evidence of teachers experiencing and openly reporting an upsurge in student violence, culminating in 'the establishment recently of an inner-city teachers' committee against violence in schools and the community (Egan, 1990a). A committee representative claimed: 'It isn't just physical violence. Teachers have been subjected to verbal abuse of a very nasty nature.' (ibid.) The violence and abuse is by no means confined to Sydney and New South Wales. In Queensland 'more than three hundred children have been suspended so far this year for discipline related problems, including assaults on teachers and other pupils' (ibid.).

The newspaper reports suggest that as far as teachers are concerned, violence and abuse in schools and towards teachers is part and parcel of a more inclusive pattern and trend of 'violence in the community' (ibid.). Thus,

[a] series of bashings, organised violence and street-crime involving school-age children – plus an increase in gang attacks on Aborigines, gays and ethnic groups – is causing growing concern among inner-city teachers. In an unprecedented move this week, the Inner City Teachers Association debated a motion warning of a 'culture of violence permeating the everyday life of inner-city children' and expressing serious 'dismay about the level of violence in the inner city'. (Totaro, 1990)

Interestingly, 'Juvenile crime directed at property is declining, figures supplied by the Bureau of Criminal Research and Statistics show. But young crime against persons is increasing [. . .] assaults and sex offences seem to be rising' (Casimir, 1990). At the same time, this particular trend would seem to be just part of a more inclusive one:

Crime in NSW rose by 43 per cent during the 1980s [. . .] But while the rates for some offences [. . .] were held in check, there was a staggering increase in NSW's figures for sexual offences and offences against the person. The rate for sexual offences [. . .] more than tripled while that for offences against the person rose by 260 per cent according to the NSW Bureau of Crime Statistics. (McEvoy, 1990)

Of course, official criminal statistics cannot be regarded as completely reliable indicators of either actual patterns and trends or underlying sources of such patterns and trends. As pointed out by the Director of the Bureau of Criminal Research and Statistics, Dr Don Weatherburn (Casimir, 1990), all it takes 'to lift the figures is an increase in the willingness of the victim to come forward [. . .] And there is always an increase whenever there are campaigns run by police and women's groups'. The issue of the reliability of official crime statistics has attracted considerable attention over a long period from sociologists, notably Steven Box (Box, 1971). Added to this is the unreliability of mass media reports and interpretations, as in the notorious case of 'the battle of Bidwill' in Sydney's west in 1981:

> 'About 1000 boys and girls from rival schools fought a bloody, no-holds-barred battle that held a Sydney suburb in terror last night. The Mt Druitt area is still reeling from the Battle of Bidwill – staggering schoolkid violence that erupted on the streets.' That is how the evening news reported an incident on October 15, 1981 that came to be considered the most outstanding example of violence among school children in Australia and used by the NSW teachers Federation as part of its argument for the introduction of electronic surveillance in schools. (Egan, 1990b)[26]

Teachers' experience, perceptions and interpretation of student resistance to the point of violence has led them to respond by increasing surveillance, protection and control facilities and arrangements, including committees 'against violence'. The same experience would seem to be, also, a major factor behind other types of response: 'A survey of teachers found the dominant reasons for stress were associated with student attitudes, values, behaviour and discipline' (Egan, 1990a). Furthermore, the way in which teachers are 'subjected to abuse and having to deal with difficult children', has been used to help account for why 'Competent teachers of many years' experience are leaving teaching in large numbers' (Nichols, 1990). Moreover, the pattern in Australia is replicated in other countries, such as Britain:

> The number of teachers leaving the profession through ill health has nearly trebled over the last 10 years, according to figures released yesterday [15 January 1991] They [. . .] show steady increases every year since the early 1980s and a big jump in 1988, the year when the Education Reform Act was introduced [. . .] the Labour [Party] education spokesman [. . .] said yesterday: 'The figures show that teaching is no longer a secure job. The three-fold increase in the number leaving for health reasons concerns the additional stress under which teachers are working.' (Bates, 1991)

It is not surprising to learn that teachers themselves are very much aware of the links between educational expansion and both student alienation and student violence. Thus, in Australia 'Some teachers feel the drive towards keeping more students until year 12 [16 years of age] could be adding to the problem, with those [who would be] better off leaving school feeling compelled to stay.' (Egan, 1990a)

The Sydney Grammar School headteacher's view about the links between student alienation and the (increasing) instrumental approach to education is consistent with a now long established analysis within sociology as propounded by, for instance, Ivan Illich (1973). He argues that education *should be* a liberating experience through students being provided with the opportunity to use, realize and develop their creative capacities, initiative and judgement in a *free* and *full* manner.[27] However, Illich claims that schools are educationally inadequate: that they are far from effective in drawing out people's talents and promoting their skills. He argues that these educational processes are best left in the hands of those people who already utilize their talents and skills in everyday life and practices. Illich views schools as repressive organizations which smother creativity, stifle imagination, stupify, indoctrinate, and induce students to conform – to comply with the interests of the most powerful members and sections of society. Herein lies schooling's 'hidden curriculum', which operates by virtue of the way students have little or no control over the content and form of the learning and teaching processes. The student is instructed within an authoritarian teaching regime, and is required to comply with the regime's demands and rules in order to be successful. What Illich regards as real learning does not flow from instruction, but from people's free *participation* within the learning process. Essentially, 'most learning requires no teaching'. The ability of schools to enforce conformity to their rules and to coerce their students into accepting instruction is rooted in their power to grant credentials which are believed to bring rewards through the labour market. Those who conform to the rules are selected to go on to higher and more rewarding levels within the educational system. Illich views the educational system as the source of various personal and social maladies in modern society. This hinges on the way schooling is crucial to the creation of mindless, conforming and easily manipulated members of society. Through schooling people learn to value and comply with the educational system and similar social services; to defer to authority; to be good consumers; to accept their alienation; to be content with not having to think very much for themselves. Illich proposes a radical solution, as the title of his book suggests: the answer lies in the abolition of the present system of education centred on schooling.

Of course, there are many issues and problems surrounding Illich's somewhat simplistic argument and solution.[28] The naivety of Illich's ideas and assumptions is perhaps indicated by the way schooling, rather than being reduced, continues if anything to be expanded and extended so as to occupy ever more expenditure and hours. The result being, in effect, an ever-increasing consolidation and a further elongation of 'childhood', in the sense discussed and discovered by Philippe Ariès (1973). That is, since its social construction, or invention, by the bourgeoisie around three centuries ago, childhood has become an ever expanding and emphasized phase of the life-span; an ever increasing distinct, separate, removed, protected, controlled and dependent phase. This development was initially centred on the family (hence the 'child-centred' bourgeoisie, conjugal family form,[29]) but more recently has been reflected in and aided by the expansion of (especially compulsory) education. This expansion has brought with it ever increasing divisions and discrepancies (along the lines indicated by Ivan Illich and Dr Ralph Townsend, among many others) between (a) the world of education and to a large extent through this the immediate (somewhat idealized) social world of childhood; (b) the outside social world of adulthood, especially in that this incorporates the labour market along with paid employment, labour and productive activities; and (c) certain underlying (and somewhat shrouded) 'realities of childhood': realities which among other things cover (i) basic human physiological, psycho-sexual, emotional and mental capacities, capabilities, potential and developments, and (ii) children's 'actual' place, participation and contribution within the full scope of social life, labour and production.

The way in which there has been an ever-widening gap between, for instance, (a) the protected, restricted and repressed pace of socialization and social development through childhood towards adulthood and (c)(i) the pace of underlying (irresistible) physiological, psycho-sexual, emotional and mental developments has given rise to much discussion pinpointing resulting personal and social 'problems'.[30] However, the same discussion has been marked by an almost blanket ignorance of what may amount to a crucial gap and discrepancy between (a) and (c)(ii), and as such has merely reflected certain everyday (ideological) assumptions which underpin the discrepancy; and thereby has in effect reinforced the same assumptions and their consequences for children, children's experiences and children's reactions.

That is, it is commonly assumed that because children are separated from the external adult world of paid employment, their work activities (including their schoolwork) are fundamentally different from that conducted by adults as paid employment. It is assumed that children's activities, wherever they are performed, barely warrant the label of 'work'; and that they certainly do not deserve the more important or technical categorization of 'labour'.[31] Essentially, according to this view, the activities performed by children within education (their study activities) do not constitute 'labour' in that they are not 'productive', at least in the sense that applies to the activities of adults within paid employment. In something of a circular fashion, it might then be argued that children's study activities are not and cannot be paid because such activities do not constitute 'labour', in the sense that adult paid-employment activities constitute 'labour' by virtue of being 'productive'.

The everyday view of (ideological assumption about) study activities as 'non-labour' and 'non-productive' means not only that students do not receive payment, but also that they (or someone on their behalf) may be required to make payment in return for being allowed to participate in education – public as well as private, especially at the tertiary level. As reported by Russ Francis (1990), 'New Zealand tertiary students [. . .] are being required to contribute directly to the costs of tuition [and the resulting] stress has been exacerbated by the new $910 tertiary fee'. Such obligatory payments in return for the opportunity to engage in study activities help explain why 'New Zealand tertiary students continue to come mainly from families with education and income levels well above average [. . .] Since [. . .] 1987, the socio-economic level of students' parents has increased slightly'.

The issue of social class differentials and inequalities with regard to educational opportunity and achievement is, of course, of the utmost importance both practically and theoretically. But this aside, the possibility arises that students of whatever social class (in New Zealand and elsewhere) are being required to pay and find 'stress inducing' amounts of money in exchange for permission to engage in study activities which (despite everyday ideological assumptions and official interpretations) are not fundamentally different from adult paid employment activities. Perhaps study activities are merely superficially different (the major difference being that study activities are ideologically denied the status of 'productive labour', and on these grounds are denied monetary reward). Perhaps, therefore, from a sociological point of view student activities would be more appropriately and usefully conceptualized as 'productive labour' alongside adult paid employment activities. Such an alternative approach to the conceptualization, categorization and treatment of study activities is consistent with the interpretation offered by Bowles and Gintis (1976) of the character, form and 'function' of schooling in captalist America in relation to the economy. Bowles and Gintis examine the nature of work and social relationships in the educational system and argue that they mirror those of the economic system. In this way young people are prepared for the requirements of the world of work. Schools are organized on a hierarchical principle of authority and control. Teachers give orders and pupils obey. Students have little control over the curriculum, the subjects they learn or the work they do. They are not involved in their work and get little intrinsic satisfaction out of it. The actual teaching process [. . .] provides the student with little opportunity for self-fulfillment in his [sic] work. Instead he is taught to be content with extrinsic satisfactions, to respond to rewards which are external to the work itself such as [. . .] the approval of teachers [. . .] rewards [which] provide teachers with a powerful instrument of control [. . .] Bowles and Gintis argue that social relationships in schools 'replicate the hierarchical division of labour in the workplace' [and mean that] pupils are prepared for their work roles 'through a close correspondence between the social relationships which govern personal interaction in the work place and the social relationships in the educational system'. (Haralambos, 1985, p. 183)

Following Bowles and Gintis, despite – and perhaps because of – the ever-increasing ideologically and institutionally based divide between the world of childhood and the world of adulthood, schooling has acquired a relational content (character or style) which very much resembles the character of what is perhaps the centrepiece and mainstay of the latter – namely, the sphere of paid employment. It is as if (in a way which echoes the Parsonian view of the educational system (Parsons and Bales, 1955) schooling has acquired a relational style which 'functionally' serves the pedagogical purpose of compensating for and bridging the gap that has otherwise opened up. It is as if schooling has become both separate from and similar to the world of adults at one and the same time: as if schooling's increasing institutional, formal and statutory separateness has required it to become similar relationally; so that despite the separateness it can continue to play a part in children's preparation for adulthood.

However, the possibility of conceptualizing study activities as 'productive labour' does not rest solely on the way in which these activities are embedded in work and social relations – are characterized by a 'work situation' (to use the terminology of David Lockwood (1958)) – akin to those associated with paid employment. The possibility rests also on the character and form of study activities in relation to the (economic) outcome of such activities. This outcome may be summarily labelled as 'labour power', the 'ability to work',[32] or the capacity created and embodied in all human beings by virtue of which they are capable of (further) work, labour and production. At the same time, the possibility on these grounds of conceptualizing study activities as 'productive' arises not simply because such activities eventually result in that labour power which is embodied in those (adults) who have left or who are leaving the educational system for entry into paid employment. It arises also because such activities currently, immediately and daily result in that labour power which is embodied in those ('children') still within the educational system: in that labour power which is immediately and recurrently being to some extent used (consumed) through study activities in the daily process of the reproduction of that labour power embodied in students. Study activities result in that reproduced labour power which is denied not only the status of 'product', but also (formally, statutorily) the chance of being used (consumed) within the sphere of paid employment activities; and so denied the chance of having its current (accumulated) exchange value realized through the labour market. In this way, the sociological value of conceptualizing study activities as 'productive labour' may be obscured, but nonetheless is perhaps worthwhile uncovering and recognizing on analytical and theoretical grounds.

Quite simply, children and students may put a considerable amount of effort (and labour) into the daily round of reproducing their own, embodied, labour power (product); but will experience the inconsistency and disjunction of having their real effort in this regard dismissed as being 'non-labour' and 'non-productive'; as not being of the same stature and 'value' as adult paid employment activities; and therefore of not being worthy of current pecuniary remuneration. At one and the same time, children and students will experience being both (a) *positively* encouraged to 'work hard', to the point of coercion in so far as they are forced (statutorily obliged, to some extent against their will) to engage in study activities; and (b) *negatively* discouraged by virtue of the way their activities are categorized (ideologically, practically and remuneratively) as 'non-adult' or 'sub-adult' or 'pre-adult'.

Moreover, this experience occurs in conjunction with the way children and students gradually and increasingly (with age, over the life cycle) pass and emerge through (by participating in) a developmental process rooted in (a) their underlying physiological, psycho-sexual, emotional and mental (human) potential; and (b) their socialization and education. At the same time, however, children and students experience having the immediate outcome of this process – namely their labour power – handled negatively by being denied and repressed on the basis of their identification and categorization as 'children'. This categorization means that children and students – despite their development, labour power and capabilities with regard to productive labour – will experience being increasingly (historically speaking) separated from the world of adults (and in particular from paid employment) within the confines of the world of children. Moreover, within these confines, their experience is compounded by their separation and division from adults (parents, teachers), who proceed to control and direct them and their labour power.

Herein (within this experience), perhaps lies a major source of growing student dissatisfaction, resentment, resistance and struggle: 'growing' in the dual sense of (a) historically and (b) developmentally (with age, over the life-cycle). The possibility that students and their study activities are artificially – but 'functionally' – distinguished, divided and denied in relation to adults, paid employment and productive labour has hardly made an appearance in sociological writings. As Jens Qvortrup has put it:

> The limited interest which sociologists have shown in childhood *in itself* reflects the assumption that children are not part of organised society. They have been marginalised and residualised – kept in a waiting position until they can be classified as 'adults', living and competing in adult society. Children are not human 'beings' in sociological literature, but only human 'becomings'. (Qvortrup, 1985)

Following the pioneering discussions by Qvortrup (see also Qvortrup, 1990), my argument is that the process of 'marginalizing' and 'dehumanizing' (or 'pre-humanizing') children takes place by way of denying and negating their productive labour activities (predominantly and increasingly) through the educational system. It is within education that children's productive labour is (a) largely performed and (b) mainly denied and negated. It is predominantly within and through the education system that children and students are separated from the adult world, in conjunction with being alienated from their own productive labour and their own product – and thereby 'alienated' from themselves in the sense of their own (basic, human) capacities, capabilities, potential and development.

At the same time, however, the negative handling of study activities is complemented by further educational features which also (together) thread through and shape student experience, and thereby have a crucial bearing on their meaningful (re)actions to their marginalization and alienation. First (following Bowles and Gintis), the work situation within which students perform their study activities closely resembles the work situation within which adults carry out their paid employment activities. Second (following Qvortrup), study activities may be not only sociologically categorized, but also socially experienced as 'labour' and as 'productive labour', despite the ideologically based classification to the contrary. Third, the educational system, whatever its limitations, does facilitate a type of human development and a degree of student opportunity, even though 'the reality' in these respects may fall far short of the promise. That is, fourth, of major importance in shaping student experience and reactions in relation to the educational system is the way the latter presents and emphasizes a promise of a positive kind *vis-à-vis* student (human) capacities, capabilities, potential and development. This promise is partly met, but only partly. The discrepancy between the promise and 'the reality' of the education system with regard to the realization of human potential is firmly demonstrated in the evidence on the way student achievement varies considerably by social class, sex-gender and race-ethnicity; and has been discussed under such headings as 'the myth of the meritocracy'. For instance, for Bowles and Gintis:

> the educational system is seen as a giant myth-making machine which serves to legitimate inequality. It creates and propagates the following myths: educational attainment is based on merit; occupational reward is based on merit; education is the route to success in the world of work. The illusion of meritocracy established in schools leads to the belief that the system of role allocation is fair, just and above board. (Haralambos, 1985, p. 185)[33]

Maybe the education system through its positive promise and degree of success does foster the (ideological) 'myth of the meritocracy', which then 'reduces discontent' (ibid., p. 185) so that in this way '"education reproduces inequality by justifying privilege"' (ibid., p. 186).[34] However, maybe also the outcome is not quite as simple and straightforward as this, given that students' experience – their direct and immersed experience – may entail the clear message (registered by Bowles and Gintis in their removed location as observing sociologists) that there is something of a discrepancy between the positive promise and the somewhat negative reality of education: a negative reality which hinges to a large extent on the way student productive labour, capacity and capabilities are negatively categorized, constrained and controlled.[35]

There is a parallel case to the possibility of recognizing children's study activities as 'productive labour', and its importance in making sense of the experiences and associated meaningful (re)actions of those involved.[36] That is, a considerable amount of scholarly, as well as more practical, attention has been given to the issue of whether and in what sense *domestic labour* – mainly of course performed by women[37] – can be appropriately and usefully conceptualized as 'productive' by virtue of its relationship with the (re-)

production (daily and inter-generationally) of labour power, as well as thereby, with capitalist production (centred on the production of surplus value, the source of capital accumulation and profits). This issue has, for instance, given rise to much writing and discussion under the heading of the Domestic Labour Debate, the result being various arguments, interpretations and conclusions.[38] The debate, which to a large extent hinges on fine conceptual and theoretical technicalities is far from settled (despite suggestions to the contrary[39]) but it has helped establish the seriousness of the issue along with attempts to transpose domestic labour into exchange equivalent or wage equivalent amounts in recognition of the possibility that, after all, domestic labour is 'productive labour' alongside paid employment labour and, in particular, wage labour.

Accordingly, there have been numerous attempts to quantify domestic labour by assessing its value – its exchange value equivalent or whatever. One such attempt has been made in Australia on behalf of the state by the Australian Capital Territory Community Law Reform Committee (Walsh, 1990). Its concern is with the issue of women's 'right to claim compensation for the loss of capacity to do housework'; and so with the possibility of matching the right already enjoyed by men to 'claim compensation for the loss of a "wife's services and companionship" if she is injured or incapacitated.' At present,

> ACT courts [measure] a husband's loss according to his needs – the hire of a housekeeper while the wife is ill, and wages lost if he has to stay at home. Courts have also been asked to quantify the loss of sexual companionship [. . .] Estimates from the ACT Justice Department set a married, employed woman's worth in the home at $19,625, or if married and unemployed, $27,044. Add two children, and the figure rises to $68,068 a year. (ibid.)

These figures compare with $8171 for a single, employed female; $15 779 for a single, unemployed female; $9141 for a married, employed male; $5403 for a single, employed male; $15 118 for a married, unemployed male; and $8498 for a single, unemployed male.

If such estimates are possible and permissible in the case of adults with regard to domestic labour, presumably they are possible and permissible in the case of children with regard to study activities.[40] Some writing has at first glance come close to acknowledging the possibility of recognizing children's study activities as 'productive labour'. Thus, in a recent newspaper article (Dawson, 1990), the following argument is outlined: 'The vital issue in education is productivity – improving and increasing the education Australia produces per unit of resource input – says a report by [. . .] the

Federated Australian University Staff Association'. The article adds that the 'keys to improved productivity in schools and universities are a commitment to co-operative output and a commitment to "smart" methods of work, says the report'.

However, this economistic, input-output approach to 'educational productivity' does not recognize, as such, the possibility of viewing study activities as 'productive' on a par with paid employment activities. This possibility is ignored in a manner which resembles the way many sociological 'reproduction theories' of education have ignored or bracketed the part played by students in affecting (contributing to and shaping) educational 'outputs'. Sandra Taylor has summarized such theories as follows:

> The related processes of cultural and social reproduction have been important areas of study in the sociology of education in recent years. Such a focus on the nature of the relationship between schooling and the social structure developed from a broad concern about the role which schooling plays in transmitting and maintaining social inequalities [. . .] In discussing the relationship between schooling and the class structure it is possible to distinguish between theories which emphasise social relations of schooling and those which emphasise content. The work of Bowles & Gintis (1976) and Gintis & Bowles (1981) is representative of those theories which stress social relations. The [important] feature of their [theory] is the structural correspondence between schooling and economic production. Thus Bowles & Gintis argue that schools allocate students, with different attitudes and skills, to different levels of a hierarchical workforce. [. . .] In contrast, Bourdieu argues that social reproduction occurs principally through the control of curriculum content by the ruling class: that is, social reproduction occurs via cultural reproduction (Bourdieu and Passeron, 1977). (Taylor, 1984, pp. 3–4)[41]

However, Taylor then refers to the limitations of reproduction approaches to education in so far as they are 'deterministic', and boil down to nothing more than 'crude correspondence theory' (ibid., p. 3).[42] The point has been otherwise made as follows:

> Until [recently], studies of educational achievement tended to assume that 'outputs' from the educational system (levels of achievement) could be explained simply in terms of the range of pupil characteristics – the intellectual, material and cultural 'inputs' – that pupils bring with them to school. But a sustained challenge has been mounted to this way of analysing education by sociologists working in social action traditions.

Drawing upon the insights of symbolic interactionism, phenomenology and ethnomethodology, they insist that an input-output approach to the explanation of the social distribution of achievement is misleading [in that it] does not give sufficient attention to the impact of schooling itself. [. . .] Social action theorists argue that analysis of the processes of interaction in schools is essential; and [. . .] stress instead the fluidity of the self [based] upon the capacity of teachers and pupils for rational [meaningful] action [rooted in] their own understanding [and] experience of school. (Bilton et al., 1987, pp. 334–5)

Assuming that students are continuously capable of a degree of autonomous and fluid, meaningful action, influence and input – that students' educational outcome (achievement or whatever) does not boil down simply to a process of interplay between the input characteristics they bring into school plus imposed system features, bypassing students' capacity for subjective experience and independent action – then as Taylor says 'the part students themselves play in both supporting and resisting reproduction', which 'the work on reproduction [. . .] ignores' (Taylor, 1984, p. 3), needs to be acknowledged. Or, as has been pointed out by Peter Musgrave.

reproduction theories have weaknesses, in particular because their predictive power is low. Reproduction sometimes does not occur and these theories give no indication of where in society this may or may not occur. One way of conceptualising this failure has been to examine resistance to reproduction. (Musgrave, 1987, p. 69)

There is a need in trying to analyse and make sense of educational processes and outcomes to take into account the degree to which the participants, by virtue of their experience and associated meaningful action, both accept (comply) and reject (resist), especially in that such processes entail control, discipline and objectification. These features reflect and facilitate an instrumental approach to education, whereby the emphasis is not so much on 'learning for its own sake, satisfactions and rewards', but more on 'learning as a means for meeting the economy's labour power requirements' – including that of a compliant and perhaps docile labour force. Students are subjected to educational processes from which they are – by virtue of their human capacities, capabilities, potential and development – alienated; and accordingly against which they react through resistance. This approach is consistent with the interpretation of 'the subject and power' as presented by Michael Foucault, for whom the focus is 'the different modes by which, in our culture, human beings are made subjects

[. . . the] modes of objectification which transform human beings into subjects [and the relevance of] power relations [. . .] in studying the objectivizing of the subject.' (Foucault, 1982, pp. 777–8)

The first set of modes referred to by Foucault is 'the modes of inquiry', entailing for instance 'the objectivizing of the productive subject, the subject who labours, in the analysis of wealth and economics.' (ibid., p. 777) However, as I have already outlined, the possibility arises of the objectivizing of the productive subject not only at the level of scholarly inquiry, analysis and theory, but also at the level of social practice, ideology and remuneration. Foucault is interested in the way power[43] and control relations are manifested in the process of shaping (or attempting to shape) individual subjectivity, such as within and through the education system: the way in which subjectivity becomes the 'subject' of the education system and educational processes; and thereby the way in which subjectivity, as 'the subject', is 'objectivized' (becomes an 'object'). At the same time, for Foucault the 'objectifying strategy' adopted within and through, for instance, the education system may provide responses in the form of counter strategies, or *resistance*. For Foucault, any attempt to make sense of 'the subject and power' in any social sphere, needs to pay attention to resistance as a crucial and highly instructive feature.

Foucault suggests that 'we need a new economy of power relations' – a new 'theoretical' (ibid., p. 779) approach to making sense of power relations within which 'the human subject is placed' (ibid., p. 778) – largely in recognition of 'the development of the state and the political management of society' (ibid., p. 779). Foucault argues for a 'theory' which

consists of taking the forms of resistance against different forms of power as the starting point [. . .] of analyzing power relations through the antagonism of strategies [. . . In] order to understand what power relations are about [. . .] we should investigate the forms of resistance and attempts made to dissociate these relations. (ibid., p. 780)

Foucault takes as a starting point 'a series of oppositions which have developed over the last few years: opposition to the power of men over women, of parents over children, of psychiatry over the mentally ill, of medicine over the population, of administration over the ways people live.' (ibid., p. 780) Presumably, Foucault would count opposition to the power of teachers, educational institutions and the state over students – as manifested in the resistance of students. Foucault proposes that in each case, the opposition, resistance and struggle is against 'not so much [. . .] an institution of power' – such as school – 'but rather a technique, a form of power' (ibid., p. 781).

Following Foucault's argument, student resistance may be viewed as a response to a particular form of power that 'applies itself to immediate everyday life which categorizes the individual' (ibid., p. 781): which, for instance, categorizes the individual in the case of children and students (in a general sense) within education as 'immature', 'incapable', 'irresponsible', 'in need of protection' (from others and themselves), 'in need of close supervision and control', 'un-socialized' (or at least pre-socialized), 'human-becomings', 'non-adult' ('sub-adult', 'pre-adult'), 'non-labouring', and 'non-productive'. If so, student resistance will be a response to a particular form of power by which they are not only categorized but also largely (perhaps overwhelmingly) negatively categorized in comparison with and in relation to adults and the world of adults. Students will be resisting a particular form of power which helps 'rationalize'[44] and thereby legitimate a particular form of education system, in which schools separate, divide and *protect*; in which teachers control, discipline and direct; and which thereby tends to operate along the lines of a self-fulfilling prophecy by rendering students (at least more) 'immature', 'incapable', and so on. Furthermore, teacher control is in this way conveniently rationalized and legitimated in terms of (at least in the first instance) 'the needs of students', rather than in terms of such less immediately appealing and palatable alternatives as, 'the needs of teachers', 'the needs of the state', 'the needs of prospective employers', 'the needs of society', and so on. The ideological conviction that 'children' have needs which are served – and 'best' served – by education, schools and teachers, and that concomitantly education, schools and teachers are primarily concerned with serving such needs rather than societal ones, usefully endows teacher control with greater conviction and certitude.

Foucault mentions those 'modes of objectification' entailing the objectivizing of the subject through 'dividing practices'. The subject is 'either divided inside himself [sic] or divided from others' (ibid., pp. 777–8). In the case of children within the education system, this may be taken to include students being divided from both adults and themselves in a way which is largely facilitated by just one negative categorization, that of the dismissal of children's study activities as 'non-labour' and 'non-productive'. Students are thereby divided from their productive selves – in the first place in that their *actual* productive labour is neither recognized nor materially rewarded; and in the second place in that by being separated from participation in *paid* productive labour they are also being divided from their full productive capacity, capabilities, potential and development.

Following Foucault, student struggles will be against that form of power which makes individuals subjects in two senses and ways: 'subject to someone else by control and dependence; and tied to his [sic] own identity by a conscience or self-knowledge. Both meanings suggest a form of power which subjugates and makes subject to' (ibid., p. 781). Thus, students (in conjunction with being divided from adults: the adult world, paid employment, and so on) are subjected to the control of – and associated dependency upon – teachers, educators, the state and employers; and are subjected to their own self knowledge as 'immature', 'non-adult', 'non-producing', and the like. However, we can anticipate that the process of objectivizing students' subjectivity will fall far short of being complete, inevitable and final; and that consequently the presence and perseverance of subjectivity will render students capable of resistance against the objectification of their subjectivity; and by way of this, of resistance against the control and dependence which characterizes their relationships with teachers.

Student resistance represents a limit on and measure of the control and power wielded by teachers, education and the state. This seems to lie behind Foucault's proposal that in trying to make sense of power relations it would be appropriate and useful to develop a theory which begins with and focuses on resistance, and more specifically on the forms or types of resistance which characterize what we might refer to as 'power-resistance relations': on the types of struggle aimed at disrupting and dislodging power (ibid., p. 780; pp. 793–4). Foucault argues that 'generally, it can be said that there are three types of struggles: [. . .] against forms of domination (ethnic, social and religious); against forms of exploitation which separate individuals from what they produce; or against that which ties the individual to himself [sic] and submits him to others in this way (struggles against subjection, against forms of subjectivity and submission)' (ibid., p. 781). Foucault proposes that, 'most of the time', one of these three forms tends to prevail (ibid., p. 782), so that 'nowadays, the struggle against the forms of subjection – against the submission of subjectivity – is becoming more and more important' (ibid., p. 782). In other words, the predominant form of what we might refer to as 'power-struggle relations' in modern society is 'a struggle for a new subjectivity' (ibid., p. 782).

However, I wish to argue that student relationships with teachers, schools and (through these) the state[45] are characterized by a (perhaps unique) unity of all three forms of power-struggle relations, involving resistance across the board against domination, exploitation and subjection, whereby perhaps no one form is predominant, and all three forms are mutually supportive and dependent. Students are (socially, ideologically, institutionally) divided from adults, and are then controlled and dominated by certain adult representatives or agents, namely teachers. Students are equally exploited by being separated (alienated) from what they produce: in that (a) they receive no appropriate recognition or remuneration for what they actually produce (their own embodied labour power): and (b) they have no (or limited) control over what and how they actually produce – for instance, within the education system they have no (or little) control over their study activities, their time and space, the formal and hidden curricula, and so on.[46]

In so far as there is a combination of domination, exploitation and subjection of students by teachers – and, through teachers, by the state – we might expect, following Foucault, education to constitute a likely (a *primed*) social location for opposition, resistance and struggle in modern society. Moreover, we might expect student resistance to be enhanced given that within and through education there is an emphasis on control rather than care; or more precisely an emphasis on 'control over', 'protection of' and 'caring for' to the relative neglect of 'caring about'. We might expect further, not only that historically speaking resistance on the part of students in general, will be on the increase, but also that at any moment student resistance will be highly socially contingent and variable. That is, student resistance will be dependent upon and shaped by certain major social themes and cleavages, especially those connected with social class, sex-gender, race-ethnicity and age-generation; so that the likelihood of resistance will be greater among, for instance, working-class students and older (adolescent) students.[47]

However, even though older, working-class students may be in practice more likely than younger, middle-class students to engage in opposition, resistance and struggle, this may not be simply an outcome of heightened, more overt, and more obvious control, domination, exploitation and subjection in relation to such students. As I have previously outlined, the matter is more complex than this. Nonetheless, the various complicating threads which run through student-teacher power-resistance relations are, as far as I am concerned, expressions of the operation of just one principal or pivotal social mechanism which is alluded to (but only alluded to) by Foucault himself. That is, Foucault argues that the struggles against subjection (ibid., p. 782) tend 'to prevail in our society [. . .] due to the fact that, since the sixteenth century, a new political form of power has been continuously developing. This new political structure [. . .] is the state' (ibid., p. 782).

Foucault's explanation of the emergent 'series of oppositions' (ibid., p. 780) in modern society 'are struggles which question the status of the individual [and] underline everything which makes individuals truly individual' (ibid., p. 781), is that they are 'struggles against the "government of individualization"' (ibid., p. 781), against 'state violence, which ignore[s] who we are individually' (ibid., p. 781). Foucault claims that the state is not 'a kind of political power which ignores individuals [in] the interests of the totality or [of] a [social] class' within the totality (ibid., p. 782). Instead, 'the state's power [. . .] is both an individualizing and a totalizing form of power' (ibid., p. 782). The modern state is unique in that it juggles and struggles with a 'tricky combination in the same political structures of individualization techniques and totalization procedures' (ibid., p. 782). In essence:

> An important [change] took place around the eighteenth century – it [entailed] a new distribution, a new organisation of [. . .] individualizing power. [The] 'modern state' [is not] an entity which developed above individuals, ignoring what they are and even their very existence, but, on the contrary, as a very sophisticated structure in which individuals can be integrated, under one condition: that this individuality would be shaped in a new form and submitted to a set of very specific patterns. (ibid., p. 783)

What Foucault appears to be referring to is the way the modern state within any liberal democracy tries to pursue the needs and interests of the individual as a priority, but attempts to do so within society centred upon itself. This is done purportedly in accordance with the principle that the individual (his or her needs and interests) are (best) served within society, by being to some extent socialized and shaped by society: by being 'subjected' by society within a process of objectivization. But, what this means is that society and the state will also be 'totalizing' (and generalizing) forces, which in subsuming the individual may well operate against (the needs and interests of) the individual (*qua* an individual). The central issue, problem or dilemma for the state in a liberal democracy is that of setting itself the task of pursuing and balancing the needs and interests of both the individual and society (and thereby itself, the state) – to which it is also committed: of pursuing the needs and interests of society up to – but only up to – the point at which it 'best' (optimally) serves the needs and interests of the individual; of pursuing the needs and interests of society by being prepared to sacrifice some of the needs and interests of the individual (or some degree of individuality) at the same time.

As Patrick Dunleavy and Brendan O'Leary put it:

> The 'liberal' component in liberal democracy derives from liberalism – a pre-democratic political ideology which asserts that there should be as much individual freedom in any society as is compatible with the freedom of others. Liberalism is an individualist creed, which mushroomed in the seventeenth and eighteenth centuries [. . .] Traditionally, liberals have wanted freedom from the state, demanding that some individual

freedoms, or rights, should be protected from the state and majority decisions [. . .] Put more formally, liberal democracy is a system of representative majority rule [through the state] in which some individual rights are nonetheless protected from interference by the state and cannot be restricted even by an electoral majority. (1987, pp. 5–6)

While assigning priority to the needs, interests and rights of the individual, liberal democratic philosophy, principles and policies favour also society, the state and 'individual subjection' – the sacrifice of, to some extent, the individual/individualism. In trying to handle the liberal dilemma in practice – in trying to pursue and (optimally) balance both individual freedom and individual subjection – the modern state establishes or feeds into a particular social mechanism which may well be the principal (key) driving force behind expressions of opposition, resistance, struggle and rebellion on the part of children and students (among others). The modern state supports, promotes and facilitates (affirms) 'individual freedom' (or the realization of individual capacities, capabilities, potential and development) through its caring policies, services and agents (such as those of an educational kind within the overall spread of social services). However, simultaneously, the same mechanisms provide the means by which the state subjugates (shapes, constrains and controls) and negates the same item – 'individual freedom'.[48]

For me, the simultaneous affirmation and negation of 'individual freedom', or individuality, means that within modern society the individual is subjected to – and subjectively experiences – a contradiction; this particular instance, spearheaded by the state through the operation of educational organizations and personnel. I wish to argue that this contradiction is the pivotal social mechanism behind the particular (contingent) social patterns and trends which characterize student resistance: behind for instance any historical increase in the breadth and depth of resistance, especially among older (adolescent), working class students; as well as among both female and 'ethnic minority', or 'ethnically oppressed', students.[49] In turn (dialectically), such resistance feeds into further social change, specifically towards the resolution of the contradiction, and therefore in favour of the progressive development of individuality.

Of course, a perspective on social change which stresses the importance of contradictions is far from new. For instance, with the prospect of social revolution in mind, Mao Tse-Tung proposed that 'the basic cause of the development of a thing is not external but internal, and lies in its internal contradictions' (1958, p. 4). In fact, the term 'contradiction' has wide currency within sociological and related (especially Marxist, feminist and other 'critical') literature, including that concerned with education.[50] The popularity of the term suggests recognition of the sociological relevance and value of 'contradiction'. However, a doubt hangs over this inference given that the term is not only widely used, but also variously defined, in so far as it is explicitly defined at all. The way in which the term appears in the literature embraces its deployment to refer to several disparate things; its frequent use with no clear or consistent social reference point or meaning; and, occasionally, its inclusion obviously devoid of any interest in the issue of meaning.[51]

The term has been used by Sandra Taylor, apparently to indicate the central argument running through what she has to say about her empirical study of a commercial studies class in a Queensland secondary school. Her discussion focuses on the issue of schooling's part in cultural and social reproduction, with particular reference to the reproduction of 'patriarchal and hierarchical relationships', through 'the structuring of school experience' (1984, p. 3). Her analysis hinges upon the proposition that 'a number of recent changes in the structure of the workforce and the nature of office work, have resulted in a number of "contradictions" in the school/work relationship' (ibid., p. 3). She suggests: 'Contradictions may be described as areas of tensions and resistance where reproduction does not occur smoothly. An understanding of the contradictions [. . .] is crucial in providing a basis for the development of a pedagogy for change' (ibid., pp. 3–4). While Taylor seems to recognize the theoretical and practical importance of being familiar with and taking into account the contradictory character of modern schooling in relation to sex-gender inequalities, she fails to indicate clearly what precisely she means (is referring to) by the term 'contradiction'.[52] The most likely possibility is that she draws a conceptual equation between (a) 'contradiction' and (b) ('areas of') 'tension' and 'resistance'. For Taylor, 'contradictions' may be synonymous with 'tensions' and 'resistance', rather than distinct from and, say, sources of the latter. Of course, Taylor cannot be dismissed as being wrong for assuming a definition along these lines. Nonetheless, certain sociologically pertinent questions arise: 'is she drawing such an equation?'; 'if she is not, what does she mean in general by "contradiction"?'; 'if she is, why is she?'; 'if she is, what is the sociological point and value of doing so?'; 'if she is, what is the point and value of employing the term "contradiction" to refer to something for which there are alternative terms, namely "tensions" and "resistance"?'; 'if she is, what is the relationship between the meaning she attaches to "contradiction" and the meanings given elsewhere?'.

For instance, with regard to this last question, the issue arises of the relationship between the meaning Taylor gives the term 'contradiction' and the meaning(s) to be found in *The Concise Oxford Dictionary.* Thus: 'contradiction, n. Denial; opposition; [. . .] inconsistency'; and 'contradict, v.t. Deny (statement) [. . .] be contrary to'. The point in the end about Taylor's handling of the term 'contradiction'[53] is that it is somewhat typical, in the sense that it represents the treatment regularly given to the issue of the meaning and definition of the term in sociological and related discourses. Michael Apple sees the importance of the notion of 'contradiction' in the way it helps overcome the determinist, reductionist and reproductionist limitations of structuralism by reflecting the parts played by resistance and struggle within educational processes and developments:

> For all the power of structuralist criticisms of culturalism, structuralism has not been immune from some important criticisms itself. Unlike the interest in the real lives and knowledge of concrete classes of actors that one finds in the work of culturalists such as Thompson, structuralist investigations have tended to be quite abstract [. . .] Furthermore, structuralism has been involved in an even more serious dilemma in that it has often reduced a good deal of the complexities of a social formation into a kind of functionalism. [. . .] That is, ideology and culture – while having a degree of relative autonomy [. . .] – 'are subsumed within a single function: the reproduction of the conditions of capitalist production' (Johnson 1979: 69; see also Connell 1979). Like some of the [. . .] work of the political economists of education, it ultimately undertheorizes struggles, disjunctions and contradictions. As Richard Johnson nicely puts it, in structuralist analysis: 'the overriding concern with outcomes – "reproduction" – suppresses the fact that these conditions have continually to be won – or lost – in particular conflicts and struggles' (Johnson, 1979: 70). (Apple, 1982b, p. 14)[54]

Apple goes on to underline his view about the sociological value of 'contradiction' by suggesting that it is 'a time of rapid advance in our understanding both of the intricate nature of the nexus which provides the connections and contradictions among the economic, cultural and political spheres and of the possibilities for organized action in each of these spheres' (ibid., p. 16). But the lucidity and impact of the point Apple is trying to make here is reduced by his failure to formulate a general, abstract definition of 'contradiction', and otherwise to give some unambiguous clue as to what he means by the term.

Within the same volume, the relationship between 'structuralist analysis and contradictions and struggles specifically in education is taken up by' both Martin Carnoy and Roger Dale (ibid., p. 14). However, Martin Carnoy (1982) apart from also failing to be explicit about what he means by 'contradiction', seems to slide into incorporating the term within a reductionist and determinist framework. Carnoy argues (according to Apple) that education is a 'state apparatus that is both the result of social and economic contradictions and the source of new contradictions at one and the same time' (Apple, 1982(b), pp. 19–20). Carnoy makes the important and critical point (consistent with a Marxist perspective) that educational institutions, processes and reproduction, along with educational (re)action, resistance and struggle – all of which belong to the 'superstructure' (ibid., p. 20) – are explicable in terms of underlying 'contradictions in the "base" ' (ibid., p. 20), but in turn feed into, exacerbate and amplify the same contradictions. Thus, 'action in education – in and outside of formal school settings – can in fact potentially make a positive contribution to labor's position [. . .] due to the close relationship that [. . .] exists between struggle in both base and superstructure' (ibid., p. 20).

Carnoy appears to be suggesting that the economic contradictions which he sees as the underlying source of what occurs within and through education are in turn (dialectically) shaped and sharpened by the latter, thereby boosting the way these contradictions drive social change (by way of social experience) towards their own resolution; and more precisely in favour of their own eventual progressive resolution. In accordance with his Marxist approach, the progressive development of the working class (both as individuals and as a collectivity) occurs essentially and eventually through the character and contradictions of the underlying economic base: wherein the human and productive potential of the working class is negatively treated and thwarted within economic (productive and class) relationships by virtue of capitalist exploitation and domination (oppression) – even though, simultaneously, this development receives a positive push through the working class's experience within education. Thus, in his discussion of an

> educational strategy, Carnoy agrees that a key element is [. . .] the creation of counter-hegemony outside the schools [and that the resulting] counter hegemonic forces can be important tools in enabling, say, working-class youth to resist the use of schools in 'maintaining and extending bourgeois dominance'. (ibid., p. 20)

In the end, Carnoy traces what happens within and through education – and more specifically what happens with regard to the working class's educational experience, resistance and counterstrategies – back to an underlying economic base. Located within the economic base is the main source of working class experience and, connectedly, the crucial strategies towards fundamental and general social change and progress. For Carnoy, the determining source of working class experience, resistance and progress lies firmly within the economic base; and more precisely within the economic contradictions which characterize and drive both the capitalist mode of production (CMP), along with its client educational system towards change in the interests of the working class.

However, as an alternative to Carnoy's approach, it may be plausibly assumed that the education system is pervaded by a specific set of contradictions which are themselves a driving force behind educational and broader social change, while not being merely reducible to – and so epiphenomena of – underlying economic contradictions. I wish to argue that there is a set of somewhat distinctive and discrete educational contradictions, which drive the educational system (by way of student experience and resistance) towards improvement (in the sense of a progressive resolution of such contradictions) and so towards the positive realization of the human potential embodied in the members of the working-class among people in general. This is not to ignore the possibility of educational contradictions being intimately tied to economic contradictions, by way of feeding off and in turn (dialectically) feeding into the latter.

In any case, educational contradictions on the one hand, and economic contradictions on the other, may merge into each other; and may even distil down to some common contradiction: perhaps that contradiction whereby 'individuality' – or individual (human) capacity and potential – is simultaneously both affirmed (promoted) and negated (denied). Any such association or assimilation between the educational system and the economy will be facilitated by the way the state intervenes in the process of individual (human) development *and* mediates between the individual and the economy through the educational system. After all, essentially, the (dual or liberal) purpose of the educational system is (a) individual (human) development – by way of some kind of institutional unity between care and control; and (b) social development and stability, perhaps centred on the requirements of economic structures and processes – requirements which include (from Carnoy's perspective) the particular needs and interests of the capitalist class.

Elsewhere, Carnoy (with H. Levin) shows that he accepts the idea of educationally specific contradictions. He lists what he counts as (what he interprets as exemplifying) educational contradictions in particular, while at the same time indicating what he means by (how he defines) 'contradiction' in general. He proposes that there are

> three types of contradictions associated with schooling, all of which result directly or indirectly from the tension that arises between the [liberal, individualist] democratic thrust of schools and their role in

reproducing the class and work structure. The first type of contradiction manifests itself in the political struggle over resources for schooling. [. . .] A second type of contradiction is internal to the educational process. The reproductive dynamic creates pressures in schools to produce a labor force with skills, attitudes and values that fit into the hierarchical division of labor and to reproduce capitalist relations of production. At the same time, the [liberal] democratic dynamic emphasizes individual liberty and democratic participation as well as equality of opportunity and occupational mobility through education. [. . .] To a large degree, establishing a curriculum, teaching process, and educational structure that support one set of requirements must be done at the expense of the other. [. . .] A third type of contradiction is imported into the educational process through the fact that the schools correspond with the workplace [. . .] Especially important is the educational manifestations of the contradiction between capital and labor.' (Carnoy and Levin, 1985a, pp. 145–6)

According to this, contradictions arise out of the liberal democratic dilemma ('tension') of trying to balance (a) the needs and interests of the individual with (b) the needs and interests of society, the economy and the capitalist class – where the resulting contradictions appear to amount to the same thing as conflicts. For instance, when Carnoy refers to the contradiction between capital and labour, he appears to mean the conflict (of interests) between the two major social classes under capitalism, by virtue of the way capitalist relations of production are exploitative and oppressive. Carnoy goes some way (but only some way) towards more explicitly drawing an equation along such lines:

Education [. . .] is set in the context of social conflict and is an integral part of such conflict. Public schools in America are an institution of the State [sic], and like other State institutions are subject to the pull of two conflicting forces over their control, purpose, and operation. On the one hand, schools reproduce the unequal, hierarchical relations of the capitalist workplace; on the other, schooling represents the primary force in the United States for expanding economic opportunity for subordinate groups and the extension of democratic rights. These forces are in opposition, creating contradictions – i.e. conflicts and internal incompatibilities – in education that result in a continuing struggle over direction. Although at any given time one of the forces may appear to dominate and achieve hegemony, the existence of underlying contradiction means that struggle continues in various latent forms. (ibid., p. 144)

This statement includes the idea that 'contradictions' are synonymous with 'conflicts'. Also, however, it covers the possibility that such an equation does not quite hold, in that (for Carnoy) 'conflicting forces' in relation to education bring about (create), perhaps distinct contradictions. What Carnoy means by 'contradiction', and sees as the conceptual and practical relationship between 'contradiction' and 'conflict', becomes even more hazy when he goes on to suggest that 'Contradiction is at the heart of educational change by generating a series of continuing conflicts and accommodations that transform the shape of the schooling process. Changes generated by educational contradictions also induce changes in the work place. (ibid., p. 144).

Here, Carnoy appears to be arguing that contradictions bring about, perhaps distinct, conflicts. The uncertainty and confusion is increased when Carnoy goes on to make a statement which appears both to distinguish between 'contradiction' and 'conflict' and, at the same time, to use the two terms interchangeably:

> Schools are characterized by contradiction and conflict through their very function of serving American capitalist expansion and the democratic political system. These democratic and class-reproductive dynamics are conditioned by the larger social conflict outside the schools. To the extent that the democratic dynamic gains ground, the educational system diverges in certain respects from the structural exigencies of reproducing capitalist relations of production and the division of labor. This divergence in turn, is capable of exacerbating or changing the character of social conflict. It is therefore not only conflict in production that can lead to crises in capitalist development, but also contradictions in reproduction. In the latter case, crisis emerges from the failure of one of the more important institutions of reproduction to reproduce properly the labor skills, the division of labor, and the social relations of production. (ibid., pp. 144–5)

From this, any distinction between 'contradiction' and 'conflict' which Carnoy may not altogether dismiss is nonetheless difficult to grasp. In the end, perhaps this difficulty simply reflects Carnoy's own problem about managing to be clear and consistent about a distinction. Perhaps for Carnoy it is sufficient to view any contradiction between democratic dynamics and class-reproductive dynamics as simply a conflict (not to mention a 'divergence', and so on) between the same two things: perhaps for Carnoy, in other words, there is nothing to be gained from pursuing any distinction in meaning. However, in this case the term 'contradiction' is rendered super-fluous and redundant. To avoid wasting a notion in this way, the alternative is to employ the terms 'contradiction' and 'conflict' to refer to distinct social processes, albeit ones which are practically, experientially and conceptually entwined. One possibility – and one which seems to me to be sociologically worthwhile pursuing – is to use only the term 'contradiction' to refer to the kind of divergent and dynamic process addressed by Carnoy with regard to education, leaving the term 'conflict' to be deployed otherwise. Accordingly, I wish to argue that the 'divergence' or disjunction occurring within, through and around education between (following Carnoy's terminology) democratic dynamics and class-reproductive dynamics represents a major structural contradiction, and as such a principal (perhaps *the* principal or pivotal) source of relational conflict associated with modern educational systems. This relational conflict is manifested in various instances and types of student opposition, resistance and struggle (as illustrated earlier). In turn, such relational conflict dialectically feeds into, promotes and sharpens the dynamic, structural contradiction between the (political) pursuit of liberal democratic individualism and the (economic) reproduction of the capitalist mode (relations) of production.[55]

In the same volume, edited by Apple, Roger Dale (1982) also examines the contradictions confronting education (Apple, 1982a, p. 20) with reference to, in particular, the dual and overlapping economic and political ramifications of educational processes. Furthermore, again like Carnoy, Dale fails to formulate a precise definition of 'contradiction', and at best merely alludes to some kind of general notion which appears again to equate the term with 'tension' and 'conflict'. Dale identifies a set of 'core problems for the capitalist State [*sic*]': problems which confront 'all state apparatus and institutions including the education system' (Dale, 1982, p. 133). He lists three such 'problem areas confronting state education systems', and argues that 'the means of their solution are mutually contradictory; this mutual contradiction provides a dynamic for education systems' (ibid., p. 130). The three 'broad core problems for the capitalist state' (ibid., p. 133) are (a) supporting 'the capital accumulation process'; (b) 'guaranteeing a context for continued expansion'; (c) legitimating 'the capitalist mode of production, including the State's own part in it' (ibid., p. 133).

Dale proposes that 'because all the problems are related to the same over-all purpose, their solutions must be complementary with each other: they are, in fact, mutually contradictory' (ibid., p. 135). He goes on to argue (as summarized by Apple):

It is [the] assemblage of mutual contradictions that provides a good deal of the driving force behind the dynamics of educational systems. Yet, as Dale notes, we cannot pre-specify either the means or the outcomes of the process by which the State may intervene to 'solve' each of these core problems. We need to analyze the role of the State in both its specificity at that historical moment and the possible resistances which may be engendered by its attempts to resolve these contradictory problems. [. . .] Dale concludes that by the very fact that educational systems are part of an inherently contradictory state apparatus, that since education is as much an aspect of the political as well as economic sphere this provides for the very real possibility for effective resistance and action. (Apple, 1982b, pp. 20–21)

In these passages, the precise meaning of the term 'contradiction' as used by Apple and by Dale is not clear. For instance, the conceptual and so practical differences and relationships between 'contradictions' and such other phenomena as 'core problems', 'the solutions to the core problems', and 'resistance' are not obvious. However, Dale does give an insight into what he probably means by the notion of 'contradiction' when he argues, consistent with a Marxist approach, that the contradictions (or core problems) associated with education can be traced to and explained in terms of an underlying, basic or central problem (or contradiction) within capitalist societies. Here Dale demonstrates that, in the end, his approach to 'contradiction' very much resembles Carnoy's. Thus:

The central contradiction is, of course, that while the capitalist mode of production is driven by the creation (through the universalization of the commodity form) and realization of surplus value, the conditions for its success and reproduction can only be guaranteed through the extraction of some part of that surplus value by the State and its diversion into non-commodity forms. This creates a central tension between the State and capital. [The] most important point is that [the provision of the conditions of capital accumulation] are not merely varied but mutually contradictory. The contradictions involved in tackling the core problems of the State are seen as intrinsic and incapable of permanent solution. For instance [. . .] the whole welfare state apparatus, which gave capitalism a much more human face, and by demonstrating that it (capitalism) could care for all its dependants, enabled the State to preserve a context amenable to capital accumulation. However, the maintenance and increase of the benefits of the welfare state became major political matters, through immense strain on the process of surplus value creation to provide the means for it to continue delivering the goods, and on the legitimating mechanisms to make up for any shortfall of such delivery. The point is that the State does not have at its disposal the means of quickly and cleanly cauterizing these contradictions. They can only be solved in ways that lay the seeds of further contradictions. Thus 'buying loyalty' in various ways is fine, but the price keeps going up as privileges become rights; creating mechanisms to disguise the nature of state activity is fine, but there is the danger that they will come to be taken at their word. ('Education for personal development' is one of the best examples of this.) (Dale, 1982, pp. 135–6)

In this account, what is contradictory? What contradicts what, and in what sense? What is meant by 'contradictory' and 'contradiction'? Again, Dale does not specify his notion of 'contradiction', leaving us unclear about what his list of contradictions are instances of in general ('contradictions' in what sense?); and for that matter unclear about the precise identity of his contradictions. There is a good chance that by 'contradiction', Dale means 'conflict' (and/or 'tension'), such as that between the state and capitalists over the distribution of surplus value. In so far as this is a valid interpretation, Dale may be misunderstanding or misrepresenting Marx's original views and notions of 'conflict' and 'contradiction' pertaining to the operation of the CMP. [56]

For Marx, conflict certainly and endemically occurs at the point of the distribution of value; but in the first instance between the capitalist class and the working-class over the distribution of the value produced by the latter. However, this point is not the location of the basic or central contradiction under capitalism (within the CMP). For Marx, this contradiction occurs prior to and underlies the distributional conflict (the relational conflict over the distribution of value) between capitalists and the state; as well as between the capitalist class and the working class. The conflict between capitalists and the state may well be over the distribution of surplus value, but that between the capitalist class and the working class occurs as a prelude to such (capitalist-state) conflict. Class conflict accompanies the process of the production of surplus value. Surplus value is the value expropriated by the capitalist class: it is the value over and above that which the working class receives and enjoys out of the total value it has laboured to produce. Surplus value is, therefore, the outcome and measure of the exploitative (and oppressive) character of capitalist relations of production: it is the sign of the inherently conflictual character of the relations between the two principal social classes under capitalism, the capitalist class and the working class. These two social classes are inherently (or objectively) engaged in relational conflict with regard to the distribution of value produced (wholly) through the labour of the working class, and by virtue of the exploitation and associated oppression of the latter by the capitalist class.

Accordingly, the resolution of the class conflict (of interests) under capitalism, following Marx, can only be resolved by way of the (revolutionary) introduction of a mechanism – the socialist mode of production – where such exploitation does not occur: where surplus value is not produced, in that the workers receive and enjoy the full value they have produced through their labour (activity) and labour power. However, despite the inherent class conflict under capitalism, there is nothing about capitalist relations of production in themselves which necessarily drives them in a progressive direction towards the socialist resolution and revolution. The drive in this direction is inevitable and irresistible – not as a result of the character of capitalist relations of production as such – but by virtue of the character of the relationship between (a) capitalist relations of production and (b) the prevailing (capitalist) forces of production. That is, the relationship between these two levels of the economic infrastructure under capitalism (of the CMP) occurs by way of, in particular, the working class's experience under capitalism (the working class's experience as human, individual and social beings; as labourers and producers; as producers of value – use value, exchange value and surplus value; as consumers of value; and so on); and moreover, this relationship and this experience are contradictory in character – perhaps as acknowledged by Dale when he refers to the 'central contradiction' under capitalism.

Under capitalism, the working class is subjected to (and subjectively experiences) a contradictory process – contradictory messages. On the one hand, it experiences an affirmative promise *vis-à-vis* its human and social development by virtue of the capacity of the prevailing (capitalist) forces of production. The capacity of the forces of production under capitalism to meet people's physiological, psychological and creative requirements has a tendency to continuously expand: is progressive. On the other hand, simultaneously, the working class experiences a negative denial with regard to the very same human and social items by virtue of the prevailing capitalist relations of production, which are thereby regressive.

Despite the promise and prospect presented by the forces of production under capitalism with regard to the working class's 'needs', the reality of the exploitative and oppressive character of capitalist relations of production prevents even its 'basic needs' from being adequately and reliably met. The forces of production under capitalism could be deployed to satisfy the human, individual and social developmental requirements of everyone; but they are deployed instead primarily for the purpose of producing surplus value to satisfy the specific requirements of (in the interests of) capitalism and the capitalist class. The forces of production are used contrary to the developmental requirements of the working class by being used to sustain another social class – the capitalist class – which exploits and oppresses it. The forces of production are used to maintain the relations of production, the mode of production and the total (capitalist) social formation within which the working class is alienated from its full potential for human, individual, collective and social development.

Following this kind of analysis, it is only a short step to the proposition that the working class's continuing alienation, oppression and exploitation under capitalism is partly achieved through a share of surplus value being utilized by way of the state's educational provision, among other social services, which 'functions' to reproduce a labour force in accordance with the requirements of capitalism and the capitalist class. Such a view may then be used to account for – or to anticipate degrees of – both co-operation and competition (even conflict) between capital and the state. Such 'tension' (to use Dale's term) helps remind us to steer clear of slipping into crude functionalism and teleology. It means that the educational system runs far from smoothly in serving up a labour force which fully meets the needs of capitalism. But, we should also remember that this limitation on the effectiveness of educational system is a result not only of the state's restricted share of surplus value, but also of the way in which to some extent state policies, practices and arrangements are shaped by 'liberal democratic' ideals centred on the individual, individualism and individual development. That is, as recognized and emphasized by both Carnoy and Dale, the educational system has not only an *economic* side, by which it is linked to the CMP and serves the interests of the capitalist class; but also *political* features, by which it promotes ideas, values and practices that are (at least somewhat) 'dysfunctional' with regard to the CMP and the capitalist class. In other words, in order to make sense of what actually happens within the educational system – with reference to such aspects as working-class experience, struggle and resistance; student-teacher relational conflict; and progressive change – we have to recognize, identify and take into account educational contradictions.

There will be a set of contradictions which are specific to the educational system (perhaps along the lines listed by Carnoy and/or Dale): a set which represents the degree to which the educational system is distinctive, separate and perhaps autonomous within the total (capitalist) social formation. At the same time, educational contradictions may be merely particular instances of some more inclusive and general social contradiction. Educational contradictions may have something essential in common with, for instance, economic contradictions – something in common which reflects the way both sets of contradictions are merely institutionally specific (either educational or economic) refractions of the same general social contradiction.

Thus, educational contradictions may represent, in an institutionally specific manner, the same global social contradiction as is also manifested (following Marx) in the central economic contradiction under capitalism which occurs within the economic base between the (progressive) forces of production and the (regressive) relations of production *vis-à-vis* the working class (its interests, needs, potential, development, experience, and so on).

Within the total social formation there may be a society-wide, core (to borrow Dale's term) contradiction – one which in the final analysis is the pivotal one behind relational conflict, struggle and resistance throughout society; and the crucial one behind fundamental and overall social change. This core contradiction – which is then variously expressed in the institutionally specific contradictions associated with, for instance, the economy and the educational system – being that whereby individuality (individual subjectivity, freedom, potential, development, needs, and so on) is simultaneously affirmed (promised, promoted) and negated (denied, constrained).

The total social formation will be driven largely by this core contradiction in a progressive direction – towards, in other words, the contradiction's resolution in favour of individuality, or an optimum balance between 'the individual' and 'society'. This will occur by way of the various institutionally specific contradictory processes and experiences, such as those within the educational system. Within education, the contradictory messages received by students will mean experiential disunity, disjunction, discrepancy and divergence, and thereby uncertainty, confusion and tension; perhaps especially as students get older and the contradiction between educational promise and educational reality becomes more acute, pressing and even threatening. The result will be a tendency for adolescent students – especially working-class, female and ethnic minority (ethnically oppressed) ones – to react in favour of the resolution of the core contradiction by resisting the regressive educational messages of denial, constraint and control. Accordingly, adolescent working-class students will tend to engage in relational conflict (with teachers, for instance); or more precisely in conflict of a progressive kind, in that it is both an assertion of individuality and a vehicle for educational and societal change in the direction of an optimum balance between the individual and society.

The core social contradiction will be expressed within all social spheres through institutionally specific contradictions, which nonetheless comprise (following Apple's terminology) a 'nexus', whereby they interrelate and articulate.[57] Perhaps a major means by which this nexus of contradictions is constructed is state activity. Perhaps such activity helps explain why contradictions are to be found not only in state run social services and state organized social spheres such as education, but also in the more 'private' social arenas, such as *the family*. As we have seen, the occurrence of family contradictions in conjunction with gender contradictions has been touched on by Lois Bryson in her remarks on domestic labour and control; and the possibility of helping to account for these contradictions and the articulation between them in terms of state mediation and intervention has been indicated by K. Saville-Smith.

Certainly, quite a lot has been written which is purportedly about contradictions within the various social spheres,[58] but this literature is still plagued by uncertainty, inconsistency and confusion over the meaning of 'contradiction'. However, there are a few contributions which are exceptional in this regard. One writer who has been explicitly and fruitfully interested in the issue of conceptualizing 'contradiction', and has settled on an approach which is similar to my own, is D.H.J. Morgan (1975).[59] In trying to clarify the notion of 'contradiction', Morgan compares it with 'conflict':

> Contradiction is [. . .] to be distinguished from 'conflict'. 'Conflict' is often too ambiguous a term: it may be manifest or latent, individual or collective, overt or covert. Conflict may also be seen as something which is pathological or residual or as something which can be overcome within the existing system. Conflict may be a manifestation of a contradiction but it is not the same thing. A contradiction may exist in a system without there being any overt manifestations of conflict. (ibid., p. 97)

Here Morgan is referring to the way contradictions are processes which are socially deep, underlying and pervasive, emerging to some extent at a more superficial level in a highly contingent, problematic and multifarious manner as *conflict*. Connectedly, in contrast with 'conflict', a 'contradiction is resolved dialectically bringing about a major change in the system of which it is part. The term "contradiction" is therefore [. . .] dynamic and includes the notion of change at its heart' (ibid., p. 97). A contradiction is necessarily, inherently dynamic: an incessant driving force behind social change, including that of a fundamental and revolutionary kind, as well as of a progressive kind. On the other hand, a conflict occurs between at least two positions or factions that are diametrically opposed to each other, being engaged in a struggle towards each other's loss, defeat and annihilation. Conflict may be not only highly superficial, epiphenomenal and ephemeral (albeit deeply rooted within contradictions), but also wholly negative in its character and consequences. There is nothing about conflict in itself which ensures positive (progressive) change, even though it may be a vehicle by way of which contradictions in resolving themselves are sources of such change.

As *The Concise Oxford Dictionary* puts it: 'conflict, n. Fight, struggle [. . .] collision, clashing (of opposed principles etc.)'. A conflict occurs when (at least) two forces clash with each other head on and across a divide; but a contradiction occurs when two forces converge at the same point represented by a social item (such as capitalism, democracy or individuality). In the case of a contradiction, one force affirms the item and the other force contradicts this affirmation by negating (or denying or constraining) the item. The social item or point, by virtue of being subjected to and thereby experiencing contradictory forces or messages, while favouring its own affirmation, becomes the *locus* of social change – prospectively in a positive or progressive direction. Morgan puts it as follows: 'Contradiction in a social system may be defined as the experience of simultaneous affirmation and negation within the system in respect of an issue' (1975, p. 96). This definition very nearly corresponds with my own general conception of 'contradiction'. However, my preference is to omit any reference to 'experience' so as to avoid the implication that contradictions occur simply at this level. For me, contradictions are in the first place societal (including structural) processes, which will consequently be *experienced* in some way – while not necessarily being perceived or recognized as contradictions as such. Experience is not essential to the existence of contradictions; experience is only essential to the resolution of contradictions, in that experience is the medium through which they are self-resolving. Accordingly, I define 'contradiction' as that term which refers to the occurrence of the simultaneous affirmation and negation of a social item or issue – such as capitalism, democracy or individuality.

Morgan's principal focus is on family contradictions, and he explains that the 'basis for there being contradictions in the modern family lies in the fact that it is at one and the same time part of a wider system and relatively bounded in its own right' (ibid., p. 97). Morgan provides an example relating to family socialization: '[in] the first place we may note the contradiction between the fact that the family is seen as the main agency of socialization and the fact that part of this socialization is in terms of roles outside the family' (ibid., p. 97). What Morgan seems to be arguing is that family socialization is simultaneously both affirmed (supported) – such as by the state – and negated (undermined) due to the way the family overlaps with, provides preparation for, and may be in competition with various other social spheres, such the economy and the educational system. While

the state may affirm, support and promote (the distinctiveness and independence of) the family and family socialization, it will simultaneously
negate, deny and undermine the same items by virtue of the way it provides
and even imposes a (compulsory) educational system. The resulting contradiction *vis-à-vis* family life, socialization and autonomy will be experienced
by parents, who will be inclined to react by resisting the negative message
of denial, constraint and control. Hence, parents may engage in relational
conflict with educational organizations and personnel in favour of progressive change. Perhaps in this way we can better understand the recent
policies and programmes of the state in many Western societies which are
– in the wake of the expansion of formal education – ostensibly intended
to allow and encourage greater parental and community participation in
everyday educational decision-making (although, of course, the full explanation for this shift must take into account the appeal to governments
of easing the financial costs of the educational system).

Such a shift has been widely recognized and attributed with considerable
significance *vis-à-vis* the distribution of power and control in relation to
formal education. Thus:

> Australian education systems would appear to be in general retreat from
> the centralised model. The United States, where school boards consti-
> tuted by parents and local communities hold much educational control,
> including hiring and firing of staff, is often cited as an example of
> democratic, relevant school education. It is towards a similar model
> which the most cumbersome of Australia's education systems are turn-
> ing. Schools councils with the power to select principals were estab-
> lished in Victoria [. . .] some 15 years ago. Their muscle was augmented
> early in the 1980s when they were given additional responsibilities for
> finance management and curriculum. (Kennedy, 1990)

However, the impression that the shift towards greater parental and
community involvement represents a more fundamental trend towards the
decentralization of power and control over education, schools and children
may be an over-interpretation – an exaggeration. The alternative and more
plausible view is that, despite and perhaps because of the shift, there has
been and continues to be a firm historical trend towards the concentration
of control over children within schools, and a concomitant trend towards
the centralization of power over education, schools and children in the state.
I wish to argue that, essentially, the shift towards greater parental and
community involvement will not weaken (it may even strengthen) the
underlying, effective centralization of power and control over the educational system in the state.

As the last few words of Kennedy's statement implies, the process of 'decentralization' being referred to is confined to the level of 'managerial' or administrative or executive control: the control which is exercised in an immediate, routine, day-to-day manner; and so the type of control which can be distinguished from that type which may be labelled 'final', 'ultimate' or 'effective'. This view becomes clearer by more closely examining the statutory roles and 'functions' acquired by parents and the community in educational decision-making processes. Thus, in the first place, Boards of Governors in Britain and Boards of Trustees in New Zealand are required by Acts of Parliament; and School Councils for secondary schools in New South Wales are prescribed within the Education Reform Act of 1990.

In New South Wales, the recommended composition of a School Council includes the school Principal along with representatives of the teaching staff, the non-teaching staff, the students, the parents and the community. However, the recommended role and responsibilities of a Council within the education system are more or less confined to a limited range of largely administrative and advisory activities. For instance, a Council is expected to assess a school's financial needs and then to pass on its results and recommendations to others (such as the school Principal) for their decisions about policy, planning and programming. Thus, a Council's specified responsibilities include arriving at 'broad budget priorities'; examining reports on expenditure; advising the Principal on a budget plan; providing guidance for the Principal on the supplementary services required by the school; and advising the Principal on various 'matters except those relating to the employment, appointment and efficiency of staff' (Simpson, 1990, p. 5).

But even though a school council (board, management committee, or whatever) may be given a greater and more direct part to play in matters to do with school financing and staffing, it still does not necessarily follow that a major shift towards the decentralization of power and control has occurred. This applies in the case of both New Zealand and the United Kingdom where school boards have acquired statutory responsibility for financial management, and consequently experience 'the domination of financial/budgetary matters' leading to '[p]arental unwillingness to continue on Boards' (ibid., p. 5). The British example has been summed up recently by a former Pastoral Manager of a school in Nottingham as follows:

School Governors [. . .] are a collection of people elected to act as a 'watchdog' committee to more or less rubber stamp the head teacher's policies. But things have changed dramatically. The Government have introduced Local Management in Schools (LMS). The Government now funds the schools direct and not via the Local Area Education Authority. So whereas schools in the past received tens of thousands of pounds they now receive over a million because they have to account for teachers' salaries. Suddenly School Governors have become aware that they have tremendous power.' (Foyster, 1990, p. 7)

However, an alternative interpretation entails viewing the shift in the financial management of schools as signifying the persistence (even the consolidation) of centralized power and control. Such a conclusion is indicated by the very ability which the British government clearly has and retains to impose an alteration in decision-making procedures on the education system. But this aside, there is the issue of how to interpret the particulars of the imposed alteration given that these include the national government adopting a procedure whereby it finances schooling directly (bypassing local government), albeit through school (management) councils.

Similar changes to those brought about by the British government have been introduced in New South Wales, such as in the area of curriculum development. In discussing these, Peter Knapp has raised doubts about the validity of (what might be referred to as) 'the decentralization thesis'. Knapp points out that New South Wales

> is following the recent trends throughout Australia for the control of the curriculum to be taken from the various departments of education and politicised under the direct control of [government] Ministers. This is generally done under the guise of decentralisation. Politicians effectively argue that [d]epartmental bureaucracies have become top-heavy, inflexible and unwieldy and need to be streamlined. Difficult and expensive functions like professional development and staffing get devolved while the more powerful functions like curriculum, accreditation and policy get politicised in the Ministries. (Knapp, 1990, p. 16)

Knapp explains that this is a 'back to basics' response to previous curriculum developments. That is, the general trend in curriculum over the past twenty years has been away from 'prescription and content' towards 'experiential, process-based pedagogies' where specific content has been left up to individual teachers. But, the 'model of school-based curriculum has tended to be an ideal that has limited success from the point of view of classroom teachers' (ibid., p. 16). This limited success has drawn concern beyond the classroom:

The community and employers [. . .] have been making quite emotive criticisms about literacy standards. The current political agenda is demanding [a] curriculum that addresses the various 'back to basics' platforms and the educators [including those in the departments] are, for sound educational reasons, resisting. Resistance, however, is a strategy that will ultimately fail. (ibid., p. 16)

Here, of course, there are echoes of Foucault's version of post-structuralism which hinges on the association between 'discourse', 'knowledge' and 'power'. For Foucault:

A discourse embodies knowledge (or, rather, what it defines as knowledge) and therefore it embodies power. There are rules within the discourse concerning who can make statements and in what context, and these rules exclude some and include others. Those who have knowledge have the power to fix the flow of meaning and define others. The world is thus made up of a myriad of power relations and each power generates a resistance: the world is thus a myriad of power struggles. (Craib, 1985, pp. 157–8)[60]

Within the discourse concerning educational (and in particular, curriculum) development in Australia and elsewhere, politicians, ministers and governments have the 'knowledge' and power – the use of which evokes resistance from educators (covering those in departments of education as well as in schools). However, following Knapp's argument, the outcome of the discourse and associated knowledge-power struggle is predetermined by the distribution of 'ultimate control' in favour of politicians:

With the ultimate control of curriculum in the hands of politicians, the ideologically motivated positions of the educators could well result in the demise of their power. Indeed, we are now witnessing this very phenomenon as the [NSW] Department is being unceremoniously stripped of its curriculum development role. (Knapp, 1990, p. 16)

In other words, the state has retained its 'ultimate' power over the curriculum, which for a while it had placed under the 'immediate', everyday control of educators. Having decided that its experiment in devolution with regard to curriculum development was a failure (as judged in terms of its own 'knowledge'), the state has fallen back on its ultimate control in order to retrieve immediate control over this aspect of education.

This example demonstrates a general feature of recent state inspired educational developments. On the one hand, a change towards decentralization, devolution and democratization is affirmed by policies, programmes and prescriptions favouring the provision of school councils; but on the other hand, the same process is limited, undermined and 'finally' checked (even reversed) due to the way in which national (central) government retains and exercises its 'ultimate' power and control. There has been, in other words, a contradictory process at work: a process which by way of the experience of parents (among others) evokes 'resistance', and thereby promotes progressive change – even though for the time being (in the face of the state's overwhelming, ultimate power) parental resistance is largely (strategically) confined to avoiding and cancelling membership of school councils.

The parents, educational personnel and others who participate in school councils, and thereby in 'immediate' school decision making, will be sharing in 'delegated power' – that is, power which is granted, guaranteed and tolerated by the state on the basis of its 'ultimate power' (and 'knowledge'). In that the state reserves and exercises 'final power', the 'immediate power' exercised by school councils will be on behalf of (in the interests of) the state. The state's retention of 'final power' is then reflected in and reinforced by the way the process of 'decentralization' has not entailed, for instance, the state granting to school councils the right of disposal over schools; nor the state relinquishing its right to adopt and implement policies which impose a complete reversal on previous trends in educational decision-making procedures (such as towards parents playing a part in the hiring and firing of teachers) simply because state 'knowledge' assumes the failure of such trends.

Essentially, the trends towards decentralization, devolution and democracy within the education system appears to have been limited to nothing more than a redistribution of delegated, immediate 'managerial control' from educators to parents and the community. The trend has not diminished the ultimate – and so 'effective' – power of the state, if anything, it may have ('functionally') secured and strengthened this power in accordance with (following Spicker) that mode of state control which relies on co-option. The creation of school councils may have been a necessary response on the part of the state in its own interests (as well as those of social stability and order; the economy and capitalism; and so on), given the reactions, resentment and resistance exhibited by parents (and perhaps even more by children) to the long-term and persistent trend towards the centralization of ultimate and 'effective' power and control.

The distinction between 'immediate control' and 'ultimate control' (and so effective power) – although hinging to a large extent on the issue of the meaning of 'power' (see Lukes, 1974) – has been employed elsewhere. John Scott, for instance, has made use of the distinction in elucidating the changes and contrasts between the feudal estate system and the capitalist social class system (Scott, 1986; Scott, 1982). Various writers have touched on the distinction in assessing the 'managerial revolution thesis' (see Giddens, 1980); and I have made use of the distinction in assessing the argument that in modern society in recent years there has been a loosening of the gender division of labour in conjunction with a diminution of patriarchal power (Close, 1989c). My view is that if anything, in recent years patriarchy has been strengthened, in the sense of men having further secured their collective power and control in relation to women, by continuing to delegate managerial responsibility for domestic labour to women while appearing to 'do' and 'help' more than they did in the past. It seems to me that a possible parallel example is to be found in what has been happening with regard to power and control over and through education, and so over children.

Now, D.H.J. Morgan's suggestion that family contradictory processes and experiences may be accounted for with reference to the way the family is both socially 'bounded' and socially 'open' (to interference, demands and pressures from other social spheres) is consistent with the arguments of Carnoy and Dale that 'educational contradictions' may be understood in terms of the way the educational system overlaps with both the economic system and the political system – the result being contradictions in relation to (the social items of) capitalism and liberal democracy. However, I wish to argue that family contradictions and educational contradictions are institutionally specific expressions, or refractions, of one common, society-wide contradiction – that contradiction in modern Western societies, whereby individuality is simultaneously affirmed and negated.

Individuality is denied or undermined within the educational system in the interests of the economy (economic production, capitalism, capital accumulation, the capitalist class)[61] and, connectedly in the interests of social cohesion, solidarity and order. Hence the emphasis within and through the educational system on control – including at the expense of care, especially of 'caring about' as distinct from 'caring for'. In addition, however, there is a considerable emphasis within the educational system on the (political) liberal-democratic ideal of 'individuality'.[62] Hence the way in which pedagogy and assessment are very largely guided by such principles as individual ability, effort, responsibility and achievement.[63] As a result, educational – together with family among other – contradictory processes and experiences[64] may all flow from a common, society-wide contradiction in modern, Western societies whereby individuality is simultaneously affirmed (promoted) and negated (constrained). Hence student resistance and student-teacher conflict in favour of the affirmation of individuality – resistance being an immediate assertion of individuality; and conflict being a vehicle for the progressive resolution of the core contradiction through the achievement of an optimum balance between care and control, and in turn between the individual and society.

Moreover, against the dispersal of discipline thesis, under the steward-ship of the state, discipline and control in relation to children in modern society has become more concentrated within the educational system, and thereby centralized in the state. It follows that the educational system – with its especially acute contradiction *vis-à-vis* individuality – may well have acquired a place at the forefront of not only educational but also broader and more fundamental social change and progress.

NOTES

1. Australian Bureau of Statistics (1987, p. 16). According to OECD data for 1988, the unemployment rates for people under the age of twenty-five in Australia were 13.1 per cent and 12.6 per cent for females and males respect-ively, whereas the corresponding proportions for the United Kingdom were 9.9 and 13.5. The 1987 figures for Japan were 4.0 and 2.0; and for the United States, 11.6 and 11.8 (OECD, June 1989, pp. 10–11). Of course, when interpreting and drawing conclusions from this information, the issue of variations in accounting procedures arises; as does the further issue of the extent of part-time employment. For instance, in Australia in 1987, almost 40 per cent of the total paid labour force were females, and the female participa-tion rate within the paid labour force was over 57 per cent; but almost 40 per cent of female employment was part-time compared with about 7.5 per cent of male employment. The corresponding figures for the United Kingdom were 41.4 per cent; 62.6 per cent; 44.6 per cent; and 5.3 per cent (ibid., pp. 10–15). This spread of figures reflects a common pattern across all OECD countries.

2. This structural approach to the conceptualization and application of 'respons-ibility' in relation to the performance and division of domestic labour has been complemented by the recent work of Janet Finch on the normative, ideological and affective aspects (see Finch, 1989). Finch uses 'the words duty, obligation and responsibility interchangeably' in recognition of the way in which 'in practice in social life they are used interchangeably' (ibid., p. 6); and in accordance with her focus on the everyday 'sense of obligation' (ibid., p. 7) and associated 'moral evaluations [. . .] feelings and emotions' (ibid., p. 7) surrounding the performance of domestic labour. See also Finch, 1987; Finch and Groves, 1983.

3. See Davies, 1983; Handler, 1973.

4. In Britain in early 1991, social security benefits (administered by the central government's Department of Social Security) included: (a) 'income support' – 'a benefit to help people whose income is below a certain level. To get it you must [usually] be aged 18 or over'; (b) 'family credit' – a 'benefit for

working families with children [. . .] To get [it] you must be responsible for at least one child under 16 or under 19 if he or she is in full-time education [. . .])', and 'you or your partner must be working at least 24 hours a week'; (c) 'housing benefit' – 'If you find it hard to pay your full rent [. . .] whether you are working or not'; (d) 'community charge benefit' – 'If you are on a low income and find it hard to pay your full Community Charge you may be able to get help [. . .], whether you are working or not', in the form of the community charge benefit (the community charge [or 'poll tax'] was introduced in Britain between April 1989 (Scotland) and April 1990 (England and Wales) to replace the traditional system of covering the cost of local government through the rates [a tax on buildings] – the community charge is a tax on people rather than on property); (e) 'social fund' payments, grants and loans – to cover such items as maternity costs, funeral costs, cold weather bills; (f) help with National Health Service charges; (g) 'unemployment benefit' – 'provides a weekly cash payment for up to a year for people who normally work for an employer but have lost their jobs'; (h) 'maternity allowance'; (i) 'sickness benefit'; (j) 'child benefit' – a regular (weekly/monthly) cash payment to 'anyone [. . .] responsible for a child [. . .] under 16'; (k) 'one parent benefit' – a 'weekly cash payment on top of Child Benefit for any single parent (whether divorced, separated or unmarried), regardless of income [. . .] It is paid for one child only'; (l) 'guardian's allowance', a 'weekly cash payment if you take an orphaned child into the family'; (m) 'invalidity benefit'; (n) 'severe disablement allowance'; (o) industrial injuries disablement benefit'; (p) 'reduced earnings allowance'; (q) 'industrial death benefit'; (r) 'attendance allowance' a 'weekly cash benefit for people (including children) who need a lot of looking after because they are severely disabled, physically or mentally'; (s) 'invalid care allowance'; (t) 'mobility allowance'; (u) 'war widow's or dependant's pension'; (v) 'retirement pension'; (w) 'widow's payment'; (x) 'widowed mother's allowance' – 'for widows of any of age who have at least one child for whom they get Child Benefit'; (y) 'widow's pension'. (See Department of Social Security [United Kingdom], 1990.)

5. Note how Simon Upton's representations of and distinctions among the poor bear a remarkable resemblance to those made by Seebohm Rowntree almost a century ago. For a discussion and assessment of this kind of approach, see Coates and Silburn, 1970. Simon Upton became the Minister of Health in the New Zealand government following the National Party's general election success during 1990.

6. For me this definition of 'social control' is appropriate and adequate for present purposes. I am aware of alternative definitions and approaches, as well as of the problematics surrounding the issue of how best to define the term for sociological purposes. Thus, John Meyer has offered a somewhat narrow definition when he suggests that social control is about 'the attempts by a social group or by society to regulate its own member's behaviour without recourse to forcible coercion' (Meyer, 1983, p. 23), thereby distinguishing between 'social control' and 'coercive control'. I find such a distinction artificial and awkward. In the same volume, Gareth Steadman Jones (1983) offers a definition of 'social control' which appears to equate it (synonymously) with 'social order'.

7. See Higgins, 1980, pp. 1–23.
8. See Janowitz, 1976.
9. See Boulding, 1973.
10. See Arnstein, 1971, pp. 176–82.
11. See Piven and Cloward, 1972.
12. I prefer the phrase 'modes of control' to 'models of control'.
13. See (a) Merton, 1968; (b) Brake, 1985.
14. 'Conformity' is used here rather than in relation to the second mode as in Spicker's list and terminology.
15. Apart from Spicker, see George and Wilding, 1984; Mishra 1977; Gough, 1979.
16. See also Stanley Cohen's and Andrew Scull's discussion of Foucault in this context ('Introduction' to Cohen and Scull, 1983).
17. See Cohen, 1985; Garland, 1985; Ignatieff, 1978; Ignatieff, 1983.
18. See Foucault, 1977.
19. An argument which would seem to come close to endorsing the view that the totalitarian state has already arrived in modern Western societies.
20. This argument represents a rejection of claims that there has been a trend towards the decentralization, devolution and democratization of power and control in relation to the educational systems in modern societies.
21. The Signatories of the Convention on the OECD (December 1960) are Austria, Belgium, Canada, Denmark, France, the Federal Republic of Germany (presumably now Germany), Greece, Iceland, Ireland, Italy, Luxembourg, the Netherlands, Norway, Portugal, Spain, Sweden, Switzerland, Turkey, the United Kingdom and the United States. The following countries acceded subsequently to this Convention: Japan (1964), Finland (1969), Australia (1971), New Zealand (1973).' (OECD, 1985, p. 2).
22. See OECD, June/July, 1989, pp. 16–17. The figures here on the share of GDP going to public expenditure on education are not wholly consistent with those given elsewhere in the same publication (pp. 18–19). The alternative figures being: Australia, 5.56; Japan, 5.04; New Zealand, 4.49; United Kingdom, 5.53; with no figure for the United States.
23. In 1981 the social expenditure share (percentage) of GDP in the same selected OECD countries (according to 'Social Expenditure in OECD Countries: 1960–1981', OECD, 1985, Table 1, p. 21): Australia – 18.8; Japan – 17.5; New Zealand – 19.6; United Kingdom – 23.7; United States – 20.8. In 1981 (according to *Social Expenditure Programme Shares in OECD Countries: 1960–1981*, OECD, 1985, Table 3, p. 24) the proportions of social expenditure going to education (as opposed to the other major social services of health, pensions, unemployment compensation) were: Australia – 30.9; Japan – 28.6; New Zealand – 23.0; United Kingdom – 24.5; United States – 26.4.
24. Alternative indicators of the importance and value attached to education in different societies are to be had in the numbers of students and teachers per unit of population. See OECD, 1989, pp. 18–21.
25. According to Peter Musgrave,

    > Teachers see the need to meet resistance, whatever form it takes. They are paid to set up situations within which their students will be socialised

along certain dimensions, academic and moral, which are acceptable to those running the schools or to those with power over the educational system. Teachers usually meet resistance in three main ways. They take disciplinary actions to bring the deviant into line [. . .] They [change] their style of pedagogy [. . .] or they [change] the curriculum'. (Musgrave, 1987, p. 79)

26.   The media's representation of the incident as a 'battle' has been heavily criticized. However, recently in Sydney there has been a sudden increase in arson attacks on schools. The *Sunday Telegraph* of 21 October 1990 reported that 'Arsonists have attacked 12 Sydney schools in the past 16 days', and came up with an explanation:

> Kids who set fire to their schools are usually misfits worried about failing in life, a leading Sydney psychiatrist claimed yesterday. 'They are lashing out, they're hitting back at the schools which embody a success in life they feel they cannot attain,' Professor Brent Waters, from the school of psychiatry [sic] at the University of NSW, told the *Sunday Telegraph*.

The issues arise as to (a) the meaning, definition and conceptualization of 'resistance'; and (b) what is to be interpreted, categorized and counted as specifically 'student resistance'. Thus, as reported by Peter Musgrave:

> In the working class schools [J.] Anyon saw resistance at work, but [A.] Hargreaves has criticised her for using the term as 'a sort of trawling device' (1982, 113). Her conceptualisation of resistance is so undifferentiated that her catch is massive and heterogeneous: arson, vandalism and 'witholding enthusiasm' are all given as examples. (Musgrave, 1987, pp. 73–4).

See Anyon, 1980; Hargreaves, 1982; Woods, 1983. As far as the issue of interpretation is concerned, there is the problem (after deciding on what counts as 'resistance') of deciding on whether for instance violence amongst students themselves, violence by students outside of school, or student violence in any social location (no matter how far removed spatially and temporally from school) can be counted and interpreted as 'student resistance' in relation to school and education. Further relevant and instructive reading is to be found in Brake, 1985; Hall and Jefferson, 1976; Willis, 1977.

Of course, the evidence I have referred to here about student violence and resistance is merely the tip of the iceberg: such violence and resistance (depending upon definitions) may be so unexceptional and so widespread as to be more or less perpetual; this greater depth of violence and resistance being reflected in the more thorough and systematic sociological studies and writings (see, with reference to Australia, Connell, 1985; Connell et al., 1982; Walker, 1988). In so far as student resistance is extensive and perhaps perpetual, we might anticipate teachers being (collectively speaking) constantly and predominantly attending in their daily activities and routines to the problems of controlling, or at least managing, student resistance.

27.   I am indebted for the following summary to Michael Haralambos (1985, pp. 187–8).

28. Not least of which is his individualist interpretation to the neglect or under-estimation of structural features and barriers, most notably those concerned with social class, sex-gender and race-ethnicity.

29. See Close, 1985.

30. Perhaps the work of R.D. Laing is especially germane here. But, of course, the huge literature associated with the psychoanalytic framework is relevant. See Morgan, 1975; and Poster, 1975. See also the feminist inspired critiques and adaptions of psychoanalysis as presented by such writers as Helene Deutsch, Karen Horney, Anna Freud, Melanie Klein and D.W. Winnicott, all of whom are discussed by Janet Sayers in her *Mothering Psychoanalysis*, 1990.

31. In the sense of 'value' producing activities. The very title of Paul Willis's book on *Learning to Labour: How Working Class Kids Get Working Class Jobs* (1977) reflects and reinforces the view that study activities do not count as 'labour' and are, at the most, only 'pre-labour'.

32. Ian Gough, 1979, p. 21. See also Murgatroyd, 1985; Close, 1985; Close, 1989a.

33. In terms of *Reference Group Theory* (see Runciman, 1969), the educational system in modern society, by promoting the 'myth of meritocracy', extends the comparative reference groups of the working class, and thereby increases the latter's (subjective sense of) 'relative deprivation'. In this way, the work-ing class's propensity for resentment, resistance, rebellion and even revolu-tion is increased. However, one of the major problems of *Reference Group Theory* is that it struggles as a theoretical scheme to cope with the social – including the educational – changes which lie behind alterations in compar-ative reference groups and thereby in 'relative deprivation'. My argument is that these changes are best understood in terms of a dialectical interplay between contradictory social tendencies and messages with regard to the working class and education.

34. This is an argument which resembles the 'safety valve' approach to the issue of 'social mobility'. See Parkin, 1972.

35. There is, of course, a good deal of child labour beyond the confines of education and school in most societies (but in some more than others) much of which is paid, but a lot of which is 'slave'.

36. Not to mention its implications for the power relationships (in this case, the patriarchal power relationships) involved.

37. See Collins, 1985; and Morris, 1990.

38. See for instance Close and Collins, 1983; Burton, 1985.

39. See Harris, 1983.

40. This is not to imply that such estimated amounts *should* be handed over to children as payment in return for their labour participation in the (re-)produc-tion of their (own, embodied) labour power. After all, prescriptive arguments are another matter.

41. See Bourdieu and Passeron, 1977; Bowles and Gintis, 1976; Gintis and Bowles, 1981.

42. See Arnott and Whitty, 1982.

43. Foucault fails to give a clear and conclusive definition of what he means by 'power', even though ostensibly he devotes a lot of space to the issue of the concept of power. He goes only as far as to mention that he 'defines the

exercise of power as a mode of action upon the actions of others' (1982, p. 790), without being explicit about what precisely is being exercised when 'power' is being exercised. Foucault confines himself to elucidating the latter by, for instance, looking at the way the exercise of power (through 'power relations') occurs in connection with 'relationships of communication' and relationships involving 'objective capacities' (ibid., p. 786), singling out the case of 'an educational institution' for particular attention in this regard (ibid., p. 787).

44. Foucault mentions, with a 'new' theory of power relations in mind, the relevance of 'investigating the links between rationalization and power' (1982, p. 779), and especially the 'relationship between rationalization and the excesses of political power [. . .] which seems to be specific to our modern culture' (ibid., p. 779).

45. Foucault argues in line with my own view that 'power relations have come more and more under state control [through, for instance] pedagogical, judicial, economic [and] family systems [so that] one could say that power relations have been progressively governmentalized, that is to say, elaborated, rationalized and centralized in the form of, or under the auspices of, state institutions' (1982, p. 793) – such as 'pedagogical' institutions.

46. In order to illustrate the manner in which power is exercised in modern society, Foucault gives the example of 'an educational institution', in which

> the disposal of its space, the meticulous regulations which govern its internal life, the different activities which are organised there, the diverse persons who live there or meet one another, each with his own function, his well-defined character [reflect the exercise of power and control]. The activity which ensures apprenticeship and the acquisition of aptitudes or types of behaviour is developed there by means of a whole ensemble of regulated communications (lessons, questions and answers, orders, exhortations, coded signs of obedience, differentiation marks off the 'value' of each person and of the levels of knowledge) and by means of a whole series of power processes (enclosure, surveillance, reward and punishment, the pyramidal hierarchy). (1982, p. 787)

On power and control processes in education, see King and Young, 1986, Chs 4, 5 and 7; Musgrave, 1987; Rutter et al., 1979, Chs 6 and 7; Saha and Keeves, 1990, Part II.

47. There is now quite a large body of information and analysis about, especially, sex-gender differences in educational 'outputs' which suggests that these are heavily influenced by ideological assumptions – so that working-class female students will be relatively mollified and passified compared with working-class male students. See, for instance, Byrne, 1978; Deem, 1978; Leder and Sampson 1989; Musgrave, 1987; Sharp, 1976; Spender and Sarah, 1980; Stanworth, 1983.

48. For a recent discussion of the dilemmas of liberal democracy see Wolfe, 1989 (briefly discussed in this volume by Don Edgar).

49. Further useful information and ideas relating to female student resistance can be found in Thomas, 1980. See also McRobbie, 1990.

50. See for instance: Apple, 1982b; Carnoy, 1982; Carnoy and Levin, 1985b; Dale, 1982; Gintis and Bowles, 1981; Taylor, 1984.

51. There are signs that the word 'contradiction' has acquired a fashionable appeal, so that it is commonly used to convey sophistication, but little else.
52. Taylor also fails to include the word again after the title and the first page of her fifteen-page article.
53. There are further queries which might be raised about Taylor's use of 'contradiction', such as that to do with the way she seems to view contradictions as highly contingent, dependent, incidental, superficial and ephemeral rather than as socially, and perhaps structurally, deep-rooted, fundamental and inherent.
54. Thompson, 1978; Johnson, 1979; Connell, 1979.
55. On the distinction between the 'structural' and the 'relational' levels of society and social experience, see Close, 1989b. See also Craib, 1984.
56. See Close, 1985; Close, 1989a; Close and Collins, 1983; Crompton and Gubbay, 1975.
57. The issue arises as to the details of the relationships between the contradictions in different social spheres, and the implications of these relationships for making sense of resistance and conflict within any one social sphere as well as within the total social formation.
58. See Bell, 1970; Corrigan and Leonard, 1978; Dickenson and Russell, 1986; Dunleavy and O'Leary, 1987; George and Wilding, 1984, Ch.7; Giddens, 1979; Gough, 1979; Habermas, 1976; Holmwood and Stewart, 1983; Lindberg et al., 1975; Mishra, 1977, Ch.5; Mitchell, 1971, pp. 156–8; O'Connor, 1973; Offe, 1984; Offe, 1982; Ramazanoglu, 1989; Sayers, 1986; Showstack Sassoon, 1987b; Wolfe, 1977.
59. In Claus Offe's use of the notion of 'contradiction' to analyze the welfare state, there are signs of some similarity with my own approach. But the degree of similarity is uncertain in the absence of a specific general definition and on the basis of, at the most, such statements as:

> Any human society operates through an institutionalised set of rules. A part of these rules determines the process by which the society reproduces itself materially, and thereby transcends the lifetime of its individual members. More specifically, these institutionalised rules of material production regulate three things: namely, the effective control over human labour power, over the material means and resources of production, and over the product itself. Numerous mechanisms of control, or modes of production, which regulate these three elements can be distinguished [. . .] A contradiction is the tendency inherent within a specific mode of production to destroy those very pre-conditions on which its survival depends. Contradictions become manifest in situations where, in other words, a collision occurs between the constituent pre-conditions and the results of a specific mode of production, or where the necessary becomes impossible and the impossible become necessary. Without a single exception, all Marxist theorems that try to elucidate the nature of capitalism are based upon this concept of contradiction. (Offe, 1984, p. 132)

60. Of course, there are several basic problems with Foucault's scheme. For instance, if 'knowledge is a power over others, the power to define others' (Craib, 1984., p. 157), the questions remain of 'why/how some and not others have (what is defined as) "knowledge" and thereby power?'; 'who/how some

people have knowledge (are able to define what they have as "knowledge") unless they already have power?'. In other words, Foucault's scheme leaves – and even invites – the possibility of power lying, in the first instance, outside of knowledge.

61. Perhaps illustrated recently in the United States where there has been 'the first big overhaul since 1974 of the Scholastic Aptitude Test, now renamed the Scholastic Assessment Test' – partly in response to 'Employers [. . .] warning of economic catastrophe if education does not improve by the next century' (Bremner, 1990).

62. Of course, this ideal has not only 'political' but also 'religious' connotations through its association with the Protestant Ethic.

63. These principles will in practice operate in something of a culturally biased way – favouring 'the bourgeoisie' rather than 'the proletariat'. Hence Pierre Bourdieu's theoretically inspired notion of 'cultural capital' (see Bourdieu, 1973; Bourdieu and Passeron, 1977); but also in Australia, for example, favouring those who subscribe to imported, European-oriented ethnicity as opposed to indigenous, Aboriginal culture.

64. It seems to me that an appropriate way of summing up the social importance and sociological value of 'contradiction' is to suggest that it is a (perhaps the principal; key) social process which articulates social structure, social action and social change by way of social experience.

2 Pursuing Errant Fathers: Maintenance Systems in Three Western Countries
Rosemary Collins

Western countries, notably the United Kingdom, the USA and Australia, are involved in a great debate about how financial support for children should be shared between custodial and non-custodial parents, and between single parents and the state. Recent developments in these countries have been similar in that the state benefits paid to single parents and their children declined in real value during the 1980s, and greater financial responsibility was placed on non-custodial parents, including those living in poverty.

Policy decisions to cut welfare spending on the children of single parents and to increase the contribution of the absent parent (usually the father) have arisen in the context of a sharp increase in single parent families in Western industrial societies. In England, for example, the number of single parent families grew by over 20 per cent to more than a million by the end of the decade, and accounted for 16 per cent of all families with dependent children (OPCS, 1989). By 1990, 27 per cent of all births were outside of marriage (OPCS, 1990a). In Australia, single parent families increased by over 70 per cent between 1974 and 1985 (Brownlee, 1990) to a total of 324 171 (Australia 1986 Census). By the mid-1980s, 15 per cent of Australian births were outside of marriage.

The USA has registered the largest increase in the number of single parent families. Between 1970 and 1987, the number of families headed by lone women jumped from 3 808 000 to 9 236 000 (US Bureau of the Census, 1989). Considerable variation in the proportion of single parents occurred between ethnic groups. Less than half (42 per cent) of all black children lived in two parent units in 1987, whereas the majority of white children (78 per cent) lived with two parents. The incidence of births outside of marriage was much higher among black women than among white. In 1986, for example, 16 per cent of births to white mothers were outside of marriage, whereas 62 per cent of black births were extra-marital (ibid.). Garfinkel (1988) has shown that by the mid-1980s, about half of all single parents in the USA were living in poverty. The predominance of black families within the single parent category means that black children in the USA are more likely than not to be economically disadvantaged.

Single parent families are far from a homogeneous section of society, and the label serves to cover a complex variety of family situations. Crow and Hardey (1990) have argued that, while some of the diversity of single parent households is more widely recognized than formerly, not every dimension has been acknowledged and, in particular, the ethnic dimension has been under-researched. Within social policy, the old distinction between 'deserving poor' and 'undeserving poor' continues to be applied, with for instance widows being more favourably treated than unmarried mothers. Crow and Hardey point out that 'Rightly or wrongly, certain groups of lone parents are more likely than others to be seen as having "chosen" lone parenthood, as being "responsible" for their situation, and this may well have a bearing on their treatment in the formal welfare system' (ibid., p. 3).

While commentators such as Paul Close (1985, p. 16) have argued that it is 'unlikely that very many one-parent households will have been created out of choice or preference', welfare provision in the United Kingdom, the USA and Australia has been premised on the idea that the conjugal family form is the norm, and the one most suited to the demands of modern industrial society (ibid., p. 40). Consequently, state benefits paid to single parents have been organised in such a way that alternatives to the conjugal family are not favoured, and that the poverty of single parent families has failed to be centrally addressed.

SINGLE PARENTS AND THE WELFARE STATE

The rise in single parent families has been accompanied by increasing dependency on the state for financial support among this section of society. In England, for instance, in 1988 two-thirds (722 000) of single parents were dependent upon the state (National Audit Office, 1990). Unmarried mothers accounted for around a third of these claimants, and in relative terms were a highly dependent category. In 1986, 93 per cent (213 000) of unmarried mothers were receiving state benefits. This is a similar proportion to that of separated mothers (95 per cent), but is much higher than the 42 per cent of divorced custodial mothers and the 28 per cent of custodial fathers (ibid.). Between 1979 and 1988, the number of divorced and separated women receiving benefits rose by 88 per cent, and the number of unmarried mothers receiving benefits rose by 225 per cent (ibid.).

In Australia, the number of single parents receiving state benefits rose considerably between 1980 and 1987 from 158 000 to 239 000 (Harrison, 1989). The absolute numbers of single parents were much lower in Australia than in the United Kingdom, yet it has been estimated that over half were supported by the state and were, like their counterparts in the USA, living in poverty by the mid-1980s (Ochiltree, 1990). It has been estimated that in the USA in 1987, almost 90 per cent of welfare cases involved absent fathers divorced from, separated from or never married to the mothers of their children (Garfinkel, 1988). Support in the form of Aid to Families with Dependent Children grew between 1985 and 1987 from eight billion to twelve and a half billion dollars (ibid.; US Bureau of the Census, 1989), and the number of households receiving means tested non-cash benefits rose between 1980 and 1986 by 9 per cent (US Bureau of the Census, 1989). In each of the three countries, state benefits to dependent single parents families are low. United States families in 1986, for example, could expect on average a monthly payment of $355 – described by Garfinkel (1988) as a 'meagre stipend'. British single parent families in 1988 received on average £50 (National Audit Office, 1990). Similarly, in Australia in 1985, a single mother and child received $118 per week (McDonald and Spindler, 1988).

The increase in the number of single parent families has been interpreted by some commentators as a sign that the family is in crisis. Trends characterized by increases in divorce, births outside of marriage, unmarried cohabitation, and the fragmentation of the family have been associated with moral decline and social instability. The welfare state has been regarded by some politicians and commentators as the enemy of the family on the grounds that it undermines the work ethic, self-reliance, resourcefulness and self respect. Reconstituted families have been blamed for an increase in social problems. In Britain, for example, The Centre for Policy Studies has argued that child abuse can be directly linked to natural mothers cohabiting with men who are not the fathers of their children. The Centre argues further that children's experience of divorce can result in they themselves becoming child abusers on reaching adulthood:

> Increased divorce has left an ever growing number of children with so little experience of how a parent should behave that they may eventually abuse their children [. . .] child abuse is largely a consequence of the decline of the traditional family. To be effective in stemming child abuse, we must end policies which encourage the one-parent family. (Centre for Policy Studies, 1989, pp. 13-14)

The CPS argument, however, is not based on any reliable statistical evidence. The CPS fails to refer to any such evidence because it is not interested in presenting and testing a hypothesis, but instead in making rhetorical claims in support of policies to minimize the dependence of families on the state. Cuts in welfare spending have been justified on the grounds of encouraging greater personal responsibility. The assumption is that cuts will lead to the eventual re-emergence of the conjugal family form as the dominant pattern of family life.

During the 1980s, both the United Kingdom and the USA were headed by right-wing governments with policies heavily influenced by New Right theory. According to the New Right's perspective, the state in liberal democracies has become over-extended and welfare policies have become too costly. If state intervention is unavoidable, it should occur at the lowest level possible. The rationale is that individuals should be free to choose the most appropriate services to meet their needs (schooling or medical care, for instance). The state should discourage the public from expecting the government to provide more than a minimal welfare service. New Right theory does not explicitly refer to the direction of public policy making, but instead is principally concerned with an abstract *welfare-maximizing* model. Dunleavy and O'Leary (1987, p. 134) describe the model as follows:

> In all interventions governments should concentrate on trying to produce a stable, predictable environment by enforcing generalised rules and sticking to them, with the minimum discretionary decision-making by administrators, and resisting all tendencies to qualify the authority of government by bargaining with interest groups.

According to Dunleavy and O'Leary, the ideas of the New Right 'almost became an orthodoxy powerful enough to replace pluralism' (ibid., p. 72) during the Reagan and Thatcher periods in the USA and Britain. The interpretation of the theory has been less closely tied to social science in Britain compared with the USA. However, in both countries during the 1980s there were reductions in centralised government authority as well as welfare provision. The state came to define its caring role in terms of personal responsibility, the free exercise of natural rights, and the freedom of the individual. The effects on single parents have been marked. In the USA, for instance, benefits declined by over a quarter between 1975 and 1985 (Garfinkel, 1988). Palmer and Sawhill (1984, p. 13) have commented:

> Lower-tier safety net programmes were generally cut by imposing tighter income eligibility limits and offseting benefits more fully from earnings and other sources of income. The result has been to exclude many of the

working poor and near poor from government programmes – to greatly reduce benefits for others, and to target a higher percentage of the reduced funds on the poor.

The budgets of 1982, 1983 and 1984 entailed a cut of about 10 per cent in social programmes. Income security benefits and expenditure on means-tested, non-cash benefits were severely curtailed (Johnson, 1987).

In 1981, the Reagan administration sought to impose a work requirement on those in receipt of benefits. By 1987, almost all major welfare reform proposals contained not only work requirements but also, in order to enable these requirements to be met, day care provisions. The aim of these inclusions has been to remove as many people as possible from the list of welfare recipients. At the same time, Burghes (1990) has shown that the US programmes set up to encourage the self-sufficiency of single parents have in practice been far from successful. Parents with children under the age of six have been exempted, while those eligible have faced restricted numbers of places and types of activity due to limited funding. During the mid-1980s, around 80 per cent of those taking part were involved in a job search programme; 10 per cent were involved in education and training; 5 per cent were in compulsory work in exchange for benefits; and only 5 per cent were in the work experience scheme. Earnings for the participants were low, resulting in an income on a par with the poverty line. Burghes notes: 'it has been suggested that the low earnings of participants reflects the fact that so many had been engaged only in job-search activities which tend to lead to work in entry-level, low wage jobs [. . .] they do not improve participants' skills and therefore their chance of higher earnings' (ibid., p. 3). Participation has been forced on parents 'for no certain and possibly very little gain'.

The situation in Britain has been different in that welfare reforms during the 1980s were aimed solely at reducing public expenditure, and accordingly various changes in social security legislation substantially reduced the income available to single parents. The changes included an increase between 1980 and 1982 in council house rents of 85 per cent; cuts in 1986 of £68 000 000 in housing benefit; the abolition in 1987 of dual tax relief mortgage interest payments for unmarried parents; and the abolition in 1989 of the additional personal allowance for cohabiting couples with children (Walker and Walker, 1987). In 1987, the Low Pay Unit announced that since the start of the Thatcher administration in 1979 those caught in the poverty trap had increased fivefold, from 90 000 to 480 000.

The biggest change came with the introduction of the Social Security Act 1986, implemented in 1988. The aim of the Act is to 'target resources on those who need it most' by redistributing the existing social security budget among groups claiming benefits. Higher, long term supplementary benefit rates were abolished together with single payments for heating and special diets. Instead, premiums for special groups such as single parents were introduced, and loans under the Social Fund replaced grants and urgent needs payments. In addition, claimants were required to pay 20 per cent of their rates (local government taxes on buildings) out of their benefits. Rather than encourage personal responsibility, the result has been only to deepen the poverty of those affected. In 1989, 116 000 households were recognized as 'homeless' – a figure more than double that for 1978. In support of the reduction in state benefits, the Prime Minister, Margaret Thatcher argued:

> It is self defeating to have systems of state provision which undermine the self-reliance of the individual. Self-reliance and self respect are precious commodities. They are the source of all our endeavour. But they are all too easily destroyed by the temptation of state-induced dependence. Government must never supplement personal responsibility. (From a speech given to the 58th Conservative Women's National Conference, 25 May 1988. Quoted in *Family Policy*, Summer 1988)

Shaver (1988, p. 392) points out that in Australia during the mid-1980s the collapse of economic growth and full employment brought a crisis of legitimacy for the Keynesian economic policy and the welfare system. From the time of the Whitlam Labour government, welfare expenditure rose: from 21 per cent of total outlay in 1972-3 to 29 per cent in 1983-4 (ibid.). In the 1986 national budget, the government announced an austerity programme involving substantial cuts in state spending on health, education and social security. The Hawke Labor government has since made further reductions in welfare spending, cutting to some extent the flow of funds to children and single parents in particular. Shaver argues that since 'the advent of the fiscal crisis the government has begun to narrow categorical boundaries and even to abolish categories of welfare provision altogether' (ibid., p. 384). For example, the maternity allowance was abolished and the period of child dependency was shortened so that supporting parents became no longer eligible for maintenance after the youngest child reached the age of sixteen.

Commenting on the cutbacks in state provision, Brownlee (1990, p. 28) says: 'neither family allowance payments, the mothers'/guardians' allowance for single parent families, nor the family-related tax rebates, the dependent spouse rebate and the sole parent rebate, were indexed linked and all deteriorated in real value over the decade.' Despite the cutbacks, a comprehensive two-year review of social security was initiated in 1986, and the Prime Minister, Bob Hawke, pledged his government's commitment to eradicating child poverty in Australia by 1990. 1987 saw the implementation of a Family Package of measures, covering more generous payments for children in low income families; a Family Allowance Supplement; Uniform Rent Assistance; a Child Disability Allowance; and a new scheme of child maintenance to be paid by non-custodial parents. How effective this scheme has been in actually eradicating poverty remains to be seen.

The picture overall within the United Kingdom, the USA and Australia is one where single parents have been both expanding within the population as a whole and struggling to maintain their families in the face of a decline in the state benefits upon which most depend. The principle of the caring role of the state has been translated into the practice of subsisting around the poverty line. In each country there has been a consistent set of assumptions about family dependence on the state. Parents are expected to support their children in the first instance, with the state stepping in with assistance only when parents cannot meet their obligations. Increasingly, the state has been concerned to 'preserve marriage and parenthood as purely private arrangements which are construed as the result of individual choice and freedom' (Smart, 1984a, p. 118). This approach is reflected in the new policies which have strengthened the procedures intended to make liable fathers pay maintenance.

MAINTENANCE AND THE LIABLE RELATIVE

The legal obligation on the non-custodial parent to maintain dependent children has a long history dating back in England, for instance, to the Poor Laws of the sixteenth century. In the latter half of the twentieth century, a variety of state assistance and social insurance schemes have been developed in the United Kingdom which improve the position of single parents by extending the rights of children to maintenance from their fathers. For example, whereas during the 1950s, husbands 'could only be made to pay maintenance if they were guilty of a matrimonial fault' (ibid., p. 11), subsequent legislative changes have given greater priority to the support of all children (whether or not their parents are married) and by extension, their mothers as primary carers.

The justification for the obligation on fathers to pay maintenance to their non-custodial children rests on two main arguments. First: parenting is for life, and therefore fathers should continue to share in the financial costs of their children. Second: women should not shoulder all of the responsibility

for rearing children, especially given that many of them as single parents
have low incomes. At the same time, the legal demand that fathers pay
maintenance is premised on structural economic inequalities within the
family connected to a gender division of labour within which men's principal responsibility is 'financial provision' and women's is 'mothering'. As
Carol Smart points out:

> Although the conditions of women's dependency have been ameliorated
> it remains the case that the law (e.g. social security, taxation, pensions)
> as well as other social and economic policies (for example, the failure to
> provide nurseries or equal pay and work opportunities to women), obliges
> women to look to men for economic security once they are married or
> have children. Women with children who live without men are amongst
> the poorest groups in contemporary society and it is extremely difficult,
> if not impossible, for them to lift themselves out of the poverty trap
> without the help of an extra income in the household. (ibid., p. 11)

This process has been described in the USA as the 'feminization of poverty'
(Weitzman, 1985).

A principal aim of the state in the United Kingdom, the USA and
Australia during the 1980s was to improve and extend the process of
making fathers pay, and this has been prioritized in comparison with equal
pay and work opportunities for women, as well as in comparison with
developing and strengthening contact between children and the absent
parent. It has been necessary to revise maintenance payments on the practical grounds that procedures based on court orders have been remarkably
ineffective. In England, studies carried out by, inter alia, Graham-Hall
(1968), McGregor et al., (1970), Finer (1974), and Carol Smart (1984b)
have demonstrated that the amounts stipulated by court orders were
invariably low and bore little relation to the cost of bringing up children.
Often, fathers were unable or reluctant to pay the maintenance, and subsequent enforcement action rarely resulted in mothers recovering the full
amount owed.

The number of custodial parents in each of the three countries in receipt
of maintenance due to court orders is small. Using data from the US Bureau
of the Census, Garfinkel reveals that in 1985 two-thirds of mothers eligible
for child support had awards. However, 'the proportion with an award
varies dramatically with the martial status of the mother. Whereas eight out
of ten divorced mothers receive child support orders, less than half are
separated mothers and less than one in five of never married mothers have
orders'. (Garfinkel, 1988)

More recent figures from the USA (US Bureau of the Census, 1989) show that the majority of maintenance orders (83 per cent) made during 1987 were to white mothers. Only 16 per cent of the orders were to black mothers and 6 per cent to Hispanic mothers. These figures reinforce the argument by Crow and Hardey (1990) that single parent families are far from being a unified section of society, and that instead there are major divisions and inequalities between different types. The figures for maintenance *actually* paid in Australia are lower than in the USA. Snider (1989) reports that before the introduction of fundamental reforms in 1988, less than one custodial parent in every three was receiving regular maintenance. Only 40 per cent had court orders, and only 55 per cent of the court orders were being paid. Custodial parents actually in receipt of maintenance averaged only slightly more than twenty dollars a week (Snider, 1989). Just over a quarter (26 per cent) of those on social security received maintenance (Wicks, 1990).

Unlike the USA, Britain has no centralized store of data showing the numbers of women by type of single parent who have been awarded maintenance, nor the numbers of orders actually paid as opposed to the numbers not received. Instead, a more restricted set of figures is available on the numbers of custodial parents receiving state benefits and also having maintenance orders (National Audit Commission, 1990). These data indicate a similar pattern to that found in the USA. That is, among the different types of single parent, divorced women are the most likely to receive payment (38 per cent). The comparative figures for separated women and unmarried mothers are as low as a 0.25 and 12 per cent respectively. The low incidence of payment made by liable natural fathers is confirmed by the further finding that only 10 per cent of all maintenance orders made by English courts during 1988 were to unmarried mothers (Judicial Statistics, 1988).

Although, as the evidence clearly suggests, most liable parents do not in practice pay regular maintenance, it does not necessarily follow that most have made no financial contribution. Some will have reached agreements with the custodial parents about lump sum payments or about transfers of property with the breakdown of relationships; and others may have made private arrangements which will not be revealed in any formal data. Nonetheless, the statistics have had an alarming effect on governments, which have been prompted to overhaul and tighten the procedures for ensuring that liable, non-custodial parents actually make maintenance payments. In the USA, new schemes have been gradually introduced in several states following the pioneering example of Wisconsin during the early 1980s. In

Australia, a completely revised scheme has been swiftly implemented; and in England and Wales, proposed reforms to the current scheme are due to take effect following the next Parliamentary general election (currently scheduled for 1992).

The Wisconsin plan was introduced in 1983 with the aim of full implementation by 1987. It requires all non-custodial parents to share their income with their children. It stipulates that a child is entitled to receive an amount equivalent to either the support which the non-custodial parent is obliged to pay under a court order or the state-assured minimum benefit – whichever is the greater. The court order awards are formula linked: 17 per cent of the non-custodial parent's gross income is paid in the case of one child; 25 per cent where there are two children; 29 per cent where there are three; 31 per cent where there are four; and 35 per cent in the case of five children. In July 1987, this formula was used to decide the presumptive child support obligation of non-custodial parents, and the appropriate amounts were to be deducted directly from wages. The orders are index-linked, so that they rise and fall in accordance with increases and decreases in the non-custodial parent's earnings. In the case of a low income family, if the amount ordered is less than the state-assured minimum benefit, the state will make up the difference. Furthermore, custodial parents in paid employment but on low incomes are given a supplementary allowance. For instance, in 1987, such parents were paid one dollar per hour worked for a first child, and one dollar seventy five cents for a second or subsequent child.

In the USA, the Child Support Enforcement programme was established in 1975 by federal legislation, creating a public bureaucracy to enforce maintenance payments by non-custodial parents. Under Part D, Title IV of the Social Security Act, payments to Aid For Dependent Children families made by the state are to be re-claimed from liable, non-custodial parents (Garfinkel, 1988).

The Australian scheme has been introduced in two stages, the first being in June 1988. It stipulates that the amounts of maintenance to be paid by non-custodial parents are still to be decided through court orders or court registered agreements, but that they are to be transferred using a new and tighter method. Now, they are to be deducted automatically from a non-custodial parent's wages and paid through a Child Support Agency, which is part of the Taxation Office. The money collected is then passed on to the custodial parent on a monthly basis in conjunction with the Family Allowance cheque. The scheme is compulsory for all new sole-parent pensioners receiving state benefits. Snider points out that Stage One is aimed at 'increasing the levels of maintenance awarded, at increasing the numbers of custodial parents with orders or agreements, and at increasing the numbers of those actually collecting maintenance' (Snider, 1989, p. 32).

The scheme's Stage Two came into operation in October 1989 as the Child Support (Assessment) Act, and is mainly concerned with introducing an administrative formula, as in the Wisconsin scheme, for deciding on the amounts to be paid by non-custodial parents. It stipulates that non-custodial parents (usually fathers) pay 18 per cent of their taxable income for one child; 27 per cent for two children; and 32 per cent for three. It defines lower limits of income below which a non-custodial parent is required to pay nothing: for instance, $Aus124.25 where the non-custodial parent is responsible for no other children. The formula is complex in that it (a) allows for an amount of income which is 'free' in order to take account of the non-custodial parent's living expenses and new family responsibilities; (b) disregards the custodial parent's income up to an amount equivalent to national average earnings plus a child care allowance; and (c) disregards the non-custodial parent's income in excess of two and a half times average earnings. Different figures apply when parents share the custody of children, where 'shared custody' is defined in terms of children spending at least 40 per cent of the nights a year with each parent (Harrison, 1989).

The Australian scheme has been acclaimed as a success. By the end of 1989, over 60 per cent of non-custodial parents were actually paying maintenance, and the proportion of those single parents who were receiving both social security and maintenance had risen between April 1988 and January 1990 from 26 per cent to 36 per cent. The average weekly amount received by such single parents had increased three-fold to $Aus67 by October 1989 (Wicks, 1990).

The success of the Wisconsin and Australian schemes in ensuring that a greater proportion of non-custodial parents actually pay maintenance has encouraged the British government to set up similar procedures. In July 1990, plans were announced for setting maintenance payments at 18.6 per cent of average earnings; a formula to take into account any non-custodial parent's ability to pay and any custodial parent's income; and arrangements which allow a custodial parent to have an increase in earnings without incurring an identical (pound for pound) loss of benefit (*Guardian*, 19 July 1990). A proposed Child Support Agency will trace and claim maintenance payments from errant fathers. In choosing a proportion of 18.6 per cent of average earnings, the British government is proposing to set maintenance payments at a level which 'would be among the highest in the world' (ibid.). The proposals are set out in detail in the government white paper, *Children Come First* (HMSO, 1990).

The British government's plans have been well signalled, and have followed a prolonged attack in the media on irresponsible fathers, on women who 'choose' single parenthood; and on the undeserving poor. In 1989, for example, John Redwood, a Conservative Member of Parliament, argued that the government 'should be generous and compassionate with those who have been widowed, with the disabled, with those who are in circumstances beyond their control. They should ask rather more questions about those who have placed themselves and their families at risk by their actions' (*Guardian*, 19 April 1989).

Frank Field, a Labour Member of Parliament, has argued that fathers on welfare benefits themselves should pay a proportion of their benefits to their children 'in order to emphasise the importance of the responsibilities fathers have towards the maintenance of their children' (Field, 1989). In a similar way, in 1990, Margaret Thatcher asserted that 'no father should be able to escape from his responsibilities' (*Family Policy*, Spring 1990), a view reiterated by John Patten, a Home Officer minister: 'fatherhood is a life-long commitment which you cannot turn your back on and should not run away from' (*Guardian*, 21 June 1990).

The negative stereotype of 'the irresponsible father' promulgated through the media reinforces the image of single parents as a social problem. Such parents tend to be blamed with impunity for juvenile crime among other troublesome and difficult societal phenomena. Taylor-Gooby (1985) provides evidence from a survey of public attitudes towards welfare provision showing that single parents are still stigmatized: 'Benefits for lone parents, the unemployed and the low paid were not popular. Two factors seem to be at work: a distinction in people's minds between deserving and undeserving groups, and a distinction between benefits for the minority of "undeserving" poor and benefits for the mass of the population' (quoted in Johnson, 1987).

Policies towards single parents, such as those concerned with maintenance, can receive considerable public support on the grounds that errant fathers are feckless and irresponsible. However, such policies ignore and fail to come to terms with the poverty of single parents families. As Crow and Hardey (1990, p. 13) argue, 'it is the poverty of the lone-parent household which is primarily responsible for the difficulties and restrictions on choices encountered'. While pursuing errant fathers can result in clear gains for families when the fathers enjoy average or above average earnings, there are limited or no gains to be had when the fathers themselves are living around the poverty line. Accordingly, the maintenance system favours only certain types of single parent. For example, an Australian mother with two children who has taxable earnings of $Aus30 000 per year and separated from her children's father who has similar earnings can expect to receive just over $Aus6000 maintenance per year (Harrison, 1989). But an Australian mother with a former partner who is earning less than $Aus6500 would receive nothing.

UNMARRIED PARENTS AND POVERTY

The data presented in this chapter show that unmarried mothers are the least likely type of single parent to actually receive maintenance. In the USA, less than 20 per cent receive payments from fathers. Since at least half of all black single mothers have never been married (US Bureau of the Census, 1989), only a very small minority of such women will be picking up maintenance. In England, only one in every twelve mothers who have never married enjoys maintenance.

The poverty of unmarried mothers has been well charted (Finer, 1974, inter alia). Research carried out by Collins and Macleod (discussed in Chapter 3 of this volume) suggests that poverty is not simply a consequence of unmarried parenthood, but that poverty tends to precede it: that is, births outside of marriage are more likely to occur within the poorer sections of society. By drawing on official unemployment, crime and population statistics for the county areas of England, Collins (1991) has established a positive correlation between extra-marital births and indicators of economic disadvantage and anomie, as indicated by patterns of unemployment and crime. The statistics show that extra-marital births peak in urban areas characterized by high crime rates and high levels of male unemployment (detailed data on female unemployment rates being unavailable).

The study by Collins and Macleod of unmarried fathers and domestic courts (ibid.) suggests that unmarried fathers who are ordered to pay maintenance are three times more likely than all men in the United Kingdom to be unemployed; when employed, are likely to have earnings which are substantially below national average earnings; have more than a one in three chance of living with their parents even though only a few are under twenty years of age; and are likely as a result of court orders to experience financial hardship to the extent that they have a genuine inability to actually pay maintenance. The following are remarks made by three unmarried fathers during court proceedings brought to enforce the payment of maintenance:

> I'm approximately £2000 in debt. I have no social life whatsoever. I don't smoke or drink. I never go out. My financial situation is appalling. I'm unable to maintain the payments. My house is up for sale. I'm not

able to work because of my state of mind.

I'm struggling. I really can't pay anything. I've been kicked out by my parents and I'm now on my own.

Enforcement procedures in English courts often result in maintenance arrears being remitted because of the fathers' inability to pay. In one of the sample courts studied by Collins, only a third of all the men whose orders had fallen into arrears in 1988 were ordered to repay the full amount to the mother (ibid.).

These findings suggest that schemes for pursuing errant fathers and making them pay maintenance are of little value to single mothers whose partners are on low incomes, and that especially they are of no assistance to the poor. The issue arises with regard to schemes which oblige both parents to support a child in a single parent family of whether they are primarily directed at improving the standard of living of the child, or instead whether they are primarily intended to help cut back the cost of state welfare provisions and reducing the tax burden of the middle class.

Crow and Hardey (1990, p. 2) point out that, in addition to their growing numerical significance, 'lone-parent households are important because certain structural characteristics of the group, such as their poverty, represent a major challenge to social policy'. However, the enthusiasm with which errant fathers have been pursued has not been matched with anything like similar determination behind schemes designed to alleviate poverty. The most promising prospects appear to be found in Australia, where the Jobs, Education and Training (JET) programme for sole parents was due to begin in November 1990. The aim of the programme is to provide counselling, training, education, job search assistance, and child care support to single parents who want paid employment. This package is being introduced in conjunction with anti-poverty trap initiatives, including an increase in single parents' extra-benefit income allowances and permission to retain full access to state health care provisions for up to six months of paid employment (Brownlee, 1990).

Yet policy initiatives such as the Australian examples continue to treat single parents as a homogeneous category to the neglect of important social differences associated with greater disadvantage for some rather than others: such as for those who are black. As governments impose more stringent controls on public expenditure and increasingly shift welfare provision towards liable relatives, so more single parent families will be driven into poverty. Unless comprehensive policy measures for attacking poverty are introduced, schemes for making fathers pay will increase the number of children brought up in poverty, and will be experienced as merely punitive attempts to reduce the cost of welfare provisions.

3 Born in Poverty:
The Social Dimensions of Births Outside Marriage
Rosemary Collins and Alison Macleod

Having a baby outside marriage became increasingly popular in Britain during the 1980s, so that by the end of the decade over a quarter of all births were to parents who were not married to each other (OPCS, 1990d). On the surface, this pattern may appear to represent a rejection of conventional marriage in favour of relationships that are not legally sanctioned and binding. However, while some single parents were rejecting the conventions of marriage, preferring to live together, official data show that as few as 4 per cent of all dependent children were living in stable cohabiting couple families (Haskey, 1989, p. 31). Moreover, although nearly three-quarters of parents jointly registered births (OPCS, 1990d), the increase in the number of mothers bringing up their non-marital children with their partners was far outstripped by the increase in the number tackling this task alone. According to the official data, 12 per cent of all dependent children were living in one-parent families, the vast majority of which were female headed (Haskey, 1989, p. 31).

This chapter presents an analysis of the shift in family patterns towards higher numbers and rates of births outside marriage in relation to the prevailing patterns of social policy and social change in Britain during the 1980s. The discussion begins with an examination of the way the new conservatism of the 1980s affected working-class youth, leading to their impoverishment and perhaps propelling them towards having children outside marriage. The possibility arises that state social policy, geared to an idealized model of family life as conjugal, patriarchal, self-sufficient and responsible for its own social and welfare needs, helped promote births outside marriage – and moreover, to do so in such a way that their increasingly common and dominant characteristic was poverty. The discussion proceeds to explore some of the social dimensions of births outside marriage within the working class. Drawing on data from an ESRC funded research project on unmarried parents and domestic courts,[1] there is an examination of the socio-economic background of a sample of parents whose custody, access and maintenance cases came before the courts at the end of the 1980s. The data are used to uncover variations in the relationships between the parents; the incidence and experience of poverty among the parents; and the various personal and social problems which afflict economically disadvantaged families. It is argued that when state intervention in the lives of poor single parents has the dual purpose of (a) meeting their basic needs and (b) limiting their opportunities for enhancing their economic resources, then many single parents are unable to escape from poverty.

POVERTY AND BIRTHS OUTSIDE MARRIAGE WITHIN THE WORKING CLASS

Since the 1970s, an increasing number of studies have shown how in Britain poverty is a common plight of mothers bringing up children alone, and how such mothers are disproportionately represented among the poor. Morris Finer's seminal *Report of the Committee on One-Parent Families* (1974) presents detailed evidence which forcefully reveals how unmarried mothers[2] usually live in poverty; Townsend's research (1979) describes the inferior accommodation that unmarried mothers usually inhabit; while Graham (1984) has detailed the ill-health and inadequate diet of unmarried mothers. More recently, Millar (1987) has argued that the poverty of mothers who are not married has become far more prevalent simply due to the sheer increase in the *absolute* numbers affected.

Of course, the issue of how 'poverty' should be defined remains wide open. However, the various commentators (perhaps led by Townsend) tend towards the view that poverty is a relative condition, and that it is signalled in the first instance by trying to live on an income at or below the level of the state's social benefits. At the same time, there is further agreement that 'poverty' in this sense is closely associated with and intimately tied to several further prominent dimensions of deprivation, most notably in the areas of employment earnings; material wealth; accommodation; and health. In 1989, official Social Security statistics showed that as many as 249 000 unmarried mothers were trying to survive on state benefits while supporting 334 000 children. Although there is general acknowledgement that unmarried mothers and children endure poverty, less attention has been paid to the precise character of the connections between (a) births outside marriage; (b) subsequent low incomes; and (c) previous resource levels. There is clear evidence that births outside marriage are far more likely within the working class than within the middle class, and that this pattern has persisted despite recent overall trends. During the 1980s, the proportion of births outside marriage almost trebled, and official statistics (OPCS, 1990a) show that by 1988 about 70 per cent were jointly registered, with the vast majority (78 per cent) of jointly-registered babies having manual working-class fathers.

However, the upsurge in births outside marriage is not confined to the working class. *Birth Statistics 1988* (OPCS, 1990a) show that 'over the last ten years (1978–88), the rate of growth has been similar (roughly four-fold) in all social classes' (ibid., p. 13). Nevertheless, proportionately more babies are born outside marriage to working-class than to middle-class parents. In economically disadvantaged areas of major cities and towns, the rates of births outside marriage is far higher than the national average of 27 per cent. Rosemary Collins (1991) has established a relationship between births outside marriage and indicators of economic disadvantage. By examining official statistics on birth, crime and umemployment rates, Collins has demonstrated a positive correlation between areas with high rates of crime, high rates of unemployment and high rates of birth outside marriage. Essentially, the evidence clearly lends itself to the conclusion that where social deprivation is the greatest, rates of birth outside marriage tend to be relatively high.

During the 1980s, the number of people living in poverty has been judged to have increased considerably (Piachaud, 1987). The growing impoverishment of society stemmed from the way the persistence of social inequalities in income, wealth, housing, education and health were exacerbated by the economic changes introduced by the Thatcher administration (1979 to 1990) to throw many more members of the working class into the category of people with no more than subsistence level incomes and resources. There is little doubt that the economic changes had a devastating impact on working-class life and opportunities in Britain. The 1980s witnessed the systematic dismantling of the country's manufacturing base, with the resulting loss of thousands of jobs and consequently a considerable rise in the rate of unemployment. Steelworks, coalmines, factories and shipbuilding yards were closed, and there was a shift of labour out of the manufacturing sector into the distributive and public sectors. Those workers who remained in manufacture were deskilled (or at least *re*-skilled) by virtue of the rapid introduction of new technology. Of course, when industrial capital is suddenly and decisively withdrawn from a locality, the social and cultural life of the community is disrupted. A very large number of families experienced unemployment during the 1980s, and children were brought up knowing that jobs were scarce and, when available, often insecure.

Young working-class adults fared especially badly through the Thatcher years. Clarke and Willis argue that during the 1980s, the usual transition from school to work became a thing of the past:

A guillotine has fallen on the traditional couplet school/work and chopped out an empty chunk of time for most youngsters: five years before their first job, or perhaps before permanent unemployment. The changed situation can be stated simply – 'there ain't no jobs'. (Clarke and Willis, 1984, p. 2)

Apart from formal academic qualifications, by the end of the 1980s there was a very limited range of routes into moderately well-paid jobs for school leavers. Apprenticeships had been all but abolished and replaced with numerous government training schemes which rarely led to permanent, secure employment. According to the youth employment charity, Youthaid, less than six out of ten young people on youth training schemes in 1986 eventually got a job and only 38 per cent of young *black* people achieved the same result (Open University, 1988, p. 29). Finn explains that young school leavers 'are not just accidental victims of the recession and economic decline [. . .] rather, having been excluded from the labour market, they are now being actively redefined as a key element in the state's solution to the crisis of mass employment' (Finn, 1984, p. 61).

Those who did get employment often managed to find only jobs which were low paid, highly monotonous and with few opportunities for advancement. Indeed, the government deliberately encouraged employers to pay low wages. Between 1981 and 1986, for example, the Young Workers' Scheme 'provided employers with a £15 weekly subsidy per job on condition that weekly wages for young workers [were] held below £55' (Byrne, 1987, p. 28).

Female unemployment grew rapidly during the 1980s, outstripping male unemployment. Between 1979 and 1986, the number of registered unemployed women rose a 189 per cent, from 346 700 to 1 001 700 (Glendinning, 1987). Since women in employment are concentrated disproportionately within the public sector, their jobs became especially vulnerable to the cuts by the Conservative government in public spending. Of course, the rise in female unemployment meant a reduction in the employment opportunities available to young women. Under the Thatcher administration, the Conservative Party became strongly committed to lowering inflation, reducing taxation and cutting back on welfare provision. Cuts in state benefit were justified on the grounds that reliance on benefits encouraged dependency on the state and undermined individual choice. Paradoxically, as Smart (1987) has noted, changes in welfare provision led to increased dependency by young adults on their parents, and thereby to a greater burden on the family.

State policies on youth employment and welfare provision affected young working-class adults in a number of ways. At one extreme, there was the massive increase in homelessness among those with the problem of being without either jobs or families on which to rely. Also, there was widespread homelessness among those whose experience of family life included conflict, violence, physical mistreatment and sexual abuse, and who therefore had compelling reasons to escape from their parental homes. Young people's long tradition of leaving home due to family disharmony and disaffection became translated into homelessness on a unprecedented scale due to structural developments and downturns *vis-à-vis* employment patterns, the housing market and the social welfare system. At another level, high house prices combined with low wages meant that the prospect of attaining the ideal of a conjugal family arrangement became increasingly remote for young adults. By the 1990s, the working class were trying to conduct their lives in terms of an all-embracing consumer culture, which portrays household goods, home ownership, high incomes, stable marriages and personal happiness as being readily within the grasp of all – or at least all those with the correct levels of motivation, determination and application. But, dissatisfaction and demoralization were the inevitable concomitants of a cultural package which promised so much while providing so little to those who had only their unskilled labour power to sell on the market.

A working-class culture and life style dominated by economic recession and massive unemployment provided the setting within which many births outside marriage occurred during the 1980s. Clarke, however, has warned of the dangers of 'collapsing "working-class culture" into some simple, expressive, homogeneous entity' (1979, p. 23), arguing that it entails a variety and diversity of cultural forms which are being constantly transformed in accordance with society-wide economic, political and ideological developments. Following Clarke, the argument in this chapter is that that aspect of working-class culture which is reflected in the incidence of births outside marriage was shaped during the 1980s not only by such perennial and personally immediate factors as family background, educational experience and racial identity; but also by more fundamental and pervasive social forces which – as a result of the particular policies of the Thatcher years – surfaced as a growing divide between the rich and the poor; an overall impoverishment of working-class life; truncated employment prospects; severe cuts in social welfare provision; and altered views about the importance of marriage.

According to Simms and Smith (1982), the frequent occurrence of births outside marriage has always been a feature of working-class life and culture. However, whereas in the past the solution to a single woman becoming pregnant was likely to have been a 'shot-gun wedding' or adoption, by the end of the 1980s most unmarried mothers remained single while keeping their babies. This reflects the way in which there has been an easing of the stigma attached to giving birth outside marriage, and an associated shift in the norms surrounding sexual conduct and its relationship with marriage – as perhaps indicated by the fact that whereas in 1977 25 per cent of women marrying were pregnant, in 1987 only 12 per cent were. Essentially, a high proportion of births outside marriage within the working class represents a deeply rooted, traditional pattern, which acquired a somewhat novel, 'modern' expression as the proportion reached 27 per cent of all births during the 1980s.

There is evidence also that births outside marriage can arise directly from the experience of poverty. In particular, an association has been demonstrated between single teenage mothers and impoverished family backgrounds. For instance, the study carried out in London by Simms and Smith (1986) has shown that teenage mothers are likely to come from large families living in poverty; to have mothers who themselves got pregnant at a young age; and to have separated parents. A study by Dornbusch and Gray (1988) in the USA reports that a high incidence of births outside marriage to young black women is linked to poverty along with a lack of employment opportunities in that country.

However, births outside marriage within the working class are far from being confined to very young mothers. In fact, the number of births outside marriage peak not among teenagers, but within the 20–24 age range. In 1989, for instance, 43 500 births outside marriage were to mothers under twenty; 70 800 were to mothers between twenty and twenty four; and 41 900 were to mothers in the range 25–29 (OPCS, 1990d). The number of births outside marriage to women in their twenties trebled between 1981 and 1989 (ibid.). The issue of why more women were having babies without marriage by the end of the 1980s requires further examination. The most obvious answer would appear again to lie in the way family life had been re-shaped by the state's social policy in relation to such matters as employment, housing and social welfare. The selective operation of the labour market as far as men and women are concerned has to be taken into account, in conjunction with both changes in the earning power of men in their early twenties and changes in the social roles and aspirations of young women. It may well be that by the end of the 1980s, quite a few working-class women were having children outside marriage in the knowledge that a conjugal family is difficult to sustain even at an average standard of living.

The increase in the number of births outside marriage within the working class was also shaped by the class's post-1950s' recomposition through the importation of immigrant labour. Second generation black youth have, to some extent, maintained patterns of family life that exist in the West Indies. Nicki Thorogood's research, for example, has shown that economic and emotional independence for black women continues to be an important factor in the way they organize their everyday personal and social lives. This independence has its roots in 'a system of production based on the separation of economically active men (and sometimes women) from their dependants' (Thorogood, 1987, p. 28). It is manifested in the practice of many black women bringing up their children outside marriage (Cashmore, 1985).

The discussion so far has outlined some of the processes which help account for the increase in births outside marriage within the working class. It is clear that the chances of the resulting children being brought up in poverty are relatively high (Cashmore, 1985; Graham, 1984; Millar, 1987). Both the custodial parents (usually the mothers) and the children are likely to experience low incomes, inadequate housing and poor health. The discussion continues with an examination of the socio-economic background of a research sample of unmarried parents, and looks at the way the common experience of poverty affects their personal and social relationships, especially between the parents themselves.

THE NOTTINGHAM AND BRISTOL STUDY

During 1989, we conducted a research project on unmarried parents in two English cities – Nottingham in the Midlands and Bristol in the south-west – based on data drawn from the respective county courts and magistrates' courts (the *sample courts*).[3] The main aim of the study was to monitor the Affiliation and Proceedings Act 1957 during its final year of operation prior to the implementation of the Family Law Reform Act 1987. Two methodological procedures were adopted. First, data were collected from the official court files relating to unmarried parents' custody, access and maintenance applications to the sample courts during 1988: there were 458 cases in all – 384 from the magistrates' courts and 74 from the county courts. Second, almost a hundred further cases were observed during 1989. Thirty-six of the observed cases were resolved with final custody, access and maintenance orders, and these particular cases were analyzed in depth.

The principal findings of the study have been comprehensively reported elsewhere (Collins and Macleod, 1990; Collins, 1991), and the purpose of the present discussion will be served by focusing on certain aspects. That is, the study generated data on the incomes, living arrangements, accommodation and family composition of just under a thousand ($N = 916$) parents who had been responsible for births outside marriage, and this data can be used to elucidate the social dimensions of such births within the working class.

The parents studied in Nottingham and Bristol cannot be regarded as a representative sample in the technical sense of all unmarried parents. In the first place, we looked at less than a thousand parents from somewhat arbitrarily selected courts. But, in any case, the study sample of 'couples' is a biased one in that it covers only those instances where one parent has taken the other to court, and accordingly where the relationships involved have 'broken down'. The sample parents were drawn almost exclusively from the working class, and typically survived on state benefits or low wages. A high proportion were unemployed; many where sharing accommodation with their own parents or other relatives; and about a third had had children with more than one partner. Essentially the data are largely restricted to certain especially deprived sections of working-class parents, but we regard them as indicative of more inclusive patterns and trends. That is, as far as we are concerned, the data represent a more general association between poverty, unemployment and low wages on the one hand and a high incidence of births outside of marriage on the other hand, especially in major urban centres, during the 1980s (not only in Britain, but also the USA, Australia and other societies).

The sample parents' backgrounds were traced through the court files and through court observation. The files provided basic details about the parents' employment, earnings, accommodation, cohabitation and number of children. The information contained in the files was not recorded in accordance with any kind of standard procedure, so that between the files there was considerable variation with regard to presentation and content, to the point that in some cases the documentation was very thin and of little use. Despite this limitation, it was possible to detect the social and economic circumstances of most of the parents. Moreover, the notes taken by the court clerks at magistrates' hearings gave some insight into the relationships between parents (as 'couples'); the written evidence in the county court files often outlined the conflict and breakdown between parents that had led to the court cases; and court observations provided an opportunity to gather further important detail about the parents.

Each of the sources of information presented a restricted view of unmarried parenthood, and because the study sample were not formally interviewed (at least by us), the Nottingham–Bristol study revealed no systematic information about unmarried parents' definitions of the situation, meanings and experiences. At the most, glimpses of the everyday lives of the parents could be gleaned from official records. For instance, the parents' addresses indicated which type of area and community they lived in. Most lived in deprived areas, and the details about their incomes placed most around the poverty line. Also, the records revealed many families in which there were children by different fathers, indicating the frequent occurrence of family arrangements and experiences which were constantly changing and highly complex.

In the first instance, the data were examined to uncover the extent to which the parents were living in poverty. Ken Coates and Richard Silburn point out on the basis of their 1960s study and account of poverty in Nottingham that 'poverty has many dimensions, each one of which must be studied separately, but which in reality constitute an inter-related network of deprivations' (Coates and Silburn, 1970, p. 45). The presence among the sample parents according to the data of low incomes provided a key for identifying those families which were trying to survive on very limited resources in general, and thereby a starting point for investigating the wider dimensions and ramifications of these families' poverty.

The data show that the majority of the sample mothers and children were receiving the state's income support, and that the total income of most of these families was no more than £64 per week. The high incidence of sample families attempting to live on nothing other than state benefits was undoubtedly due to the effects of the prevailing policies, rules and regulations which restricted the mothers' paid employment.

In 1988, the year covered by the court files data, the rules relating to the receipt of state benefits firmly discouraged unmarried mothers from seeking paid employment. Whereas in 1980, parents had been able to work in paid employment for up to twelve hours before incurring a reduction in their state benefits, in April 1988 the period was reduced to just five hours (National Audit Office, 1990). During 1988, about 230 000 single parents had 'transitional protection' against any reduction in the state benefits they had been receiving before the April changes relating to paid employment. However, most of these parents would have then gone on to lose the protection by remaining in paid employment for more than eight weeks, when they could earn a mere £15 above their benefit payments before incurring a reduction. Furthermore, if the single parents who owned their homes took a temporary job for more than eight weeks, they were penalized by having help with their mortgage interest payments reduced by a half for the first sixteen weeks of any new claim for income support.

When considering the possibility of taking on paid employment, single parents in receipt of state benefits have to weigh the expected level of earnings against any job-related expenses and state benefit loses or reductions. They will need to assess whether the additional net income they will acquire through paid employment will outweigh the reduction in housing benefit. They will need to calculate whether entering paid employment will entail childcare costs which will result in a weekly income which is lower than their current income support levels.

Most of the sample mothers and custodial fathers were receiving state benefits, but this does not necessarily imply a lifetime of dependency on the state. Various studies have shown that low income families tend to have periods in receipt of state benefits interspersed with periods of paid employment. In the USA, Dornbusch and Gray (1988) carried out a ten year longitudinal study which shows that single parent families frequently depend upon the state for about two years before entering employment followed by a further return to welfare.

Although paid employment represents independence for many single parents, any decision about taking on a job will be conditional upon considerations relating to the state benefits system and also the local availability of jobs and of childcare. Millar (1987, p. 167) has shown how the unequal position of women within the paid labour market translates into single mothers facing considerable difficulties with trying to maintain stable, full-time employment. Given that women's gross weekly average wages are still only two-thirds of men's and that women often become progressively deskilled due to their somewhat intermittent participation in the paid labour force (Martin and Roberts, 1984), then working-class single mothers are likely to find the task of keeping their family incomes much above state benefit levels almost impossible even when they are receiving wages.

The presence of gender associated inequalities within the labour market serve to reinforce the poverty of single parents. Among the magistrates' courts sample, only a minority of the mothers were in paid employment: forty eight mothers worked full-time and twenty-six worked part-time. Earnings were very low, averaging only £4800 gross per year for those in full-time jobs – compared, for instance, with averages for all women employees and for all manual employees at the beginning of 1986 of £7134 and £5590 respectively (see *New Earnings Survey*, April 1986, Table A.14). The mothers tended to be employed in manual, service and clerical occupations in factories, shops, catering establishments and offices.

The financial position of the magistrates' courts sample of fathers was better than that of the mothers, but still compared badly with that of men in general in 1988. A quarter of the sample were unemployed, and those who were employed earned low wages – on average, £7629 per year compared with an average for men in general in England of £12 220 (*Regional Trends* 23, 1988). The fathers' occupations ranged from being unskilled labourers on building sites and in factories to being semi-skilled tradesmen in plumbing, plastering and similar crafts. The sample included several bus, lorry and van drivers, and some of the fathers were employed in the catering industry or as store assistants. Most fathers were concentrated in the secondary labour market, being employed in the least well paid, desirable and protected jobs.

The fathers' employment profiles indicate that they had low levels of qualifications and skill, so that their market situation was reminiscent of the male employees in Nottingham described by Coates and Silburn:

> Even in a city as relatively prosperous as Nottingham, there are large groups of workers whose wages are extremely low: many of these men depend upon crucifyingly long hours or regular overtime to secure themselves a decent income. (Coates and Silburn, 1970, p. 50)

Coates and Silburn's findings highlight the continuity in class inequalities over a period of years, given that their study was conducted in the mid-1960s. They explored the connections between low wages and poverty, and argued that the dimensions of poverty include gross environmental deprivation – represented by inadequate housing, high density population, pollution and a lack of privacy; social deprivation – in the form of inadequate public facilities and services; and 'impoverished states of mind' – in the sense that the poor are dominated by feelings of powerlessness and fatalism.

Consistent with Coates and Silburn's findings, the poverty of single parents is strongly reflected in the quality of their accommodation. Various studies have confirmed that single parents tend to be in accommodation which is sub-standard and overcrowded compared with two-parent families. For instance, Peter Townsend's major study of poverty has revealed how lone mothers endure a cluster of deprivations largely centred on inadequate housing. Moreover, Townsend's findings have been amply supported by the data derived through the *General Household Survey* (1983) which show that almost two-thirds of lone mothers are local authority tenants, compared with only a quarter of two-parent families. A fifth share accommodation with other adults, compared with only a twentieth of two-parent families.

The sample mothers in our study had accommodation which was in line with the general pattern. Relevant information was available for 206 of the 384 mothers who went to magistrates' courts. Nearly half of these mothers (N = 98) were living with their own parents (in their parental homes) or with other relatives. Only a sixth (N = 34) reported living with a partner – although this figure has to be viewed alongside the possibility that some mothers will not have admitted cohabiting for fear of losing their state benefits. Ninety one of the mothers reported living alone with their children, forty seven in local authority accommodation. The remainder of the study sample were in rented or 'other' (including women's refuge) accommodation. The data show that only a fifth of the mothers about whom information was available were living in local authority housing (although with regard to this figure, it is important to note that the data on housing refer to the parents' situation at the time of their court applications, often made soon after there had been a failure in financial support or a breakdown in cohabitation. Later in their personal histories, more of the parents are likely to have been living alone with their children, perhaps in local authority housing).

Townsend's research (1979) provides evidence showing how overcrowded accommodation can result in considerable tension and stress among household members, a finding confirmed by other sources of information, such as reports on homelessness. In *Social Trends* 20 (1990, p. 133), for example, the claim is made that the 'main immediate reason for statutory homelessness is that parents, friends or relatives are no longer willing or able to accommodate'. Homelessness is especially acute in Nottingham: in 1989 the city ranked among the 'top-four' cities and towns outside London in the homeless household tables (*Local Housing Statistics*, 1990). Although the statistics do not specify how many homeless households are headed by single parents, it is reasonable to assume that many single parent families living with relatives will become homeless through a combination of the relatives being unable to cope and alternative accommodation being unavailable.

The housing situation of mothers who are not married can change dramatically over a short period of time. For instance, breakdowns in relationships with cohabiting partners are common, resulting in mothers frequently returning to their parental homes – at least for a while, until they leave to either again cohabit or take up local authority tenancies. Local authorities provide the principal channel through which mothers acquire independent housing, reflecting the mothers' frequent paucity of financial resources.

It is striking how the accommodation of the sample fathers in our study was of a similar range and standard to that of the mothers. Information was available for 204 of the fathers who went to magistrates' courts, and this showed how over a third (N = 76) were living with their parents, again representing to some extent transitional accommodation following the breakdown of relationships with cohabiting partners. It is clear that some fathers were experiencing considerable overcrowding, as indicated by the details of one case observed in court:

> Clyde, Alisha and Winston lived in a three-bedroomed council house with their parents. Alisha, who was sixteen, slept in one bedroom with her sixteen month old baby. Clyde and his brother shared a bedroom with Clyde's daughter, also sixteen months. Clyde and Alisha were both unemployed. Clyde had come to court for a custody order after his daughter's mother had left the baby with the social services, stating she never wanted to see her again.[4]

A third of the sample fathers were cohabiting with new partners, and only a fifth of them were living alone. Few of them (N = 26) were in council accommodation, but as many as forty seven owned the homes in which they were living (were 'owner occupiers'). Unfortunately, the data in the court files did not include information on the parents' history – their passage between different types – of accommodation. For instance, the data did not indicate the length of time which parents lived with relatives before, say, moving into local authority accommodation.

Since the publication in 1970 of Coates and Silburn's study of poverty in Nottingham, the slum housing on which they focussed has been largely removed by a wholesale slum clearance programme. However, the slow-down in the rate of public housing provision during the 1970s, combined with the virtual absence of local government accommodation specifically for single parent families, has exacerbated the degree to which families with few resources are disadvantaged within the housing market.

The data were examined further for evidence about patterns in the parents' relationships as 'couples', with particular attention being given to periods of cohabitation. The national investigation by Haskey (1989), based on data from the *General Household Surveys* for 1986 and 1987, detected a clear upward trend in the incidence and popularity of unmarried co-habitation within Britain as a whole during the course of the 1980s. For instance, whereas in 1979 11 per cent of all single women in the age range 18–20 years were cohabiting, by 1987 the proportion had risen to 19 per cent. Haskey's data show that a high proportion (over a half) of those couples who got married during 1987 had done so following a period of cohabitation. The data also suggest that there is a strong tendency for couples to cohabit as a prelude to marriage, and moreover for couples to live together for quite short periods of time before getting married. In other words, while unmarried cohabitation had become a lot more popular by the end of the 1980s, it was frequently being used as a temporary, transitional and preparatory stage between being unmarried and being married. A further finding was that within the age range 25–29 years, non-married women with children accounted for 29 per cent of cohabiting women; while non-married women with children accounted for 19 per cent of all single, non-cohabiting women. Haskey states that it is difficult to unravel 'the dynamics of fertility and cohabitation behaviour' (ibid., p. 30), but nonetheless was able to estimate that in 1987 4 per cent of all dependent children were living in cohabiting couple families compared with 12 per cent living in one-parent families.

Relevant information about our study sample of magistrates' courts parents (as 'couples') was available for only 60 per cent (N = 165), but this revealed that 72 per cent of parents had sustained a cohabiting relationship for a period of between one and three years. The evidence indicated that cohabitation had been the norm among the smaller, county courts sample, with 98 per cent of the seventy four 'couples' having had a period of living together. These findings are consistent with Haskey's analysis which suggests that the chances of the child of an unmarried couple living with both its parents within a stable, long-term cohabiting unit are slight. Our study sample of 'couples' had had periods of cohabitation which were quite short, lasting usually for between one and three years. Since over two-thirds of the couples had an eldest child under the age of three, few of the sample children would have lived with both their parents for more than one or two years; and some (a quarter of the children covered by the magistrates' courts sample) would have had no experience of shared parenthood.

The data show considerable variation in cohabitation patterns, with some couples having split up prior to their babies being born and others separating shortly afterwards. Some couples had experience of previous cohabitations, while others had been through divorces and separations with previous partners. Some couples had cohabited intermittently, indicating that they had been neither fully committed nor fully separated arrangements. Unfortunately, incomplete information in the court files means that it is impossible to explore those patterns thoroughly and systematically.

The data on cohabitation suggest channels for further investigation into family diversity and change, and show that births outside marriage occur to partners across a wide range of living arrangements. The overall conclusions that can be drawn from the data on the study sample of single parents' socio-economic background are that the parents are relatively disadvantaged in terms of income, housing and stability of relationships; and that they tend to have a lower standard of living than that enjoyed by conjugal families bringing in average wages.

BRINGING UP CHILDREN OUTSIDE MARRIAGE

The study data indicate both the presence of a variety of routes into the experience of having a baby outside marriage and a range of socially constructed problems that can arise as part of that experience. This can be illustrated by turning to details of particular cases, the first entailing oral evidence presented at a contested paternity hearing. The mother had had an unplanned pregnancy following a short-term relationship with the father:

Joanne worked in a hairdressing salon. She liked going out with her mates and having a good laugh. By the age of twenty two she still hadn't found a regular boyfriend. One night she went to the pub with her friend and found herself standing next to Martin and his friend. The foursome started talking and a couple of days later Joanne and Martin went out drinking together. At the time, he had a well paid job as a construction worker but was on a short term contract.

They started meeting regularly and soon began a sexual relationship. It was difficult for them to meet privately because they both lived with their parents. One evening, Joanne managed to stay the night with a friend and Martin came to join her after he had finished his evening shift.

Shortly afterwards, Joanne had a pregnancy test which was positive. The couple had only known each other two months and Martin's initial reaction was outrage. He got drunk, met Joanne, swore at her and demanded that she had an abortion. He apologized the next day and asked how he could help. Joanne told him to leave her alone and stopped seeing him. Their daughter was born eight months later.

Joanne carried on living with her parents and the baby. She thought Martin was irresponsible, describing him as 'a terrible bloke really who's been done for drunk driving and all sorts'. She was glad she no longer saw him. After the baby was born she'd stopped going out drinking and lived a more housebound life.

Joanne's case confirms how women are able to land themselves an unplanned and unexpected pregnancy despite the range of effective contraceptive methods and devices available during the 1980s. At the same time, she stressed her delight with her child once born, even though she had found it difficult living merely on the income support she had been receiving since giving up paid employment. Moreover, the case shows how the experience of birth-outside-marriage is shaped by the two factors of a limited housing provision and a low level of income.

The notes in the court files suggest that only a minority of the study sample of mothers had had babies following short-term relationships, even though a quarter of the magistrates' courts sample are known not to have cohabited. The following relates to a case in which the couple had had a relatively long term, but nevertheless fragile, arrangement:

> Linda and Stephen were in their early thirties and had lived together for three years. Linda had two children from her previous marriage and she and Stephen had a baby about a year after cohabitation began. After the relationship broke down, Linda was in severe financial difficulties as she was unable to find accommodation for herself and three children with reasonable rent.

A few cases involved long-term relationships between parents which strongly resembled formal marriages:

> Jennifer and Terry lived together for eight years from the time of Jennifer's pregnancy. After separating, Jennifer stayed in the council flat with her son and continued her part-time job. Terry moved back in with his parents and remained on good terms with Jennifer. He continued to do football training with his son every Wednesday and spent one day of the weekend with him.

Only twenty-nine study sample parents' living arrangements included a period of having lived together for more than five years.

The three cases so far reflect the diversity which characterizes the formation of non-marital families. However, while there was considerable variety in the circumstances which had surrounded the births of the children, all the families had come to share the common experience of conducting their lives in poverty. The study data provide many examples of the way poverty constrained and constructed the parents' relationships. Some couples were simply unable to cope with the task of bringing up children on low incomes. That is, the break-up of relationships was often rooted in the lack of financial resources, as the following case illustrates:

> Karen was seventeen and Anthony was nineteen when their son was born. They began living together after the birth and continued to do so for three years until Karen found a new boyfriend. Karen worked long hours in the day as a factory worker and Anthony worked nights as a dye-house operative. The little boy was variously looked after by the parents, a childminder and grandmother. When they broke up, Anthony had £10 000 worth of debts.

Despite their efforts, Karen and Anthony were unable to remain financially solvent, and the court files record how debts were a contributory factor in bringing their relationship to an end.

The connection between having children outside marriage and having an impoverished life is illustrated in the details of another case. Dawn was interviewed in Middlesbrough in the north-east of England during a pilot investigation in preparation for the Nottingham and Bristol study (Collins, 1989). The case is referred to here because it exhibits a number of features that recurred among those study sample mothers who were teenagers when they first gave birth: low occupational skill; a long period of unemployment; and an unpredictable, violent partner.

Dawn lived in a 1950s semi-detached council house about two miles from the town centre. The front garden was neglected. The house was sparsely furnished, clean and tidy, but the uncarpeted stairs were blood-stained from the time Danny attacked her. Dawn had been unable to scrub the stains away. The living room was bare and cold, containing a sofa, carpet, television, gas fire and wall unit. Dawn was pleased with her attempts to redecorate the kitchen. She had covered the damp walls with cheap wallpaper. Some damp was already showing through. The cracked backdoor window pane provided more evidence of Danny's violence.

Dawn was in her early twenties. Her relationship with Danny was turbulent. They had two daughters. The eldest, Raquel, was born when they were both teenagers and Gemma arrived four years later. Sometimes the family lived together amicably. At other times, Danny would attack her, imitating his father's behaviour with his mother. Following these outbursts, he would leave the home for weeks. He had snatched Raquel from her mother twice when meeting them in the street. On the first occasion, the police found him crying in his car in a strange city two hundred miles away. He did not know what to do with the baby or to do next.

Dawn dreamt about a man who loved her and wasn't violent, living in a privately-owned house on a new estate, having a regular income and luxury goods like a car, a dining-table with matching chairs and new toys for the children.

In the meantime, her life was drab and monotonous. She wanted a job but couldn't find one that paid enough money for the children and Danny was no help because he was unemployed. She had hardly any friends and her family had cut themselves off when she took up with Danny. Every evening was spent watching television and dreading the possibility that he might arrive drunk on the doorstep. Living in the same street as prostitutes meant that the nights were noisy because of all the cars arriving and departing outside.

Dawn described her situation as a nightmare. When I called to interview her, she cried for several minutes before she began to talk.

The Nottingham–Bristol data show that when parents are cohabiting, their relationships vary between coping with an atmosphere of misery and domestic violence and being largely amicable until the break up. The problems faced by the mothers are sometimes compounded by having had children by more than one partner. The data indicate that a relatively large number of the parents in the study sample had had children by other partners. In the magistrates' courts sample, 42 per cent (N = 65) of the fathers (about whom relevant information was available) had such children; whereas a slightly lower figure of 36 per cent of the mothers (N = 64) had. One case observed in court illustrates the resulting complexity of arrangements:

> Carlton was a skilled manual worker taking home about £150 per week. He had lived with Rosaline intermittently for about six years: their daughters were six and eight. When he met Gillian, he alternated between living with her, or Rosaline, or his father who lived in a small terraced house Carlton had bought. When Gillian's son was two, he met Maxine and she became pregnant fairly quickly.

Carlton appeared in court on two separate occasions in consecutive weeks. The first appearance concerned Maxine's child and his second concerned Gillian's child. Carlton distinguished between his 'proper' family (Rosaline and her children), the family he saw occasionally (Gillian and her child), and the family he wanted nothing to do with (Maxine and her child). Meanwhile, all the families lived on income support, and a proportion of Carlton's relatively low earnings were distributed between them.

This particular case underlines the predicament a woman may face when she becomes involved with a man who is unwilling to commit himself to the relationship. It also illustrates the way some men actively avoid and even reject the conjugal family form in favour of a more varied, looser form of family life which allows them continuing sexual relations and access to their children, while freeing them from daily family obligations.

Cashmore's research (1985) covered mothers who had had children by more than one father, and it indicates that the pattern is quite common. Moreover, his findings, based on interviews with single parents, show that mothers find considerable difficulty establishing lasting relationships with men who are not their children's fathers after they have had more than one child by different partners. Some women are likely, therefore, to experience many years of single parenthood.

Debts, domestic violence and uncommitted partners were some of the main factors running through the lives of our study sample of parents leading to the break-up of the relationships they had had with their partners. In a minority of cases, the problems were so overwhelming that mothers had walked out of their homes. Three cases were observed in the Nottingham magistrates' court, one of which involved Angela:

> Angela and Graham were both unemployed and had spent some time as 'travellers'. Eventually, they returned to Nottingham with their baby and moved in with the paternal grandparents. The relationship between Angela and Graham became difficult. She moved out for a while, returned and then left again. Graham applied for custody. By the time the case was heard, Angela was pregnant and homeless. In a dispirited way, she said she was happy for Graham to have custody.
>
> Graham, who was twenty-four, was working as a kitchen porter.

In this particular case, homelessness, lack of employment and difficulties between the parents combined to press Angela into feeling that she could no longer continue bringing up the child.

Other files revealed that cohabitation, like marriage, can entail unstable, disturbed and violent patterns of family life. For instance:

> Carolyn and Brian met when she was a teenager. He had a long criminal record and was unemployed. They lived together with their two children for five years. Brian often hit Carolyn and their relationship was bitter and acrimonious. She left him for Alan, who had children in [local government] care. Carolyn's children had speech problems and were quiet and withdrawn. The daughter described as 'dead eyed' by her teacher, was on the at-risk register [a list of children deemed by the social services to be at risk of non-accidental injuries from parents or other household members].

A further file was about Denise and Dean:

> When Denise met Dean, she was fifteen and he was seventeen. He already had a criminal record and was violent and abusive to her from the start. Despite these circumstances, she became pregnant straight away. Between the child's birth and second birthday, Dean was sent down [to prison] for burglary. On release, he bullied Denise into working for him as a prostitute [. . .] She carried on working until the night he assaulted her for bringing home only £20. Denise fled to a woman's refuge with her daughter.

These three cases from among the study sample suggest that having a baby outside marriage can be an integral part of an impoverished way of life: that is of a life which has little to offer when judged in terms of the goals set by an achievement-oriented society. Unlikely to meet prospective husbands with the kind of occupational skills which bring a comfortable life-style, women like Angela, Carolyn and Denise with very few marketable skills of their own may be tempted into settling for and risking cohabitation with unreliable partners. Carolyn's case reflects clearly how state intervention is targeted at the individual rather than at the underlying social structural forces which help shape and construct the social problem presented by 'at-risk' families. Denise's case illustrates how one outcome of limited employment opportunities for young women can increase their dependency on their families – which for Denise's case means her cohabitee. The difficulties faced by Denise were compounded by the scarcity of rented accommodation; the rules relating to the receipt of state benefit (when pregnant, she was too young to claim); and the fear of her violent partner.

Angela, Carolyn and Denise were all teenagers when their first child was born. Commenting on teenage pregnancies, Cashmore has remarked:

> the phenomenon is not just about more girls having sex at earlier ages without taking precautions. It is also about disturbed family backgrounds, deteriorating job markets and different cultural traditions. (Cashmore, 1985, p. 173)

The phenomenon will also be characterized and fashioned by the sense of powerlessness and fatalism that accompanies the experience of living in poverty. Cashmore makes the further point that few women actively choose and plan to become lone parents, yet even before becoming pregnant their futures are constrained by the limited opportunities and constraining social structure that encompass their lives (ibid., p. 173).

This chapter has shown how the experience of unmarried parenthood – usually unmarried motherhood – is socially constructed in a number of different ways. Unmarried parenthood is often subjected to regular transformation as different partners enter and leave the family lives of the mothers and their children. At the time of their court hearings, most mothers are struggling to support their families on very low incomes, and so live in poverty with its associated inadequate accommodation and other related problems.

Cashmore suggests that the common situation whereby fathers fail to provide their families with regular financial support indicates the 'weakening of obligations and "honourable" ties that bind fathers to the women that they make pregnant in a moral and possibly legal relationship' (Cashmore, 1985, p. 172). While Cashmore's analysis and argument may be valid, the account in this chapter has focused on showing how the 'weakening of ties' between unmarried parents is shaped by the material circumstances of society along with the social policies of the state. The lives of the young working-class parents which we have touched on were strongly conditioned by the process of economic restructuring which occurred during the Thatcher years, leaving many more people unemployed or employed but in receipt of low wages. Once children are born, the lives of the custodial parents are circumscribed even further by social policy decisions on employment, housing and welfare provision.

The data suggest that when births outside marriage occur to parents with few skills, and with either low or no wages (through being unemployed), the resulting multiple economic disadvantages mean that they have considerable difficulty sustaining the viability of any alternative to the dominant conjugal family form (see Close, 1985). When state policy is directed at preserving the dominance of the conjugal family form, as it was in Britain during the 1980s, non-marital families become economically and socially marginalized. However, when such families have 'problems' that turn them into a 'social problem', thereby inviting state interest and intervention (through social work activity, for example), the ethos of intervention involved targets the individual. In this way, the state manages to disregard and by-pass those features of society's social structure which contribute to the deprived, impoverished and restricted lives of non-marital families. Moreover, while the state exercises control over non-marital families through social workers, state benefits, the law and other mechanisms, it also contributes to their expansion through its commitment to economic liberalism. In basing social policy on the need for, and so needs of, one particular family form (conjugal and patriarchal) – as the linchpin of social order – the state in effect reduces the ability of the poor to become self-sufficient and thereby enlarges the number of non-marital children being brought up in poverty.

NOTES

1. We are grateful to the Economic and Social Research Council for supporting our project.
2. We are familiar with the doubts surrounding the label 'unmarried mother', but are nonetheless using it on the grounds of convenience and consistency.

3. In England and Wales, magistrates' courts represent the preliminary level of the legal system. They are presided over by magistrates (or Justices of the Peace) who are not trained and qualified lawyers, and who usually work just part-time (there are about 29 000 JPs). These courts deal with minor (or 'summary') criminal offences, amounting to about 96 per cent of all criminal cases in England and Wales (about two million cases each year). The more serious criminal offences – involving rape or murder, for instance – are dealt with by higher courts (initially Crown Courts) presided over by legally trained and qualified 'circuit judges'. Magistrates' courts also cover a wide range of non-criminal, or 'civil', cases including family disputes, such as those in which women attempt to gain maintenance payments and in which local (government) authorities attempt to take children 'into care'. County courts also deal with civil disputes, but are presided over by legally trained and qualified 'circuit judges' (there are 94 Crown Courts).

4. All the personal names in what follows are fictitious.

4 Benign or Sinister?
Parental Responsibility and State Intervention in Britain
Sonia Jackson

All major political parties in Britain are committed to 'supporting the family'. The value and importance of the family was a consistent theme throughout the twelve years of the Thatcher administration, and was if anything reiterated with increasing vehemence. The same period saw a series of government measures combine to shift the costs of childrearing from society as a whole to parents in particular. But, rising expectations were not matched by material support; and within the government, conflicting positions were reflected in legislative decisions and administrative arrangements. For substantial sections of the population, parenting has steadily become more difficult. However, it is only when the family is eventually overwhelmed that the state acknowledges its own direct responsibility: at which point the state's intervention is likely to be perceived less like support and more like punishment.

Janet Finch, in her penetrating analysis of the concept of 'family responsibility' as applied to people who are either older or disabled, describes the commitment to supporting the family as 'a curious mixture of the benign and the sinister' (Finch, 1989, p.115). This phrase is equally apt with regard to parents in relation to children. Thus, in the middle of 1990, Margaret Thatcher delivered a frequently quoted speech in which she asserted that 'government must be concerned to see parents accept responsibility for their children'. Mrs Thatcher proceeded to make it clear that the way parents went about meeting this responsibility was their own affair and problem. The state was seen as having no part to play in the task of childrearing, which thereby became a matter for the family. Yet the same government carried through 'the most comprehensive piece of legislation which Parliament has ever enacted about children', the Children Act 1989 (Department of Health, 1989). This Act appears to represent a very different view of the relationship between the state and the family: it emphasizes a partnership between the two in an attempt to strike a balance between on the one hand, family autonomy and on the other hand, the protection of children.

In contrast with the simplistic pronouncements of politicians, the Children Act and its associated voluminous regulations and guidelines show considerable sensitivity about the way people's behaviour towards their children is heavily influenced by a complex mix of demographic, ideological and economic forces. However, on the issue of the financial and other resources required for its effective implementation, the Act manifests a curious reticence. We might speculate that the good intentions reflected in the Act will in practice founder on government determination to hold down public expenditure. In a sense, as I demonstrate later, the Children Act is a product of the British preoccupation with child protection, and thereby of the low level of state support for ordinary, non-deviant families with children. For the vast majority of families, the children of which do not come into contact with state agencies except within the educational system, the effect of government policies is less visible but just as pervasive. For the purpose of the ensuing discussion I will take for illustrative purposes the impact of government policies on gender roles within the family and on women's opportunities for participation in the paid labour force.

THE CHANGING BRITISH FAMILY

As the Children Act recognizes, the apparently straightforward question 'who are the child's parents?' is not as simple to answer as it would have been twenty years ago. As New and David (1985), among many other writers, have pointed out, the 'typical family' consisting of husband in paid employment, wife at home and dependent children now accounts for only a minority of households.[1] The incidence of divorce has risen enormously from 27 000 in 1961 to 151 000 in 1989 (OPCS, 1990c). The increase in divorce in Britain has been greater than in any other European country, although the trend has been the same everywhere. The evidence strongly suggests that more than one in three marriages currently being contracted will end in divorce. Over half of divorcing couples have a child under sixteen years, and the current prediction is that 7 per cent of children will experience the divorce of their parents by their fifth birthday; 12 per cent by their eighth birthday; and 24 per cent by their sixteenth birthday (OPCS, 1990c). The immediate effect is the creation of a large number of lone-parent households, mostly headed by women. However, since four out of five of those divorcing under the age of thirty remarry within five years, it is likely that increasing numbers of children will have the additional experience of living in a stepfamily.

There has been an even more dramatic upsurge of births outside marriage: the present proportion is 28 per cent of all births, representing a threefold increase over ten years. But also, it is possible to deduce from further published data that well over half of extra-marital births occur within stable parental relationships. For instance, 70 per cent of the births are jointly registered by both parents (OPCS, 1990a) (see Chapters 2 and 3 in this volume for further examination of this and related matters). Although all European countries have shown an increased tendency for couples to live together outside marriage, this trend has been more marked in Britain than anywhere else except for Sweden.

Married or not, women are choosing to have their children later in life. Thus, in 1989 the average age of women giving birth was 27.3 years, and this figure is projected to rise to 28.7 by the end of the century (with a corresponding decline in average family size). Economic pressures, combined with the growing assumption that women in two-parent families will be in paid employment outside the home, are likely to feed into the tendency for couples to have fewer children. The consequences for population patterns as well as for the paid labour force have been well recognized and much discussed, such as in the recent government Training Agency report on *Defusing the Demographic Timebomb* (NEDO, 1989). However, rather than having produced a pro-natalist response (along the lines of French policy), or a redistribution of resources in favour of parents, the British government's approach seems to have been dominated by nineteenth century apprehensions about a feckless underclass irresponsibly reproducing itself.

It has been argued that any changes in the profile of the British family have been exaggerated. For example, Pugh and De'Ath (1984) point out that four out of five children will spend the years from birth to sixteen at home with both their natural parents. Also, the rise in the divorce rate is partly a function of the popularity of marriage; and cohabitation regularly leads to marriage. In any case, cohabitation is frequently indistinguishable from 'marriage': the main difference being that the couple have not gone through a formal ceremony (Fletcher, 1988). Nevertheless, taking a longer historical view, it cannot be denied that ideas about what constitutes normal family life in Britain have been revolutionized. It is instructive to note that the undoubtedly enlightened and farseeing *Beveridge Report* of 1942, which laid the foundations for the system of social welfare and social security in Britain, contained the assumption of the permanence of marriage, so that it treated divorce and separation as minor issues. The *Report* viewed women in the unchanging roles of wives and mothers, who like their children are dependent upon their husbands for financial support. Many of the problems faced by parents in Britain today can be traced to the persistence in government thinking of this traditional model of family life, a model which hardly resembles social reality (Deakin and Wicks, 1988).

FATHERS AND MOTHERS

The allocation of gender roles within the family is an issue which attracts considerable research and popular interest in Britain. There seems to have been a significant ideological shift with regard to the appropriate pattern, as evidenced throughout both media reporting and attitudinal surveys. However, the degree to which such a development has been matched at the level of behaviour is in doubt. For instance, Lewis (1986) has argued that the 'emergent' father as popularized in the United States by such writers as Lamb (1976) and Levine (1980) is a myth, similar to that which tends to arise with each new generation. In practice, the vast majority of men and women still play roles very much along traditional lines, a conclusion which has been increasingly supported by United States research (Hochschild, 1990).[2]

One clearly demonstrable alteration, however, has been in the proportion of men attending the births of their children. Fathers were not allowed in the labour wards of British hospitals until 1970, but by 1974 around 40 per cent of them were attending. Brian Jackson (1984) found that 81 per cent of his sample of first-time fathers had attended the birth of their children, and a further 14 per cent said they intended to be there. More recent surveys have reported a figure as high as 94 per cent for London; and one of 87 per cent for Dublin, which was much slower to admit fathers. The attendance of fathers at the birth of their children in Britain has been given the royal seal of approval – Prince Charles was present at the birth of each of his two sons. He had not been similarly attended at the time of his own birth.

Most men report that witnessing a birth is an intense experience which brings them much closer to the mothers and their children (B. Jackson, 1984; Woollett, White and Lyon, 1982). The studies suggest that the experience often motivates fathers to be highly involved in childcare, not only after the child has grown enough to talk and be played with (as indicated by previous evidence), but also over the first few weeks of life. Brian Jackson (1984) argues that men's apparent withdrawal from childcare is a consequence of the insensitivity within the world of work to men's (as well as women's) desire to be closely attached to their young children.

This interpretation contrasts with that proposed by Charles Lewis (1986) according to which the attendance by fathers at the birth of their children is simply a socially prescribed ritual which has no bearing whatsoever on the fathers' subsequent involvement in childcare.

Perhaps whether and to what extent men are participating more in childcare will be established only when the results of research being conducted at present can be compared with those from enquiries in, say, ten years time. Major methodological problems arise by either asking men to compare their own parenting role with that of their fathers or comparing data collected in studies of fathers in previous generations with those obtained recently. People vary greatly in what they can remember about very early childhood; few can recall much before their fourth birthday; and most have a strong tendency towards conflation (Morton, 1990). Also, until the late 1970s, most researchers interviewed women only, and in any case asked questions which were framed in very vague terms. However, Lewis (in collaboration with John and Elizabeth Newson, 1982) has managed to generate research data which allows a systematic comparison of father participation in infant childcare in 1980 with that in 1960 in the city of Nottingham.[3] His conclusion is that there has been little change in the extent of fathers' participation in the care of very young children, with putting them to bed being the only activity showing a marked increase.

Similar comparisons have yet to be provided in the case of older children. However, in 1970 a longitudinal study (CHES) centred on the city of Bristol was begun and has provided some data on the childcare involvement of fathers in over 13 000 two-parent families when children are five years old (Osborn, Butler and Morris, 1984). Each mother was asked if in the previous week the father had (a) looked after the child for part of the day to allow her to do other things; (b) put the child to bed; (c) taken the child to school or nursery; (d) read to the child. Of course, this list of items represents a limited and somewhat crude guide to participation in childcare activities. However, it does tap into fathers' involvement beyond physical care; and the character of the questions does allow for reasonably accurate reporting of actual, concrete activity rather than merely overall perceptions or impressions. The results of the study tend to support Lewis's claim that the extent of fathers' involvement in childcare following the perinatal period has been exaggerated. In Bristol, no more than half the fathers helped with each of the activities; and only 4 per cent of them helped in all four ways.

Socio-economic variations appear to be less significant than might have been expected. There are almost no differences between socio-economic categories in the proportion of fathers who look after their children for part of the day; and only a shallow downward gradient from the most to the least privileged with respect to the extent to which fathers both put their children to bed and take them to school or nursery. The fourth item in the list, reading to children, showed by far the greatest differences. Brian Jackson (1984), by re-analyzing the same data, has shown that there are closely aligned differences among fathers in (a) their participation in the four activities and (b) their educational backgrounds. Of fathers with no formal educational qualifications, 39 per cent had read to their children during the previous week; for those with university degrees, the figure was 70 per cent; and for those with teaching qualifications, the figure rose to 76 per cent.

One interpretation of these findings, supported by various observational studies, such as that by J. McGuire (1982), is that fathers simply have greater freedom of choice over whether to participate in 'non-essential' domestic activities, and that therefore fathers choose to participate in what they regard as more important and find most congenial. At the same time, it seems that fathers' contribution to 'essential' activities varies to some extent in response to various practical considerations, such as the number and the ages of the children.

All empirical studies seem to confirm that the responsibility for the everyday essential childcare activities remains firmly with mothers, so that fathers provide help more or less as they choose (S. Jackson, 1987). Moreover, the majority of women appear to accept this situation. Backett (1982) shows that for men to ensure their wives' marital satisfaction, it is not necessary for them to actually do any childcare whatsoever. The crucial factor seems to be for women to simply perceive that their husbands would be willing to help with childcare activities if asked.

There is an interesting parallel here with male and female roles at the other end of the life cycle. Lewis and Meredith (1988) studied women who had cared for their elderly mothers and found that most of the women had made enormous efforts to prevent their caring activities and sense of obligation in this regard from encroaching on their husbands' lives. Even when the women's overall load was overwhelming, they nevertheless struggled to maintain the accustomed marital and household routine, such as by providing an unaltered pattern of meals for their husbands. Lewis and Meredith comment: 'There was no sense among our married respondents of sharing the tasks of caring with other family members, particularly husbands. Husbands received an excellent press and a majority of cases seem to have been genuinely supportive, but none was reported to have helped in the actual work of caring'.

THE IMPACT OF PAID EMPLOYMENT ON FATHER PARTICIPATION

The CHES study (Osborn et al., 1984) clearly demonstrates that for men, paid employment takes precedence over childcare. Fathers fit childcare around their paid employment commitments, in contrast with mothers, who organize their labour market participation around their childcare obligations. Brian Jackson (1984) has shown how even those men who to begin with strongly wish to be closely involved in the care of their new babies are, nonetheless, readily distracted by the requirements of their paid employment. Jackson has reported the amount of time that a hundred prospective first-time fathers intended to take off for the birth of their children. For over 20 per cent, the intention was to take two days at the most, but the average was about a week, taken as part of the fathers' annual holidays. Afterwards, the men's plans entailed a return to their jobs, probably to work overtime in order to bring in extra money to cover the underestimated costs of having children, while compensating for the wives' lost earnings. Jackson shows how initially both a father and the mother may well lack confidence in handling their child, simply because the majority of new parents have no experience of babycare. But, the mother, due to constant practice, quickly becomes much more competent than the father, who may see his child only briefly at the end of his working day. As this happens, it makes sense for the mother to eventually take over all the 'essential' caring activities, while the father slips back into the male's traditional role.

It is certainly the case that men in full-time paid employment, whether manual or managerial, tend to have little time to spend with their children at least prior to the weekend. With the middle class, one influencing factor is the way in which the period of childrearing tends to coincide with the principal stage of career-building. At this time, men will experience the need for intense paid work involvement (much of which will be conducted outside of paid work time) in order to prepare the ground for future career prospects and promotion.

A man's position in the occupational system has not only practical but also symbolic significance with regard to limiting his participation in childcare. This becomes clear when we look at those cases of men's involvement in childcare within families that do not conform with the standard pattern. The most obvious instance here is where men are not in paid employment. The number of unemployed men in Britain almost doubled in the four years between 1979 and 1983 to stand at over three million, and despite numerous official attempts to launder the figures the trend remains firmly upwards. However, because of government regulations

covering the payment of unemployment benefit and income support, families will not necessarily gain financially if unemployed men's wives go out
to work instead; and accordingly unemployed men's wives are only half as
likely to be in paid labour as married women in general. The requirement
that unemployed men must be instantly available for employment in effect
prohibits them from assuming the role of primary caregiver. But, Morris
(1990) suggests that husbands and wives who are without paid employment
and consequently tied to the domestic arena will be inclined to define their
gender roles in an especially clear and consistent manner along traditional
lines. The point here is that unemployed men's already undermined self-
esteem will encourage them to resist the further threats posed by performing
'female' tasks; and their wives will resist having their expertise within and
control over the domestic arena challenged and reduced. Bell and McKee
(1984) agree that unemployment may well promote a polarization of male
and female domestic activities instead of a convergence between them.

Even when wives are in paid employment, the evidence suggests that
little change takes place in the allocation of domestic roles. Brian Jackson
points out that none of the unemployed men with employed wives in his
sample became conspicuously nurturing fathers: the 'blockage was that
they were with the child reluctantly, and they held on as strongly as they
could to their old sense of identity – an identity defined by [paid] work'
(1984, p. 108). Mattinson (1988), from a psychoanalytic perspective, after
studying the impact of unemployment has come to a similar explanation for
men's withdrawal from childcare, often with disastrous marital and family
consequences. Such interpretations are then highly consistent with the
conclusion Graham Allan draws out of a review of a number of studies of
unemployed men: the 'ideology of the domestic division of labour is suffi-
ciently embedded into everyday life for it to be hardly threatened by the
male's lack of employment' (1985, p. 166).

Caution needs to be exercised about attributing too much weight to the
research findings in that unemployment is not, after all, evenly spread
through the population. Unemployment is concentrated within the older
urban centres of heavy industry, where we might anticipate traditional
views and values to persist more than elsewhere. Most studies have found
that manual couples are slower to subscribe to shared parenting compared
with non-manual couples. At the same time, however, a study of a different
family type, that based on cross-class marriage, has also revealed evidence
which illustrates the firm grip of traditional gender roles.

Of course, it is usual for husbands to enjoy occupational status and
earnings superior to those of their wives, this providing a common explanation by couples – including many subscribing to the egalitarian ideal of

marriage – for their decision that the wives should relinquish paid employment to look after the children. But, it is then of special interest to learn what happens in those cases where the wives are in higher status and earning jobs. Susan McCrae (1986) in her study identifies thirty couples in this category and shows that such an occupational profile does have some impact on marital roles. In the area of decision-making, McCrae's findings are a replication of Stephen Edgell's: when women are the primary income earners, they take the financial lead and make decisions about such matters as major domestic purchases, holidays and moving house. Otherwise, women of this kind, some of whom are in very demanding professional occupations, plan their lives to interfere as little as possible with their role as conventional wives. When these women bring work home, they try to make it invisible to their husbands, perhaps getting up at six o'clock in the morning or waiting until their husbands have fallen asleep to do it. Only one husband out of the thirty in McCrae's study participated anything like fully and equally in childcare.

Typically in cross-class marriages, the wives assume almost all the responsibility for the provision of care within and outside of working hours. As with fathers in general, cross-class fathers tend to restrict their participation in childcare to the more pleasant side (playing; reading books; helping with homework), leaving the mothers to feed, dress and wash their children, as well as arrange substitute care as necessary. McCrae remarks that fathers who do not dominate their families occupationally, do not compensate by assuming an increased part through fatherhood: 'in cross-class families, child care remains women's care'. McCrae's findings are especially interesting in so far as they show the persistence of traditional gender roles even when what might be regarded as the underlying economic support has been removed. In the study, with few exceptions (resulting in divorce in one case), this pattern appears to have occurred just as much due to the women's choice as to the men's. Such findings indicate how often women are reluctant to relinquish their control of domestic territory in response to their husbands' willingness to take on a greater share. Only two couples in McCrae's study are reported to have shared an ideological commitment to equality.

The behaviour of those couples is very similar to that exhibited by 'dual career families' as studied by the Rapoports (1976). When each partner has a professional job, the wife nonetheless retains the bulk of the responsibility for running the household and taking care of the children, albeit that she may manage to get other family members to share in what is done. Accordingly, what the husband does is to 'help' the wife. This pattern is far from unique to Britain: many studies conducted in the United States have arrived at similar conclusions. Hochschild (1990), for instance, estimates that American women tend to work in the home for about fifteen hours more than their partners, and to take a disproportionate share of the more essential tasks. Only 20 per cent of the men in Hochschild's study performed an equal share of the housework. The effect is widespread simmering resentment felt by women, putting considerable strain on marriages, which as a result often break down.

However, the unequal load between men and women does not signify simply exploitation. Women's own attitudes appear to play some part in the persistence of traditional roles within the family. Both Brian Jackson (1984) and McCrae (1986) have noted the tendency for women to emphasize their superior competence within the domestic arena, including with regard to childcare; and connectedly to disparage and actively discourage men's attempts to participate. This type of behaviour has been observed among highly qualified women in professional and managerial occupations in both Britain and the USA (Hochschild, 1990).

These women have been brought up by mothers who may have been just as capable as themselves, but were confined by prevailing social attitudes to remain tied to the family and home. Cognitive dissonance theory would predict that the older generation of women will be likely to subscribe to the traditional view that any woman is best fulfilled by caring for children and supporting her husband, whose role is that of financial provider. Such traditional women are supposed to take pride in their competence in home making, cooking, cleaning, washing and at all times being available to serve their families. Conversely, it is assumed that women who distance themselves from such activities cannot be good wives and mothers. These messages may be so strongly transmitted from mothers to daughters that the latter find them difficult to discard, even when the messages do not suit their particular family and occupational circumstances. This possibility aside, women may find that in any case shared parenting, not to mention role reversal, is so socially unusual or abnormal that it is difficult to sustain, as Graeme Russell's Australian studies have vividly illustrated (Russell, 1987).

As has been indicated, the British government's social policy does not play a neutral part with regard to the gender division of housework and childcare. Despite various formal gestures towards equal opportunities between men and women, the state strongly reinforces traditional gender roles, divisions and inequalities. It does this by making difficulties for women with children to gain paid employment in accordance with the view that it is normal for mothers to remain in the home and be supported by husbands in paid employment. Men's family responsibilities are taken to be almost exclusively financial. For instance, in Britain there is no statutory right for men in paid employment to take paternity leave or time off, with or without pay, to care for sick children (Cohen, 1988). Just about the only family-related matter in which the 1980s' British Conservative government has taken any serious interest has been the issue of securing child support from absent fathers (see Chapter 2 in this volume). However, although more realistic and regular maintenance payments from fathers will be helpful to the minority of lone mothers who are in full-time, paid employment, the majority of lone mothers will gain nothing because of the way maintenance is deducted from social welfare payments (not to mention the loss of other benefits). Moreover, the fathers will often have another family, with the result that their other partners and children will be adversely affected by their maintenance payments. Essentially, the measure merely masquerades as supporting family values: more accurately it amounts to an act of punitive intervention in family and personal life. The overall net effect will be to do little more than redistribute small amounts of money from some poor families to some other even poorer families; to create additional financial pressures which may result in the breakup of second marriages; and to confirm lone mothers in the position of dependency. But, the development is clearly in line with other government social policies which aim to shift the burden of child support from the state to parents.

MOTHERS IN THE PAID LABOUR FORCE

The contradictions of British government policy are nowhere more obvious than in the area of day care for the children of mothers in paid employment. After the Second World War, ideology and economic expediency coincided. Ministry of Health officials were able to argue for the closure of large numbers of day nurseries, which had been set up originally to enable mothers to join war-related production, not only on the grounds that the jobs were needed by the returning armed forces, but also supported by the views of John Bowlby on maternal deprivation (Bowlby, 1948). The gains that had been made by mothers were lost and have never been fully recovered. Some of the day nurseries did survive, and a few more have been set up since by local authority (local government) social service departments and voluntary organizations, mostly in urban areas. However, the number of nursery places falls far short of demand, and their geographical distribution is largely a result of historical accident. In most parts of Britain, the current provision of nursery places is mainly reserved for children who are severely disadvantaged; who are at risk of neglect or abuse; or who have been taken into local authority care. The day nursery service is no longer available to children simply because their parents are 'working parents'. Local authorities are not statutorily obliged to provide pre-school childcare places, and some have no day care nurseries whatsoever. Nursery schools and classes are similarly unevenly spread around the country, and in any case operate for short hours with long holidays, making them of limited use to mothers in paid employment.

Nonetheless, 60 per cent of married women with dependent children have paid work outside the home, as have 31 per cent whose youngest child is still under five years of age. But, most women of this kind face a highly restricted choice of jobs due to the limited range of childcare arrangements available, and many find themselves employed at levels well below their capacities and capabilities. As a result, the increase in the numbers and proportions of mothers within the paid labour force cannot be taken to necessarily indicate a fundamental alteration in women's experience and view of their primary role. The rise can be almost entirely accounted for by an expansion of part-time employment, so that the proportion of mothers in full-time jobs has remained more or less static at 17 per cent. Part-time employment is usually low paid, lacking in security and undertaken in order to fit in with family demands. It may serve the important purpose of raising family income, but it is unlikely to provide a basis by which married women are able to challenge the position of their husbands as the main breadwinners.

The situation in Britain is in marked contrast with most other European countries, where nursery education (often with extended hours) is almost universal, and where state-subsidized day care is provided as a service with no stigmatizing connotations (Meluish and Moss, 1990). Understandably, there has been concerted pressure for an alteration in British government policy, on the grounds not only of promoting equal opportunities for women but also of the economic advantages.

Increasingly, industrial and commercial organizations have come to see women with children as an important pool of reserve labour, which will be of use as labour and skill shortages emerge in line with anticipated changes in demographic patterns (Institute of Personnel Management, 1990).

There is no doubt that attitudes towards employed mothers have altered radically. Recently, surveys have shown that many women without paid employment would keenly seek jobs if suitable childcare arrangements were available (Hardill and Green, 1990). But, despite support and pressure from its own political constituency – the business community – the British government has consistently confirmed its view that the provision of day care for employed parents is not to be confused with its policy of 'supporting the family'. The government argues that if women want to enter the paid labour force, it is their responsibility to find alternative care for their children. During the 1980s, while some government ministers were trying to encourage married women with children to enter paid employment, Mrs Thatcher spoke disparagingly of 'the creche society'.

In contrast with the negative side of the government's approach to publicly provided or subsidized day care, the 1989 Children Act specifically imposes a duty on local authorities to provide day care, not only for pre-school children but also for older children out of school hours (Department of Health, 1989). Local authorities are also required to carry out an immediate review of day care services for children up to eight years of age, and subsequent reviews every three years. At first sight this development may seem like something of a victory for childcare campaigners. However, on closer inspection the Act stipulates that local authorities are obliged to provide day care only for children 'in need', which could mean for children who are already in the 'priority' category for day nursery places or with sponsored childminders. Local authorities are given the option of also providing day care for children not 'in need'. However, given that local authority budgets are under exceptional pressure due to cuts in central government funding, to difficulties in collecting the new community charge (the 'poll tax'), and to the imposition of strict limits being placed on the level of the community charge, there is likely to be only a modest extension of the current patchwork of pre-school services. Certainly, there will be nothing like the comprehensive services which have been achieved in various other European countries, including France and Sweden.

It is obvious that the government has hoped that the gap will be filled, as in the United States model, through private day care centres along with workplace nurseries. Indeed, the last two years have witnessed a very rapid increase in private provisions in Britain. But, the major stumbling block here is that such private childcare is usually too expensive to be used all day by mothers, except those in well paid professional and managerial jobs. In the case of workplace childcare, so far in Britain far more has been promised than has emerged in practice. Interestingly, 'private' workplace provision lags behind 'public' workplace provision. A 1989 study has revealed that only 2 per cent of the 'private' industrial and commercial employing organizations surveyed are offering childcare, while a further 7 per cent claim to be contemplating it. The respective figures for 'public' (state; local government) employers were 12 per cent and 48 per cent (Institute of Personnel Management, 1990).

Several categories of women are especially hard hit by the lack of affordable day care in Britain. They include women in minority ethnic groups, who relatively speaking are likely to be in full-time employment at low wage levels and to be using unregistered (unofficial) childminders (Jackson and Jackson, 1981; Mayall and Petrie, 1983). Two other susceptible categories are the wives of unemployed men and lone mothers. Both of these find themselves in a trap created by the operation of the state social benefits system which means that they are very likely to be financially disadvantaged by getting paid employment. Jane Millar (1989), with particular reference to childcare, has spelt out what then happens in the case of lone mothers who remain dependent upon state income support given that the latter is barely sufficient to pay for basic food, housing and fuel. The picture painted by Millar is consistent with the finding that state income support allows for nothing more than 'an extremely restricted and drab lifestyle' (Bradshaw and Morgan, 1987). In effect, the assumption that 'supporting the family' means keeping mothers at home to look after their young children not only conflicts with the principle of discouraging welfare dependency, but also imprisons families within disadvantaged circumstances, making it difficult in practice for them to be self-reliant.

Also, lone mothers experience strong financial disincentives when it comes to another possible escape route: entering a partnership with a man. The difficulty here is that the state penalizes lone mothers suspected of cohabiting by withdrawing benefits. The state operates with the view that the man should assume responsibility for the financial support of the mothers and children. This is the case even though the 'partnerships' may be in the very early stages, exploratory and fragile; the men may not have much interest in the children; and the men do not see themselves and are not seen by others as in any sense the children's fathers (see Faith Robertson Elliot, 1986).

The British approach is almost uniquely harsh in its treatment of lone mothers in relation to social benefits. Other countries take the view that the mothers of very young children should be allowed the option of staying at home to care for their children with the assistance of generous financial allowances. While Sweden and Denmark encourage lone mothers to be in paid employment, there are well developed employment practices for reducing women's disadvantage in the labour market along with comprehensive systems of child support covering financial assistance and day care provision. Likewise, both France and (the old) West Germany encourage self-reliance through paid employment by applying a combination of financial incentives and childcare services. Even the USA, which scores low marks in the areas of public child support and day care, allows childcare expenses to be tax deductible.

The poverty into which many lone parents are forced makes it difficult for them to fulfil their responsibilities and obligations as parents. The result is the strong chance that such families will be subjected eventually to direct state intervention. For instance, the chances of a child from a lone-parent family being taken into care are many times greater than a child from a two-parent family (see Bebbington and Miles, 1989).

PROBLEMS IN PARENTING

This brings us onto the issue of child abuse and its links with state interventionism. While child abuse was assumed to be a rare occurrence, perpetrated by adults who are 'mentally ill' or 'morally depraved', the problem could be treated as a simple one to deal with, involving for instance the removal of children from culpable parents in order to place them in new homes to receive loving care. This approach was sustained by, in particular, the very influential writings of Goldstein, Freud and Solnit (1973). Both scholars and practitioners focused their attention on how to ensure stable substitute care for children whose natural parents were seen to have 'failed' them. Holman (1980) has pointed out, however, that what for the most part this meant in practice was removing children from the poor and transferring them to the middle class. Nonetheless, the 1975 Children Act in Britain, which eased the process by which children could be adopted without parental consent, commanded widespread support: it seemed self-evident that the parental rights should be removed from those who had shown they could not be trusted to use them properly.

More recent research has confirmed Holman's argument. Packman (1986), for instance, detected a shift away from children being placed in care at the request of their parents towards them being taken coercively into care by local authorities under Place of Safety orders. The power bestowed on local authorities to forcibly remove children from their parents was intended to be used in cases of emergency, but Packman's research shows that it had come to be deployed as much more of a routine measure.

Perhaps the clearest instance of the over-zealous use of Place of Safety orders occurred in the so-called Cleveland Affair, when a large number of children were removed from their parents on suspicion of sexual abuse, only to be kept in squalid, crowded conditions in a children's hospital. The event turned into a major scandal, occupying much media space for many weeks. It aroused strong feelings in part because it demonstrated how powerless parents can be when confronted by an alliance of medical and social service personnel. There is evidence that some of the children who were separated from their parents for several months only to be found not to have been abused, suffered damaging experiences as a result. The local Member of Parliament, who supported the parents' cause, later compared the Cleveland Affair with the witch trials in seventeenth-century Salem (Bell, 1988).

On the other hand, while the inquiry (conducted by High Court judge, Lord Justice Elizabeth Butler-Sloss, 1988) into the Cleveland events concluded that many mistakes had been made, it confirmed that most of the allegations of abuse had been substantiated. In the wake of the Cleveland Affair, in almost every other part of Britain there have been steep increases in reported incidents of child abuse, especially sexual abuse. Several explanations have been proposed for this occurrence. For example, it has been argued that much abuse existed in the past that was simply not recognized or even tolerated. Connectedly, it has been suggested that the apparent concentration of child abuse within the poorest sections of society is largely a reflection of the way that child abuse which takes place in middle-class families tends not to come to light, and in particular not to come to the attention of public agencies. Such views give credibility to the conclusion that child abuse is, in practice, more or less evenly spread between social classes.

However, a more convincing analysis of the incidence of child abuse suggests that we should view the phenomenon (at least in its less extreme forms) as simply representing one pole of the full spectrum of regular parenting behaviour. The quality of parenting in particular cases may then be viewed within this social perspective, and explained in terms of factors beyond merely the personal characteristics of the parents involved. Parton (1985) has argued cogently in favour of an ecological interpretation of child abuse, relating the phenomenon to the lack of public support for parenting. In accordance with this view, the apparent increase in child abuse in Britain can be understood in terms of the government's fiscal and economic policies (which have made couples without children better off but those with children worse off) combined with public spending cuts – which have required local authorities to make reductions in the various services relating to children in general (Andrews and Jacobs, 1990).

As far as family finances are concerned, decades of research led by Peter Townsend and the Child Poverty Action Group has shown that the most effective way of channelling resources to the poor is through the universal (non-means tested) child benefit, paid to mothers through post offices. While the government has not taken the final step to abolish this benefit (a move which would be unpopular through the range of political opinion in Britain), it has steadfastly refused to increase its value in line with the rate of inflation. Consequently, child payment benefits have lost a lot of ground relative to the cost of raising children.

In addition, government housing policies have resulted in a steep decline in the amount of low-cost rented accommodation. For instance, there have been policies which have obliged local authorities to sell off its own stock of 'public' housing and which, at the same time, have imposed strict limits on how much they can spend building replacement stock. Consequently, there are many homeless families that have no alternative but to accept accommodation in miserable, overcrowded 'hotels'.

Some public housing remains unsold, but therefore is usually in a dilapidated condition in the least desirable districts. Accordingly, the poorest families become concentrated in such areas. For those families which depend on state benefits, their income is barely enough to guarantee subsistence essentials, but there is an absence of public childcare facilities which would enable the women – often lone mothers – to take on paid employment. Private childcare is of little help because of the prohibitive cost, especially given that if the women were to enter paid employment they would lose state benefits: hence, the 'poverty trap'. In the face of this, the government maintains its claim that women enjoy the freedom to choose to work outside the home, and that thereby they should bear the responsibility for making arrangements for substitute childcare.

Discussion of childcare often carries the implication that the issue over the balance between family responsibility and state responsibility lasts only until children begin school, or at least until children can be safely left without constant supervision. But, its continuation beyond this stage is exemplified in the way any state sponsored shifting of the upper boundary of childhood can have considerable consequences for child–parent relationships. In Britain, although the statutory minimum school leaving age is sixteen, it is possible to stay on 'free of charge' until the age of eighteen. However, this upper limit translates – by way of financial considerations – into a built-in bias against the children of poorer families. That is, the various 'hidden costs', the falling value of the child benefit, the absence of compensatory maintenance grants, and the loss of potential employment earnings combine to make it difficult for poor children to stay on.

There is income support for sixteen to eighteen year olds, but it is paid to only those who accept places on youth training schemes, and is set at levels which prevents the young people involved from living independently of their families. The same kind of constraints afflict those eighteen to twenty-five year olds without jobs who receive unemployment benefit. In addition, however, those in this age range have become liable to pay 'poll tax' (local government community charge), which has replaced the previous household rates ('property taxes').

There is no doubt that the shift from the state to the family in the cost of maintaining young people has had, in turn, consequences for parent–child relationships, in particular by exacerbating tensions between parents and adolescents. Such an inference is evidenced in the enormous increase in the numbers of young people who are not just homeless, but have become street beggars. It has become common in British cities – in a way which is unique in most people's memories – to see young people slumped pathetically in doorways displaying placards proclaiming that they are 'homeless and hungry'. The official view that these young people have chosen their street life due to their irresponsibility and laziness has chilling Victorian overtones.

There is much evidence that the quality of parenting within a society is largely shaped by the degree of stress suffered by people in carrying out that role, and that in turn such stress is dependent upon the character of social policies in relation to parenting, especially those social policies which impinge on the pool of family resources available for parenting (see Steinmetz, 1988).

SETTING STANDARDS FOR PARENTS

Parental stress is enhanced not only by declining resources but also by rising expectations about parenting. Recent research has indicated that in Britain there does exist a degree of consensus over what constitutes 'good parenting' practices, despite variations by social class and ethnicity. A group of childcare researchers has been involved in an inquiry into what 'good parenting' means in conjunction with a study of 'the state as parent' (Jackson, 1989). In Britain, about 70 000 children are in the care of local authorities on the grounds that their parents are unable to provide a satisfactory home life, but the picture generated by the research on the lives of these children has lent itself to the conclusion that the state cannot be a 'good parent': that, at the most, the state can merely stimulate good parenting. It is not possible for a public agency to provide the total, lifelong emotional commitment which is the principal characteristic of parent–child relationships. The 1989 Children Act acknowledges this by stressing, for instance, the continuing responsibility of both parents for their children, wherever their children may be living.

The inability on the part of the state to substitute for the family as far as parenting is concerned does not, however, imply a policy of non-interventionism. The debate persists between, on the one hand, those who advocate detection and punitive action against those deemed to have fallen below society's childrearing norms and, on the other hand, those who argue for a major redistribution of resources in favour of families with children. At one extreme has been the Thatcherite position, which stands in contrast with the view that children represent a resource for society as a whole and, therefore, a public as well as a private responsibility. Those who subscribe to the latter approach argue that the most effective way to improve standards of parenting and to fight abuse is to provide adequate day care and after-school facilities.

The inclination of the British government has been to favour the American approach which leaves childcare largely to the play of market forces, the result being that the most vulnerable children receive the least satisfactory care and that in general quality is subordinated to profit-making (Melhuish and Moss, 1990). The main force pulling in the opposite direction is Britain's increasing immersion within the European Community, which has a greater commitment to equal opportunities and to social policies which genuinely support children and their families. In addition, demographic trends – which have meant prospective shortfalls in the numbers of people available for technical and professional training – have led employers (Institute of Personnel Management, 1990), encouraged by increasing government support (Beavis, 1989), to persuade mothers to remain in or to re-enter paid work.

Moreover, there are signs of a fundamental change in attitudes to the issue of men, masculinity and fathering which has found its way into the school curriculum. Personal and Social Education in British schools includes the topic of 'becoming a parent', and firmly favours the symmetrical rather than the segregated pattern of parental roles. However, perhaps ironically, the very strength of the message along these lines brings with it the risk of rising expectations being unfulfilled, especially in view of the government's social policies which continues to pull in the opposite direction. The outcome could be to increase the frustrations and tensions of family life, to the detriment of children especially.

I have argued that the policy of encouraging family responsibility for children can only work in conjunction with a firm policy of family support, taking into account a changing family structure and a new balance of parental roles. The way people operate as parents and the quality of care they can give their children are profoundly influenced by government policies, even those which at first sight may appear to have nothing to do with children. The state cannot choose non-intervention in family life: its only choice is to intervene in a fashion which is either benign or destructive.

NOTES

1. For further discussion of the nuances and problematics of the relationship between family form and household composition, see Close, 1985.
2. For further evidence and analysis concerning gender roles, divisions and inequalities associated with the performance of housework and childcare (domestic labour) in Britain, see Close (1989c); Collins (1985); Close and Collins (1983).
3. See J. Newson and E. Newson (1963, 1968, 1976).

5 The State and Social Welfare in Japan: Patterns and Developments
Ryuji Komatsu

The social welfare system in Japan has, compared with other modern societies, a distinctive history and connectedly retains a distinctive pattern of profiles and relationships among its principal players. In particular, the Japanese social welfare system today is characterized by a balance between the state as represented by national government, local (prefectural) government and private participants (private practitioners). The outcome is an effective social welfare system which reflects and reinforces distinctive, underlying traditional Japanese cultural values. This is exemplified by the foster care system in that, for instance, the foster parent role in relation to the national and local government roles can be understood in terms of the persistence of traditional values concerning family life.

When examining social welfare in any modern society an obvious focus of attention is the part played by the state. If we were to ignore the state, we could hope to gain only a partial and highly fragmented picture of the social welfare system. The state tends to be to the fore – perhaps necessarily so – in providing and organizing the services designed to help meet a broad and comprehensive range of social welfare requirements within a complex set of social arrangements, as well as social problems. Historically, however, the leading role played by the state within the social welfare system is not only recent but also has taken much longer to emerge in some societies compared with others. In Japan, for instance, the state has belatedly become a central participant within the welfare system. Essentially the Japanese state has been slow to accept any responsibility for (any obligation to help satisfy) people's welfare requirements, reflecting the fact that it has been reluctant to accept people's rights to enjoy some kind of minimum standard of life.

From the standpoint of global history, initially the state maintained a third-party-like position in relation to social welfare, participating in its provision in a highly limited, unsystematic and discretionary manner: its approach to social welfare can be summed up as fitting in with the general charitable perspective which operated at the time. The state did not acknowledge any rights to welfare; and especially, it did not recognize any rights in this regard for which it was responsible. The state did not assume that it had any obligation to meet people's welfare requirements; but that instead the family bore the main burden of responsibility in this regard. Accordingly, the state's practical involvement – by way of both contributing substantively to social welfare provisions and organizing the social welfare system – was marginal and meagre.

But this initial phase in the historical evolution of the social welfare system was eventually superseded by a further one linked to broader and underlying social changes. With the development of capitalism, the state gradually enlarged its practical involvement in the social welfare system even though it continued steadfastly to resist the assumption that it had a duty to be involved at all. However, yet another phase emerged in the early twentieth century: a phase marked by the state's acceptance of people's right to certain minimum standards of life and of its own responsibility for helping maintain these standards. One of the most important and influential events in this context occurred with the close of the First World War. In 1921, the newly formed League of Nations adopted a Declaration of Children's Rights which prompted a number of countries to introduce various laws and regulations concerning children's *rights* to welfare. Accordingly, the state's conceptualization of – or guiding principles concerning – welfare needs, rights and responsibilities changed in such a way that it came to assume an obligation to help maintain certain minimum standards of life. Thereby, the state's practical participation in the provision of social welfare increased: it began to contribute more substantively; to expand the 'public' social welfare measures and services; and most important to acquire and accept a leading role in organizing and spearheading social welfare overall.

This general historical pattern applies very much to the particular case of the way the Japanese state's participation in social welfare has unfolded, but with one signifiant proviso. Whereas the turning point for the progressive evolution of social welfare in Europe and the USA coincided with the period around the First World War, that in Japan occurred in conjunction with the end of Second World War. In other words, the state's acceptance of an obligation to meet people's welfare needs in order to help maintain a minimum standard of life through the provision, organization and leadership of social welfare activities and services occurred earlier in much of Europe and North America compared with Japan. The Japanese state's acceptance of welfare involvement and responsibilities on a par with the 'modern model' first developed in Europe and North America had to wait until the impact of the special conditions surrounding the end of, and Japan's emergence from, the Second World War.

Prior to the Second World War, the Japanese state showed no interest in assuming any responsibility for social welfare, so much so that it cannot be attributed with what may be usefully referred to as a 'social welfare policy'. Its approach to social welfare was aloof and begrudging, *ad hoc* and piecemeal, patchy and uncoordinated. However, this changed as a direct result of the end and outcome of the War, and in particular with Japan's adoption of a fresh national Constitution. This Constitution was designed to sharply transform Japan into a fully 'modern democratic society' along the lines of the leading Western societies of North America and Europe. It was consistent with this particular constitution that from then on the Japanese state would accept that citizens have various minimum rights, including those to a minimum standard of life and so a minimum level of social service provisions, for which it had not only some but also central, overall responsibility. Accordingly, soon after 1945, the Japanese state began to formulate a comprehensive social welfare policy; and began to introduce, expand and improve on a wide range of social welfare measures, activities and services.

Essentially, therefore, the Japanese state suddenly and radically altered its stance on social welfare: from one in which it assumed a position of 'peripheral non-responsibility' to one in which it accepted more or less the converse position of 'central responsibility'. Crucially, whereas prior to the Second World War the most characteristic feature of the state's involvement in social welfare was the absence of any initiative in promoting and developing provisions and services, subsequently it strode into the lead by assuming the role of overseeing, co-ordinating and spearheading the evolution of the social welfare system. In Japan, since the Second World War, the state has undertaken a concerted programme of social welfare expansion, centred on its own 'public' activities and services, but more specifically under the stewardship of local government. The national government, in other words, has adopted and applied a policy of realizing the state's responsibility for social welfare through social service provisions at the district – or prefectural – level. The national government has tended to construct a statutory framework within which prefectural government has the immediate responsibility for, authority over and resources to cover the social welfare needs, provisions and services *vis-à-vis* local populations.

Having given the foregoing sketch of the historical drift of the state's changing role within the Japanese social welfare system, I will proceed to examine somewhat more closely the profiles and relationships among the principal players within the system. This will be exemplified with reference to the pattern and development associated with one particular sector of the social welfare in Japan, that of the foster care system.

THE PRINCIPAL PLAYERS IN JAPANESE SOCIAL WELFARE

Looked at comparatively and historically, it is evident that what might be referred to as 'the players' in social welfare systems change and vary considerably. Thus, the identity of the players change and vary, as do the profiles (or relative prominence) of and, connectedly, the relationships among them. However, it is possible to characterize the social welfare systems of modern (advanced, Western) societies in general as having just four principal players in the sense of constituent components, which in changing and varying degrees participate in the provision and receipt of social welfare; among which social welfare contributions and benefits are distributed so that each has a particular profile within the overall pattern; and between which there are the all important, determining relationships of rights, responsibilities, authority, power and so on. Moreover, it may be argued that the particular pattern of participation among these players both reflects (being contingent upon) the prevading dominant cultural and institutional features of a particular society, while in turn feeding into these features. At the same time, perhaps a range of patterns are possible – and identifiable – in modern societies, giving rise to speculation about a further possibility: that one particular pattern is more appropriate, efficient and effective than others. The four players I have in mind are (a) beneficiaries, recipients or clients; (b) the state (which for the purpose of discussion can be equated with national government); (c) local government; and (d) the private sector – made up of a range of 'non-governmental' benefactors (individuals and institutions; groups, organizations and agencies) acting in accordance with a charitable inclination to help the poor, the needy and so on.

Of course, the one constant in all systems of social welfare will be the presence of beneficiaries – those members and sections of society who exhibit disadvantages or handicaps, thereby attracting care, assistance and protection in the form of the social welfare provisions and services. However, there are considerable and highly significant variations which occur between societies and over time in the number, identity and the profile of the beneficiaries, and connectedly in the social relationships between the beneficiaries and the other social welfare players. This applies in the case of, for instance, foster care children. In general, the attention and interest shown to such children has grown considerably over the years within

modern societies, as has (as a result) the attention shown to foster parents.
In effect, the foster care system has increased its relative importance within
the social welfare system overall – ensured by the private sector, the state
and local government's increased attention and interest. In particular, this
development has hinged upon an increase in the concern about, care for and
rights of foster children – or more precisely those children who would be
deprived of a private home and family if it were not for foster parents.
However, there are considerable variations between societies in this regard.
In Japan, prior to the Second World War, not only prospective foster
children but actual foster children lacked rights within society and in particular within the relationships they had with their foster parents. Statutorily
speaking they were wholly subordinate to their foster parents, being denied
the right of independent choice and action. Foster parents, by contrast, had
considerable rights over their foster children to the point of enjoying almost
complete authority and control. Concomitantly, foster parents had to
shoulder all the responsibility for foster children – for their care and upbringing; their welfare requirements; and so on. The state neither at the
level of national government nor at the level of local government assumed
any responsibility; and accordingly failed to provide any supporting services or assistance of any kind.

Today, in contrast, in most modern societies, foster children have acquired officially sanctioned rights and enjoy an officially guaranteed standard of life below which they will not be allowed to fall. As a general rule,
foster children enjoy statutory rights on a par with foster parents; and
accordingly each type of beneficiary tends to have a similar, prominent
profile within the social welfare system. It is reasonable to argue that
modern state policies and practices in relation to foster children and foster
parents are essentially very similar within all modern societies.

But, there remain notable differences among societies with regard to the
particular manner and arrangements by which the state plays a part in the
lives of foster children and foster parents. For instance, in some societies the
state plays out its responsibility for foster children in a direct manner
through its policies, practices and centralized provisions and services: through
retaining its authority and control over the immediate operation and organization of the foster care system, rather than passing its authority in this
regard to local government. However, in other societies the state at national
government level plays hardly any direct part at all within the system,
having delegated the authority required to manage the system to local
government, which accordingly comes to assume a high profile within both
the foster care system and the social welfare system overall. This particular
distinction is important when examining and trying to make sense of the

state and the social welfare system in Japan; the historical development of the social welfare system overall; and the features of the foster care system in particular.

SOCIAL WELFARE AND THE STATE DURING IN THE EARLY MODERN PERIOD

Historically, the development and expansion of the state in Japan has followed the pattern set by the state in modern societies in general by eventually assuming overall responsibility for social welfare and guaranteeing a minimum standard of life for all. Today in Japan, everyone whether fit and healthy, ill, handicapped, young or aged is covered by the state's guarantee. Accordingly, the state has formulated a range of social welfare policies, and has introduced a variety of welfare measures, laws and regulations within which the modern Japanese social welfare system operates: a system designed to ensure the practical implementation of its guarantee of minimum standard of life across the board. For instance, an important piece of social legislation in this regard is the Livelihood Protection Law, passed immediately following the Second World War.

However, the process through which the current social welfare framework has been built and secured has been slow in comparative terms, linked to the fact that it was only as long ago as the 1860s that Japan became a 'modern society' along the lines set by many European and North American countries by way of, for instance, the industrial revolution, continuing industrial progress, and the march of capitalism. Whereas by the 1860s Britain and the United States, for instance, had a well-developed centralized state which acknowledged a range of citizenship and welfare rights for which it was responsible and which it guaranteed, Japan still had a long way to go in these respects. The point at which Japan entered the category of 'modern society' can be precisely located as occurring in 1868 – it was in this year that Japan bade farewell to its all-embracing feudal social system. However, this does not mean that in 1868 Japan managed to shake off all of its feudalistic past – far from it. For instance, in a way which was consistent with feudalistic values and institutions, the Japanese state placed considerable emphasis on the place and importance even in modern society of family life, relationships and responsibilities. The state was unequivocal in its view that people's standard of life was a matter for them and their families; that people's needs, poverty, health, disabilities, unemployment, family disintegration and so on were personal and family problems; that these problems were in no way due to the operation of society, capitalism or the state; and therefore that they were not the responsibility of the state. The state was not guided by any sense of duty to assist, care for or protect 'the needy', potentially needy or anyone.

At the same time, however, while the state assumed no sense of responsibility or obligation, the choice was made not to ignore the needy completely: to become involved marginally through statutory acts and measures, such as the Rule for the Relief of the Needy which was passed in 1874. This piece of legislation provided very rudimentary assistance to the needy, and thereby represents an elementary form of *standard of life protection*. The Rule focused state assistance on those whose physical, material and social circumstances were so impoverished that they were living around the subsistence line. Essentially, the state's social welfare provisions were fixed at a level designed to do no more than prevent starvation and death.

Guided by the conviction that it was not obliged to provide any social welfare assistance at all, the state gave the minimum which was consistent with an extreme 'safety net' approach. The level of its assistance was meant to catch and support people hovering on the line between life and death, and moreover only some people who were enduring such circumstances. That is, in accordance with its view that the needy's problems were only personal and family ones, and that at the most it was prepared to engage in discretionary and charitable assistance, the state was highly selective about who were legitimate recipients. The state distinguished between types of needy, so that only those who were barely alive, who were ill or handicapped, who were over seventy years old, and who had no family to support them were eligible. As a result, state assistance went to only a very small and narrow band of elderly people, leavng many younger people to cope with dire poverty.

However, in the second half of the 1880s, there began to emerge a growing interest on the part of politicians and other political leaders, the intelligentsia, and further sections of the population – not only in expanding and improving charitable and discretionary social welfare but also in a much more comprehensive social welfare system entailing 'minimum standard of life' protection. This development can be linked to the continuing development of industrial capitalism and its associated social changes. Most important, the 1880s and 1890s saw an ever-expanding industrial labour force and thereby urban-based working class, which in turn meant the ever-increasing experience of capitalist-related exploitation, alienation, harsh working conditions, low wages, uncertain employment, high unemployment, and so on. It became clear that the circumstances of the needy could not be regarded as just personal and family problems after all – that they could be attributed to the various social developments centred upon the progress of industrial capitalism. There was more and more acceptance of the view that greater state intervention in and development of the social welfare system was called for in the interests of both justice and continuing economic and social progress.

From the end of the nineteenth century there was growing popular and state interest shown in the development of, in particular, labour policy specifically concerned with worker protection. This culminated eventually – albeit belatedly – in 1911 when the national government passed the Factory Act. This piece of state legislation (which was similar in its purposes to the Factory Acts passed in Britain up to eighty years before) represents the first practical step on the part of the Japanese state towards guaranteeing a minimum standard of life and, connectedly, towards a comprehensive social welfare system.

On the other hand, the 1911 Factory Act represented only a partial and half-hearted step in this direction, reflecting the way in which the state was primarily concerned with the labour force and with worker protection in the interests of the economy and capitalism, in contrast with its very limited concern about other distinguishable ('non-economic') categories such as 'the poor', 'the hungry', 'the sick', 'the disabled', and so on. The state was still reluctant to provide assistance to anyone other than 'workers' in the form of 'worker protection'. It was still committed to an approach where the needy's problems were largely their own and their families'; where otherwise the needy would have to rely on charitable and so discretionary gifts; and where most charity was to be provided by private benefactors, individuals and organizations.

It was during the second half of the 1880s that the first children's orphanages and young people's reformatories were established in Japan. However, all such social welfare facilities were privately created, financed and organized. This was followed during the 1890s by the first homes for mentally handicapped children, and at around the turn of the century by the first nursery schools for the needy. In general, the various homes, orphanages, reformatories and schools were of good quality, and all due to the charitable activities of the private sector of the social welfare system.

The state's relative detachment from the social welfare system – and especially from the development of a comprehensive system in which it accepted a responsibility for guaranteeing a minimum standard of life to everyone – remained very much the mainstay of its general approach to social welfare right up until its sharp about face straight after the Second World War. However, just as there are signs of the state relenting somewhat

given its decision to introduce and implement worker protection legislation
in 1911, there are even earlier signs by virtue of its decision at the turn of
the century to get centrally and directly involved in that sector of social
welfare concerned with juvenile delinquency. Moreover, just as the state's
worker protection policy can be understood as a response to the growing
(threat of) economic and social problems associated with the progress of
capitalism and the expansion of capitalist society's working class, so the
state's interest in juvenile delinquency can be understood in terms of the
growing threat posed by this phenomenon.

Thus, in response to the spread and pressure of juvenile delinquency, in
1900 the Japanese state decided to take the initiative away from the private
sector and its attempts to cope with the problem by introducing the Reformation Law. In this way, the state shifted from a tentative involvement
in social welfare through 'charity work' to a firmer and more direct involvement through 'social work'. That is, the Reformation Law allowed the
state to play a part in establishing and running juvenile reformatories: it lead
to a co-operative venture between national government and local government, whereby the former guided and oversaw the latter's role of setting up,
organizing and managing the reformatories. In this way, the Reformation
Law marks a major step in the state's participation as a player in social
welfare, from lurking on the sidelines to moving closer towards its eventual
role as a central and leading player; to more clearly creating and defining a
'public sector' of social welfare; and to turning charity work into social
work. The state's player profile within the social welfare system through its
intervention in juvenile delinquency was further enhanced by the passing of
the Criminal Code in 1909 and the Juveniles' Reformation Law of 1923.

At the same time, the state did not neglect its involvement in social
welfare by way of charity work. In fact, the state increased its player profile
in this regard also by taking the lead in 1908 – through the Ministry of
Home Affairs – in founding the Central Charity Association, a national
federation of private charity benefactors. This public body was set up with
the purpose (like its equivalents in Britain and the USA) of overseeing,
monitoring and co-ordinating charity work as carried out by the various
private benefactors, the aim being to ensure that the work would be conducted in a more efficient and effective way. With this in mind, the state
through the Central Charity Association began to undertake and otherwise
encourage research, study and training in matters served by charity work.
In all of this, however, the state still insisted on preserving its own op-
tional and 'voluntary' participation in assisting 'the needy', rather than in
any way assuming any kind of responsibility for them and duty to deal with
their problems.

THE STATE AND SOCIAL WELFARE AFTER THE FIRST WORLD WAR

The period around the First World War represents a major turning point in the development of Japanese social and political life given the unprecedented influx and impact of ideas and values from the modern societies of Europe and North America which, in particular, strongly encouraged the spread of 'liberal democratic' principles and practices. This was accompanied by an associated spread of interest in and support for socialism and the Labour Movement. In the area of social welfare, there was an increasing amount of popular pressure on the state to improve its social welfare policy, to develop a comprehensive social welfare system, and concomitantly to turn 'charity work' into 'social work' – pressure from which the state did not remain immune. Moreover, the gradually changing posture at the level of national government was matched to some extent by a similar alteration at the level of local government. The latter began to introduce, expand and promote its own district level provisions and services under the auspices of the 'district committee system', the forerunner to the current 'welfare officer system'.

In addition, within the private sector of the welfare system, purely charity work was giving way to 'social work' at an increasing pace. In 1921, the Central Charity Association had its scope enlarged, in recognition of which it was re-named the Central Social Work Association.

The emergence and growth of social work provided another source of pressure on the state for a change in its approach to social welfare. The increasing number of progressively-minded social workers urged the state to alter its approach from one of non-obligatory, selective and scattered assistance to that of a comprehensive system of services to all people as a right, in order to guarantee a minimum standard of life. The demand was for the state to take the lead in helping prevent 'need' rather than merely reacting to 'need' in a piecemeal, ameliorative and largely inconsequential manner once it had arisen. In any case, according to social workers, the state should acknowledge its duty and responsibility in relation to the needy, whose circumstances and problems were, after all, largely attributable to the character of modern society. Similarly, the growing band of socialists within Japan located people's deprivations in the operation of the capitalist system and thereby the (capitalist) state itself. At the same time, in the absence of being able to persuade the state to accept and follow through its full obligations to the Japanese people, socialists began during the 1920s to assist the needy by establishing their own range of social services, such as in response to medical and childcare (nursery) requirements.

Also during the 1920s, Japan was afflicted by the world-wide economic depression, the result being a huge increase in unemployment along with a general lowering of incomes, living standards and well-being. By 1927 the depression had become so severe that the state was moved to update the Rule for the Relief of the Needy given that it had been introduced over fifty years before to help only a very limited range and number of people. Thus, the state passed the more generous and encompassing Relief and Protection Law (1929), itself the precursor to the even more improved Livelihood Protection Law which was to be passed immediately after the Second World War. In effect, the Japanese state's decision to increase its assistance in recognition of the prevailing social and economic circumstances amounted to a tacit acknowledgement of its responsibility in relation to the needy and their problems. At the same time, however, the Japanese state was still falling far short of realizing – especially in a practical sense – its full responsibility: its obligation to maintain a minimum standard of life for all.

Yet further political events and developments were to prove influential on the state's gradually evolving approach to social welfare. In particular, the hostilities associated with the China Affair of 1937 and the outbreak of the Pacific War in 1941 had a regressive and detrimental impact. That is, whereas the course of social welfare and social work had been steadily advancing, the international conflicts which broke out in the late 1930s and early 1940s led the state to shift its attention from general welfare support and needs by giving priority to the requirements of economic and armaments production – especially the requirements with regard to labour power. Accordingly, the state's concern was mainly with policy and practice in relation to industrial workers to the neglect of its involvement in the social welfare system in relation to, for instance, the physically handicapped with their restricted labour potential. Significantly perhaps, what had been known as 'social work' was re-labelled as 'welfare work' (*Kosei-jigyo*). The state's emphasis on the needs of industry and industrial workers rather than those of the Japanese people in general remained firmly in place until the conclusion of the Second World War.

STEPS TAKEN BY THE STATE AFTER THE SECOND WORLD WAR

Until the conclusion of the Second World War, the Japanese state – at the levels of both national government and local government – had at the most only alluded to its responsibility for the social welfare of the general population. The state was prepared to leave the bulk of social welfare provisions to the activities of the private sector of charity work, social work and eventually welfare work – and thereby to only a rudimentary version of a modern system of social welfare services.

The conclusion to the Second World War brought a radical change to the circumstances underlying the Japanese social welfare system, and thereby to the overall thrust of and player profiles within the system. With its defeat, Japan was obliged to change from a society in which power was highly centralized and concentrated in the hands of the Emperor to one in which power was more broadly distributed in accordance with democratic principles and institutions. As a result of the post-war Constitution, sovereignty and political decision-making was statutorily transferred to the people, and accordingly a radical change took place in the formal relationship between the state and the people. In particular, the state acknowledged the concept of basic human rights, and (as stipulated under Article 25 of the Constitution) accepted that it had a responsibility for the people's well-being and a duty to guarantee a minimum standard of life.

The state proceeded to follow through its newly acquired sense of responsibility and obligation by introducing rules and regulations specifying and ensuring people's rights, along with several measures designed to guarantee in practice the achievement of minimum standards of life. The various pieces of legislation included the Livelihood Protection Law which was concerned with the general issue of need and preventing need; various Health Insurance Laws to help the ill and injured; the Child Welfare Law; the Law for the Welfare of the Physically Handicapped; the Welfare Law for the Mentally Handicapped; and the Old People's Welfare Law.

At last, the state realized both in principle and in practice its responsibility and obligation *vis-à-vis* the provision, adequacy and development of social welfare. Accordingly, suddenly and radically the player profile of the state at national level was increased considerably immediately after the War. However, the state underwent the change in a way whereby it still retained a degree of distance from the immediate circumstances and problems of people's lives. That is, national government accepted principles, passed legislation and set frameworks in favour of satisfying people's social welfare rights and requirements, but left the immediate task of providing, operating and organizing the social welfare assistance and services to local government. Essentially, national government delegated the state's responsibility, authority and control in relation to the social welfare system to local government at district, or prefectural, level. In this way, almost by proxy, local government also acquired a position as a prominent player within the Japanese welfare system.

Consequently, since the Second World War, the three players of the state (or national government), local government and the private sector have been similarly prominent within a co-ordinated and co-operative arrangement for meeting the welfare requirements of the Japanese people. However, this is not to say that the arrangement has at all times operated smoothly. For instance, in the years immediately following the War, the national government failed to provide the kind of finance which would have allowed local government to offer adequate assistance and services. As a result, the quality of the social welfare system in Japan was far below that of the systems in many European and North American countries, and remained so for around twenty years. There was only a gradual improvement in the level and adequacy of the services in line with the pace of Japanese economic recovery up until the close of the 1960s. Then around 1970, Japanese economic growth took off, and with it so did the expansion and improvement of the social welfare system. By the early 1980s, the Japanese system of social services and assistance had attained a standard on a par with most of its counterparts in Europe and North America.

During the progressive development of the social welfare system in Japan, the private sector played a not inconsiderable part, especially with regard to certain services. However, the major force behind this development overall towards a comprehensive system has undoubtedly been the state. The state has played and continues to play the leading role in the social welfare system and its drive forward – in particular by constructing the overall framework, limits and constraints within which the services are provided. Most important, national government is the main source of finance: by the late 1980s national government contributed about 90 per cent of the total cost of all local government managed social services. Local government is required to offer a particular range of nation-wide services within certain financial limits set by national government, but it is allowed to boost or add district services out of its own coffers.

Since the Second World War the state has both expanded existing social services and introduced new ones, and has ended up overseeing, financing and managing (albeit largely at local government level) a public sector which has become much greater than the private sector. Whereas at around the period of the First World War, only about 10 per cent of social welfare facilities (such as childcare facilities, nurseries, orphanages, reformatories, homes for the handicapped and homes for the aged) were 'public' (being operated by the state), by the late 1980s the proportion had increased dramatically to 64 per cent, as indicated in Table 5.1.

By the late 1980s, almost twice as many social service facilities were 'public' in the sense that they had been set up and were being run by the

Table 5.1 Distribution of social welfare facilities, personnel and beneficiaries in Japan, 1987

	Facilities	*Personnel*	*Beneficiaries*
Public	30 170	270 286	1 141 643
Private	16 561	299 087	1 126 010
Total	48 731	569 363	2 267 653

Source: Department of Health and Welfare, Japan, *Annual Report on Facilities* (Tokyo: Department of Health and Welfare, 1989).

state largely through local government, even though the numbers of 'public personnel' and 'public beneficiaries' were similar to those found within the 'private sector'.

The changes which have occurred in the state's participation in the social welfare system in Japan since the Second World War entail four main 'improvements': (a) the state has come to accept its responsibility for the general well-being of the Japanese population and therefore its duty to maintain a minimum standard of life for all; (b) the state has come to accept that people have a basic right to social welfare; (c) the state has adopted a social welfare approach, policy and programme which ensures that everyone in some way or another is the object of its protection; (d) the state when assessing people's particular social welfare rights and requirements has adopted criteria which are less about economic and labour power considerations and more about basic humanitarian concerns.

In Japan at the end of the twentieth century, the social welfare system is that social arena involving a set of principal players and relationships which has undergone considerable – radical – change in terms of relative prominence, profiles and power. There are four principal players – the first being 'receipt and rights oriented', and the other three being 'provider and practitioner oriented'. These are (a) the general population with not only 'needs' but also 'rights' and thereby (comparatively) recently acquired consumer power; (b) the state at national government level which directs the overall thrust of the social welfare system, constructs the general social welfare framework, provides the bulk of social welfare finance, gives basic social welfare guarantees, and wields central power; (c) local government which manages the immediate provision and everyday operation of the 'public' sector of the social welfare system at district level, and wields executive power; and (d) the 'private sector' of remaining charitable individuals and organizations which yields residual power. The four players relate to one another in a largely balanced (if not equal) and co-operative manner around the flow of care, assistance and support. The key to the recent patterns and trends in the relative profiles of the players within the social welfare system is the power, initiative and drive of the state at national government level, albeit by way of local government managed services, facilities and person-nel, and under the influence of the continuing presence of the private sector, along with the growing power of the general population.

THE STATE AND THE FOSTER CARE SYSTEM

The prominent part that the state has come to play in the Japanese social welfare system in general is exemplified in the operation of the foster care system in particular. The national government oversees the foster care system as the major provider while local government manages the system as the major practitioner. Of course, there are the foster children whose role within the system is recipient-rights oriented. But, this leaves foster parents whose role is perhaps complex and ambiguous. On the one hand, foster parents play a part which is recipient-rights oriented; but on the other hand, they play a part within the private sector of social welfare as providers-practitioners. Foster parents are private citizens who voluntarily, and in a charitable manner, provide a home and care for foster children. In this way, foster parents share in those practical activities by way of which the state follows through the social welfare responsibility and duty it has come to accept with regard to people in general and to foster children in particular. The state at national government level sets the framework of rules, regula-tions, rights and responsibilities within which both local government (within the public sector) and foster parents (within the private sector) deal with the needs, welfare and care of foster children. In effect, the responsibilities assumed by the state (by national government on behalf of the state) in practice are played out (managed, executed) by a combination of local government and foster parents in practice – through the practical, everyday provision of social welfare services.

While the Japanese system of foster care entails the same four principal players – the state (national government), local government, the private sector (and in particular foster parents) and beneficiaries in the form of foster children – as are to be found in any modern system, player profiles and relationships of the Japanese system have acquired a pattern which is somewhat specific and special.

Originally, as is the case with the Japanese social welfare system in general, the foster care system emerged within the private sector. When, towards the end of the nineteenth century, Japan began its processes of modernization, industrialization and capitalist development, the private sector initiated a foster care system from which the state remained, on principle, completely detached. The state's approach to social welfare was that people's well-being and needs were the problem and responsibility of themselves and their families. Accordingly, as far as the state was concerned, children without parents or caring parents or a home was not its responsibility: the state was not going to stand in the way of private sector charity and initiatives, but nor was it going to provide, assist or support in any way whatsoever. The state, therefore, left all the provisions, costs, responsibilities, rights, authority and control with regard to foster children to private providers-practitioners.

At that time, the private character of foster care often meant in practice that a child (as a result of family/household breakdown or loss) became a foster child through the *ad hoc*, haphazard and unregulated intervention of a 'caring' volunteer, such as a nearby relative, neighbour or other benefactor. Thus, a private individual would act as the child's foster parent out of charity and without any kind of financial or other support from the state at either the national level or the local level. Due to the lack of facilitating resources, legal framework, conventional guidelines, specialist theory, and so on, foster caring and parenting practices varied considerably. There is evidence of some foster parents lavishing a luxurious standard of living on their charges, while others tended to mishandle, mistreat and abuse. Some foster children were treated as full kin and so family members, while others were regarded as nothing more than another pair of hands for work and bringing in extra income. In other words, due to the absence of state involvement and intervention the foster care process and outcome were highly uncertain and precarious.

The ill-defined character of the foster care system symbolized the overall character of the social welfare system, which in turn reflected the lack of state interest and intervention. It took quite some time for fostering to attract recognition as a useful and valuable means of ensuring childcare and child protection, especially when it is not left wholly to chance and 'nature'. Over time, the accumulated experience of child welfare activities indicated that there is a place for foster care so long as it receives appropriate and adequate social support and guidance. In other words, gradually foster care acquired theoretical respectability, especially through the experience of and as an alternative to care in orphanages and similar facilities. In this context, the lessons learned by Juji Ishi, who in 1887 founded an orphanage at Okayama, were especially significant and influential. He came to the conclusion that child welfare and development depends not just on the quality of facilities such as orphanages, but also on the social relationships entailed – on whether or not these were or closely resembled those relationships found in households and families. On these grounds he became a strong advocate of developing and improving the foster care system.

However, despite this encouragement the state remained unmoved in leaving the foster care system fully to the private sector until after the Second World War. The system attracted little attention and interest except in such exceptional circumstances as those of war and 'natural disaster' in so far as these events resulted in a large number of orphans and homeless children.

Immediately after the War, as part of the radical change in the social welfare system overall, the foster care system was given a considerable boost as a result of state intervention and leadership. In accordance with the state's acceptance of its responsibility for people's rights to a minimum standard of life, it proceeded to ensure that children without parental protection would be taken care of and accommodated either within social service facilities, such as orphanages, or within foster homes. Thus, with the passing of the Child Welfare Law in 1947, the state brought the foster care system into the public sector of social welfare for the first time (at least partially, given that foster parents necessarily remain *private* providers-practitioners). Most important, the state introduced a scheme of financial assistance to foster parents, albeit through local government. Local government, as is the case with social welfare assistance and services in general, was given the task of implementing the scheme as part of the overall operation and development of the foster care system.

The state removed the foster care system from its location wholly within the private sector based on voluntary action and charity and lodged it firmly within the public sector which it oversaw, organized and led. It laid down various principles, rules and standards for the guidance of the system; the managerial activities of local government; the selection, conduct and assessment of foster parents; and the rights of foster children. In particular, the process by which people became foster parents was tightened up, so that it was no longer an arbitrary matter dependent solely upon self-selection, but instead guided by strict requirements with regard to parental values, attitudes and behaviour.

Essentially, in 1947, the roles, profiles and relative power of the players within the foster care system were drastically altered by being statutorily shaped into a clearly defined pattern within the public sector. In this way, the foster care system very much represents the general features of the post-War social welfare system. However, the foster care system also has certain distinctive features due to the emphasis which has been placed on the issue and importance of the formal rights of the players involved. Connectedly, the state has urged local government to exercise considerable flexibility in its expectations and requirements of foster parent–child relationships by being sensitive to the particular kind of relationships entailed; the local cultural conditions (associated with family and personal life, for instance); and the personalities involved.

In Japan in recent years, there has been a considerable expansion in the presence and place of the foster care system within the overall social welfare system, in the numbers of foster children and parents, and in the diversity of foster parent–child arrangements and types. At the same time, however, there is no doubt that the system has a long way to go before it achieves the stature of those systems in various other countries, such as Britain and New Zealand, where there is an even greater emphasis on the use and value of foster care compared with facility-based care. In Japan while the state has strongly supported family-based childcare in theory and principle, it has been relatively slow to provide backing in practice. The outcome is a balance between family-based care and facility-based care which remains firmly tipped in favour of the latter, and which therefore is out of touch with the general trend of modern societies.

This difference is perhaps both surprising and understandable at the same time in view of the state's commitment to the family. On the one hand, this commitment lends itself to the state promoting family-based care, not merely in principle but also in practice. On the other hand, the same commitment also inclines the state to keep its distance so as to allow family-based care to emerge 'naturally' along traditional lines and in accordance with traditional values. That is, the state's posture can be understood in terms of its commitment to the particular features of the traditional Japanese family – its strength, cohesiveness, autonomy, and pattern of parental independence, authority and control. In other words, the state finds it culturally compatible – not to mention financially convenient – to intervene as little as possible in the everyday conduct of foster parent–child relationships; to treat foster parents as if they are 'traditional national parents'; and therefore to give minimum practical support to foster parents. In Japan, more than in other modern societies (such as Britain and New Zealand) foster parents are treated as full parents, and thereby not only experience considerable independence, rights and authority but also have to face high expectations and heavy demands as a result of being placed at the forefront of the process by which the state implements its acknowledged responsibility for the welfare of all children. Foster parents are, in effect, placed in the position of having to shoulder and realize in practice the responsibility accepted formally by the state. Foster parents are required to be responsible on behalf of the state, but without the kind of practical support that is supplied in other countries. In Japan, more than anywhere else, foster parents are squeezed between low practical support on the one hand and high expectations on the other.

The prominent profiles in Japan of foster parents and of local government (through each local Child Consultancy Office) as players in the form of provider-practitioners within the scope of the social welfare system can be accounted for in terms of the way the state, at the level of national government, has accepted obligations with regard to minimum standards of life, while at the same time remaining reluctant and distant from the immediate provision of services, care and protection. In effect, the state at national government level has implemented its obligations in relation to children by passing its responsibility on to (first) local government and (second) foster parents. This approach very much reflects and, in turns, reinforces traditional Japanese assumptions and expectations about welfare linked to values about, for instance, family life. The emphasis has been and firmly remains on (private) family support and self-reliance. As a result, the social welfare system in general in Japan may in terms of quantity and quality match the systems in other countries, such as Britain and New Zealand. However, it also remains comparatively distinct. The state in Japan allows and promotes a system whereby national government, local government and the private sector have similarly prominent profiles within a co-operative enterprise. This compares with the situation in Britain and New Zealand where either national government or local government has by far the highest profile.

In Britain, the state not only places a high value on foster care as opposed to facility care for 'children in need of protection'; it also provides considerable practical support – the result being that over 50 per cent of such children are in foster homes. At the same time, the state at national government level (as in Japan) provides the overall statutory and financial framework within which the foster care system operates, and within which local government not only implements more practical support, but also assumes more rights and plays out greater responsibilities in the everyday lives of foster children. Accordingly, in comparison with Japan, in Britain foster parents have less independence, rights and responsibilities.

In New Zealand, compared with Britain and Japan, the state at national government level has the highest profile within the foster care system. National government through the Department of Social Welfare and its social workers is the most prominent player in the everyday implementation of the system at the immediate practical level. Accordingly, the independence, rights and responsibilities of both local government and foster parents are comparatively limited, even though (again as in Britain) foster care is highly valued and given a lot of practical support.

The particular character and operation of the foster care system in Japan very much represents the character and operation of the overall social welfare system, and can be accounted for to a large extent in terms of the particular cultural values and traditions in Japan as they apply to, for example, family life, relationships and responsibilities. That is, the state in Japan has accepted its basic responsibility for the welfare of all people – so that it is obliged to ensure a minimum standard of life for all. However, just as the Japanese state was in a world-wide sense comparatively slow in arriving at this position in principle and theory, it remains somewhat tentative – even reluctant – in practice. The Japanese state's major practical involvement is to provide a statutory and financial framework within which local government, private benefactors and recipients have much greater and more 'equal' profiles than is the case in other societies – such as Britain and New Zealand.

Of course, it is open to debate whether the distinctive development of the Japanese welfare system not only fits in with the traditional Japanese cultural and social patterns (such as those associated with family and parents), but also ties in with other major changes which have been taking place, such as those connected with the economy. It is unclear whether the Japanese approach to state care through the social welfare system could provide a model for other societies: one which could be adopted as a means of providing an improved balance between ensuring a minimum standard of life for all in conjunction with economic progress. Certainly, many Western political parties and governments, under the influence of New Right theory, have been in recent years tempted by policies and practices (such as those which come under the headings of 'decentralization' and deinstitutionalization') that would appear to be based on the assumption that something resembling the Japanese model can be implemented elsewhere. It remains to be seen if this experiment in trying to impose such a model on societies with value systems very different from that to be found in Japan will be successful.

6 The State and the Survivors of Hiroshima

Katsuya Kodama

Almost half a century ago, in 1945, the first nuclear weapons ever to be used in warfare exploded above the Japanese cities of Hiroshima and Nagasaki, reducing them and and many of their citizens to ashes, with nearly 130 000 people in Hiroshima and 70 000 in Nagasaki dying before the end of October. The atomic bombs dropped caused unprecedented destruction and death simply through the enormous energy which was unleashed in the multiple forms of blast, heat and radiation. However, the horrors of the bombing are not confined to the immediate impact. They have persisted to the present, handicapping and haunting the survivors. For the majority of the survivors, the bombs have meant a forty-five year period of considerable difficulties, hardships and suffering. As a result of the physiological, psychological and social damage, the survivors' daily lives have turned out to be, and very much remain, arduous and miserable.

The following discussion is concerned with the way in which the state has played a part in the everyday lives of the survivors of the bombing; the way in which the state has responded to the personal and social consequences of the bombing, including the wants, demands and pressures expressed by the survivors themselves; and the extent to which the state has responded in a 'caring' fashion by helping to meet the needs and improve the circumstances of the survivors. The argument is that rather than easing the difficulties, suffering and hardship of the survivors, the state has exacerbated these things by pursuing an approach characterized by a notable absence of care, interest and help. Connectedly, the history of the Survivors' Movement (a multifareous assortment of groupings) has been a long and tortuous experience of attempts to gain, in particular, medical and financial assistance from the state, but with only limited success. The struggle by the survivors and their Movement may then be traced to a series of factors and events, some of the main ones being: state disinterest rooted in a lack of motivation; state reluctance to accede to – and to be seen to accede to – the survivors' demands and pressures; instead, an inclination by the state to curtail and control the Survivors' Movement; and the policies and practices of the Occupation Forces, which soon after the end of the war issued through the General Headquarters (GHQ) one particular command with especially troublesome consequences for the survivors – that of the September 1945 press code.

While both the original Japanese invasions within the Asian-Pacific region along with the event which brought the Second World War to a climax and conclusion, the dropping of the atomic bombs on Hiroshima and Nagasaki, have been frequently, firmly and vociferously condemned, the lack of care shown by the Japanese state towards the atomic bomb survivors has gone relatively unnoticed. My concern is to draw attention to the 'crimes' of the state which have contributed to the damage and suffering endured for so long by the remaining victims.

THE PRESS CODE OF THE OCCUPATION FORCES

Following its defeat which brought the Second World War to an end, Japan came under United States occupation. On 6 September 1945, the Occupation Forces GHQ issued a statement claiming that all the victims of the Hiroshima and Nagasaki bombs had died by the beginning of that month: that there was no one left suffering from bomb related diseases. Thirteen days later the same authorities issued a press code designed to suppress activity which might reveal the actual picture of the bomb damage and its aftermath. The press code prohibition covered all investigations, reports and commentaries about the bombing; and it even extended to accounts of the medical procedures used to treat atomic bomb related diseases. The code remained in place and was rigorously applied until the signing of the San Francisco Peace Treaty in 1951.

One major consequence of the press code was that the survivors of Hiroshima and Nagasaki were seriously obstructed in their efforts to make sense of and cope with the damage and pain from which they continued to suffer. The code meant that not only the victims of the bombs themselves, but also their doctors had considerable difficulty in acquiring information about the precise character of the bombing, and about procedures for treating radiation related diseases. The survivors were simply left to accept their condition as some kind of tragic but inevitable misfortune along the lines of a natural disaster. At the same time, the code ensured that the general population of Japan were prevented not only from getting to know about the extent and depth of the damage and suffering, but also from realizing that the survivors even existed. In turn, this widespread ignorance may be seen as one of the major factors behind the tardiness of the Japanese government to introduce measures to relieve the suffering. Moreover, the impression on the part of the survivors that they were not recognized and cared about had deeply disturbing psychological effects. The phenomenon of 'psychic numbing' or 'psychic closing-off' as discussed by Robert Lifton (1967) is, in my view, at least partly the result of the survivors' feelings of being ignored and their sense of not existing in the consciousness of the Japanese population and state.

However, in contrast with the general tendency towards compliance, there are some noteworthy exceptional instances of opposition to the press code from among the victims. In particular, certain literary figures and other intellectuals who had survived, courageously reported on the bombing casualties in conjunction with their involvement in various peace activities. Thus, in December 1945, a poet (Ms Sadako Kurihara) established the Chugoku Cultural League (Chugoku being the name of the region in western Japan at the centre of which is the city of Hiroshima) which then published a monthly magazine called *Culture of Chugoku*, the first issue of which was devoted to an account of the bombing victims. Also, in 1947, Professors Tatsuto Morito and Arata Osada, among other intellectuals, formed the Hiroshima Culture and Peace Association and proceeded to seek poems of peace. The result was that the citizens of Hiroshima presented the Association with 10 000 contributions. However, such organized activities were both relatively rare and heavily restricted, ensuring that the survivors were left with having to cope in the face of very little state interest, attention and care, at least until the signing of the San Francisco Treaty.

THE SURVIVORS' MOVEMENT AND THE STATE

After the signing of the San Francisco Treaty, which brought an end to the press code, the survivors of Hiroshima and Nagasaki began to organize themselves into support and pressure groups. These groups were small, being restricted to the bombed areas and populations. For example, in 1951 the Hiroshima Atomic-bomb Victims Rehabilitation Society was formed in order to promote the process of self-rehabilitation through mutual help; and its membership was composed of twenty-five young girls all of whom had keloids or other severe facial scarring. Their self-help took them to receive plastic surgery in the United States, where they became known as the 'Hiroshima maidens'. In 1952 several literary figures, including Sankichi Toge and Tomoe Yamashiro, founded the A-bomb Victims' Association of Hiroshima. This organization proceeded to appeal widely to the Japanese population for help in meeting the medical and subsistence requirements of the survivors, as well as in supporting research into the atomic bomb damage. However, the size and composition of such groups meant that their impact, and in particular their influence on the Japanese government, was only very slight. Consequently, the practical benefits of these groups was largely confined to that which came from facilitating mutual help and friendship.

But, the Survivors' Movement was suddenly transformed from being more or less exclusively concerned with mutual help and self-rehabilitation into pressing the government for medical assistance, examinations and treatment as a result of one particular event, the 'Bikini incident'. In 1954 a US hydrogen bomb test at Bikini Atoll, in the Marshall Islands about 4000 kilometres south-east of Japan, irradiated the crewmen of a Japanese fishing vessel. This incident had a huge impact by shocking the Japanese public, inflaming sentiment against nuclear weapons and focussing attention on the plight of the remaining victims of Hiroshima and Nagasaki. In effect, the Bikini disaster is responsible for a sudden heightening of Japanese awareness of the existence and needs of the survivors of Hiroshima and Nagasaki, and connectedly gave a boost to the Survivors' Movement.

In response to a surge of public interest and concern, the first World Conference Against Atomic and Hydrogen Bombs was held in Hiroshima on 6 August 1955. This mass gathering gave rise to the formation of several new groups of survivors. For instance, in September 1955, following the initiative of Professor Seiichi Nakano, a youth group called 'Ayumi' ('moving on') was created. Ayumi had a membership of almost eighty atomic bomb orphans, and it was concerned with not only providing self-help but also with pressing for government assistance and with promoting world peace. October saw the emergence of the Nagasaki Atomic Bomb Youth Association, and its aims included tackling the issue of health care and promoting the investigation of atomic bomb damage. Of particular importance was the formation in 1956 of the Japan Confederation of A-bomb Sufferers Organizations. This confederation pursued the following goals: to achieve an international agreement banning all nuclear weapons; to establish an A-bomb Victims Relief Law in conjunction with a system of health supervision for the remaining victims; and to promote a scheme of vocational training to facilitate the survivors' personal and social rehabilitation.

Apart from these groups formed from among the Hiroshima and Nagasaki survivors, in September 1955 the first national peace organization, the Japan Council Against Atomic and Hydrogen Bombs, was created. The Council had a genuine, nation wide mass appeal, and it was supported by large numbers of survivors and the general population. Following the repeal of the press code and the impact of the Bikini incident in generating widespread concern about nuclear weapons, the Survivors' Movement and the anti-nuclear movement enjoyed solid support from among those at both ends of the political spectrum – radicals and conservatives alike. This reflected the way in which each movement was at this time politically independent, having no affiliation or association with any particular political orientation or organization. The government and governing party, the Liberal Democratic Party (the Liberal Democrats) expressed their sympathy and support for the Survivors' Movement, albeit in a limited and cautious fashion. The Movement attracted even greater encouragement from the other, non-governing, political parties, such as the Japan Socialist Party (the Socialists). The Movement's broad political support was turned into a practical gain during 1956 when the Lower House of the National Diet (parliament) approved a resolution setting up a system of medical assistance, and in the following year the A-bomb Victims' Medical Care Law was implemented.

However, after enjoying several years of expanding membership, sympathy and support, the Survivors' Movement along with the anti-nuclear movement reached a crucial turning point. By 1958 the anti-nuclear movement was unable to avoid acquiring a stronger political colour given that Japan was preparing to be re-armed in a world that was increasingly resorting to nuclear arms within the context of the gathering Cold War split between the Western-capitalist and Eastern-socialist camps. In particular, the revision in 1960 of the Japan–US Security Treaty sparked a severe confrontation between the national peace organization – the Council Against A-H Bombs – and the Japanese Liberal government. In order to block the Japan–US Treaty, the Council became aligned with the Socialists along with the General Council of Trade Unions of Japan, and in response the government and governing party formed an alliance with other conservative factions against the Council. In 1961, as part of its attempt to counter and suppress the Council, the conservative alliance created a parallel – but essentially bogus – 'peace' organization, the National Council for Peace (NCP). This organization represented a blatant attempt to disrupt and dismember the peace movement which had been forged around the now politically aligned Council Against A-H Bombs.

The NCP was allied with the Liberal Democrats; the Japan Democratic Socialist Party (the Democratic Socialists), which despite its title is located on the political right, being even more conservative than the Liberal Democrats on issues relating to national security; and the Japan Confederation of Labour. The NCP was composed largely of people of religious and humanitarian persuasions, and ostensibly its main aim was to promote world peace through human love and fellowship. On the other hand, at the core of the organization, some of the leaders were first and foremost anti-communists and, in practice, against peace movements and in favour of nuclear armament. In reality, the purpose of the NCP was to inflict as much damage and disarray as possible on the peace movement and its prospects. Moreover, the strategy turned out to be quite successful in managing to disrupt the peace movement by specifically targeting and damaging the credibility of the Council Against A-H Bombs. The Council was identified as being associated with communism, the result being to persuade many people – bomb survivors and others – to distance themselves from the Council and the encompassing peace movement.

Partly due to the growing antagonism between the peace movement and the Japanese government, the latter began to draw back from helping the survivors of Hiroshima and Nagasaki; and in particular, governmental aid to the survivors was reduced to the minimum level guaranteed by the A-bomb Victims Medical Care Law.

Within a few years of the formation of the National Council for Peace, the Council Against A-H Bombs broke up into two separate organizations (in 1964). A section of the membership of the Council split off in order to form a new peace organization, the Japan Congress Against Atomic and Hydrogen Bombs. The immediate causes of this division were differing stances over whether nuclear testing by any country – capitalist or socialist – should be opposed; and over how to evaluate the Limited Nuclear Test Ban Treaty. The faction which emerged as 'the Congress' aligned itself with the Japan Socialist Party; insisted that nuclear testing by all countries should be condemned; and supported the Treaty as a step towards the total prohibition of nuclear testing. On the other hand, the remaining Council Against A-H Bombs allied itself with the Communist Party; adopted the view that nuclear weapons in socialist countries were defensible on the grounds that they benefited world peace; and dismissed the Treaty as a ploy in the interests of American Imperialism.

The anti-nuclear movement in Japan had, in effect, experienced two splits within a period of five years, resulting in three competing organizations: the National Council for Peace, supported by the conservative portion of the political spectrum; the Council Against A-H Bombs, supported by the Socialist Party; and the Congress Against A-H Bombs, supported by the Communist Party. As these events unfolded, the Confederation of A-bomb Sufferers managed to remain somewhat aloof and more or less intact. However, even though the Confederation managed to avoid serious rupture, it did not go unscathed. Both the peace movement and the Survivors' Movement were drained of much of the commitment it had so far enjoyed from the general population. The politicization and multi-polarization of the peace movement provided the Japanese government with an excellent excuse for opting for a cold-hearted approach to meeting the welfare needs of the Hiroshima and Nagasaki survivors. In other words, as on the one hand the peace movement became marked by mainstream politics and marred by competition and conflict, so on the other hand the remaining bomb victims were pushed aside and left without anything like the kind of assistance and care their continued suffering invited.

The antagonistic and confrontational relationship between the peace movement and the Japanese government has not abated: today it is as prominent as ever. Moreover, although the Confederation of A-bomb Sufferers is officially politically unaffiliated, the bulk of its core members and leaders are sympathetic to either the Socialists or the Communists. Consequently, the Confederation has been regarded and treated as, in practice, belonging squarely alongside the opposition parties. Connectedly, issues concerned with the welfare and care of the remaining Hiroshima and Nagasaki victims have became a source of acrimonious debate along party political lines; and have been caught up and exploited within the party political power game.

In the late 1960s, the Survivors' Movement won a partial victory in its battle with the government. In 1966, the Confederation of A-bomb Sufferers published a booklet entitled *Special Features of the A-bomb and the Demand for the A-Bomb Victims Relief Law*. This publication challenged the Japanese government to clearly spell out the problems being faced by the survivors, and fuelled public interest in and concern about especially the difficulties remaining for the victims in the areas of health and maintaining an acceptable standard of living. During 1967 in Tokyo, the Confederation staged three public campaigns demanding government action on the A-bomb Victims Relief Law. Such activities, in conjunction with the increase in popular sympathy, persuaded the government in 1968 to introduce the A-bomb Victims Special Measure Law. Nonetheless, both this piece of legislation and the earlier (1956) A-bomb Victims Medical Care Law represent merely partial victories for the survivors. They fall far short of the kind of measures that are required to adequately deal with the breadth and depth of the difficulties and suffering that continue to be endured. Most survivors express strong dissatisfaction with the statutory provisions gained so far, and many continue to demand the introduction of the A-bomb Victims Relief Law.

TWO LAWS AND THEIR SHORTCOMINGS

Two laws have been passed specifically concerned with the care and needs of the survivors of Hiroshima and Nagasaki, or more precisely of the *certified* survivors: on 31 March 1956, the A-bomb Victims Medical Care Law provided free medical examinations and subsequent treatment; and on 20 May 1968, the A-bomb Victims Special Measures Law was introduced to contribute to their general welfare.

The Medical Care Law covers four categories of survivors: (a) those who at the time of the bombing were within approximately four kilometres of an epicentre or within a black rain area; (b) those who entered a two-kilometre zone (around an epicentre) within two weeks of the bombing; (c) those who participated in one of the rescue teams or who were involved in disposing of the corpses; and (d) those offspring of survivors who at the time of the bombing had not been born but had been conceived. At the same time, however, only those people who are able to corroborate their claims to be survivors on the basis of the testimonies of two witnesses, neither of whom can be family, are accepted as certified survivors and therefore entitled to the Medical Care Law provisions. Certified survivors receive A-bomb health books to signify their certification and record their medical details and treatment. However, actual survivors often face considerable, and some-times insurmountable, difficulties when trying to obtain certification. The stumbling block for many people is the requirement to find two non-family witnesses to identify them as survivors, given especially the effects of the bombing and the passage of time. Survivors may discover that by the time of their application for certification no suitable witnesses have themselves survived; or survivors may simply not know the fate or the whereabouts or how to track down suitable witnesses. The bombing's destruction and devastation led large numbers of people to leave the areas affected in order to settle elsewhere, and in the process to leave behind for ever the neigh-bours and acquaintances they had lived among in those areas. The upshot is that a large number of genuine survivors, who may need substantial and urgent medical attention, cannot satisfy the requirement with regard to suitable witnesses, and so remain uncertified and unable to make use of the Medical Care Law provisions. A further, incidental, consequence is that the available official statistics on the survivors will be inaccurate.

On 1 August 1985 the number of people who possessed A-bomb health books was 366 957. According to a survey of these certified survivors carried out by the Ministry of Public Welfare (1987) (the survey having a response rate of 86.7 per cent) the ratio of male to female survivors was 43:57. The proportion of certified survivors in category (a) under the Medical Care Law was 63.3 per cent; that in category (b) was 27.5 per cent; that in category (c) was 7.9 per cent; and that in category (d) was 1.6 per cent. The average age of the survivors was 59.9 years (59.4 for men and 60.3 for women). Table 6.1 shows that the largest number of survivors was in the specified age range of 50-59 (for both males and females); that a majority of survivors were in their youth (roughly early teens to mid-twenties) at the time of their irradiation; and that in 1985 this majority had recently entered the so-called 'cancer age'. While the links between nuclear radiation and cancer are still being researched so that no final conclusions are possible, evidence on the survivors indicates a notable increase in the incidence of cancer with time and age.

Whereas the Medical Care Law provides medical assistance to all the certified survivors of the atomic bombs in recognition of their physical injuries, the A-bomb Victims Special Measures Law has introduced a system of financial allowances designed to help victims in various particular circumstances. The range of allowances includes ones to cover 'medical care', 'health maintenance', 'health protection', 'nursing', 'burial' and 'special'. However, from the point of view of the survivors, there is a considerable problem when it comes to them taking advantage of this piece of legislation. Access to the allowances is heavily restricted by eligibility regulations linked to income and income tax considerations, so that only a portion of the survivors is receiving each of the allowances. According to the Ministry of Public Welfare's study (1987), in 1985 only 61.2 per cent of those people who had qualified for the A-bomb Health Book were receiving the health maintenance allowance; only 5.5 per cent were receiving the health protection allowance; and less than 1 per cent were receiving the medical care allowance or the nursing allowance. Over a quarter of

Table 6.1 The age distribution of A-bomb survivors in 1985*

Age	Male	Female	Total
Under 49	9.4 (29 604)	11.2 (35 150)	20.7 (64 751)
50–59	15.5 (48 541)	17.8 (55 936)	33.3 (104 477)
60–69	8.5 (26 557)	15.1 (47 222)	23.5 (73 779)
70–79	6.6 (20 745)	9.1 (28 424)	15.7 (49 169)
Over 80	2.9 (9049)	3.9 (12 258)	6.8 (21 307)
Total	42.9 (134 496)	57.1 (178 991)	(313 499)

* Percentages. Figures in brackets are corresponding absolute numbers.

Source: Ministry of Public Welfare, *Report of the 1985 Survey of the Survivors of Hiroshima and Nagasaki* (Tokyo: Ministry of Public Welfare, 1987).

certified survivors were receiving none of the allowances made available by the Medical Care Law. On the other hand, for most of the survivors the allowances, and in particular the health maintenance allowance, is the only means they have to alleviate the everyday hardships of life linked to the bombing.

However, a further problem for the survivors is that, once obtained, allowances turn out to be meagre and insufficient. For instance, for most of the survivors, the only Special Measures Law allowance which is open to them is the health maintenance allowance, and its value is just 29 050 yen (approximately US$ 208) per month. The value of the health protection allowance is only 14 530 yen (US$ 104) per month; but that of the *special* allowance rises to 118 260 yen (US$ 845) per month, at least for those survivors whose certified disease has not been cured. In the case of those survivors whose certified disease has been cured the value of the special allowance drops down to 43 580 yen (US$ 311) per month. The 'uncured' special allowance is relatively generous, but is received by few survivors due to the restrictive definition of 'certified disease'. Just 672 people were receiving this allowance, and merely a further 740 people were receiving the 'cured' special allowance, out of a total of 366 957 registered survivors of Hiroshima and Nagasaki. This leaves two further Special Measures Law allowances, the nursing allowance which varies between 12 380 and 40 500 yen (US$ 88 and US$ 289) per month; and the burial allowance. The latter is paid when anyone who has been granted an A-bomb Health Book dies. It is paid to the deceased's family to cover funeral expenses, and its value is 130 000 yen (US$ 929). The inadequacy of the range of Special Measures Law allowances in assisting with the daily living (and dying) expenses of the survivors of Hiroshima and Nagasaki reflects the exceptionally high commodity prices in Japan, the result being that a large proportion of remaining victims are left to suffer considerable economic hardship.

THE CONTINUING STRUGGLE FOR THE SURVIVORS

One of the outstanding aspects of the damage wreaked by the 1945 bombing is its persistence, so that it is a mistake to conceive of the disasters of Hiroshima and Nagasaki as being in the past. The havoc and horrors brought by the atomic bombs are, for the survivors, very much matters of the present as well as for the future. Forty-five years may have gone by, but many survivors still suffer considerable hardship which can be directly or indirectly related to the bombing. Further statutory measures are urgently required to help meet the needs of the remaining victims, as becomes clear if we examine details of what it means to be a survivor today in Japan.

In the first place, the atom bombs caused a range of specific physical injuries and diseases. These so-called A-bomb diseases may be variously attributed to the three basic destructive features of the bombing: blast; thermal rays; and radiation. However, it is mainly the effects of the radiation which continue to spoil the health and bring physical suffering to the survivors. There were differences between the bomb dropped on Hiroshima and that dropped on Nagasaki: apart from anything else the former was a uranium device while the latter was plutonium based. Nonetheless, in each case, the view is that gamma rays and neutrons were the main agents in the radiation emitted by the fission at the moment of explosion, by the resulting fission products, and by the subsequent induced-radioactive materials in the surrounding areas (Hiroshima Prefectural Office, 1976).

The set of symptoms which emerged within the first few months following the bombing have been referred to as 'acute injuries', and they include (apart from the external wounds and burns) malaise, susceptibility to fatigue, headache, nausea, vomiting, loss of appetite, diarrhoea, fever, eropharyngitis, leukopenia, menorrhagic diathesis, anaemia and epilation. After a time, perhaps as the acute injuries began to show signs of healing, another set of disorders emerged. These after effects include keloids, blood disorders, ocular lesions, liver troubles and cancer. Most keloids developed during 1946 and 1947, and today have flattened out, even though they are still signalled by scars. Several types of blood disorders, such as leukaemia, have been widespread among survivors as a result of being exposed to the radiation. The occurrence of new cases of leukaemia was greatest during the period 1950 to 1954, since when the number has steadily declined. Another disease common among survivors is ocular lesions, the first incidence of atomic bomb cataract being detected about two years after the bombing, and cases are still occurring. The radiation also caused liver ailments and cancer; and several investigations have clearly shown marked higher levels of deaths due to these diseases among survivors compared with the remaining, unexposed population.

A troublesome issue surrounding the lives of the survivors is that of the impossibility of deciding whether a particular case of a disease can be attributed to the atomic bombing. There is no doubt that the likelihood of contracting the kind of diseases listed above is much greater among the survivors than among the general population; and this ties in with the findings of animal experiments according to which there is a strong correlation between such diseases and radiation exposure. However, this evidence does not by itself tell us the 'cause' of disease in a particular case.

After all, it is not only A-bomb survivors but also members of the general population who contract these illnesses. It is because there is uncertainty about discerning the actual source of a disease that the state has fixed the allowances paid to A-bomb survivors under the Special Measures Law at low levels.

As well as the direct physical consequences of the bombing there are, however, more indirect effects on people's lives. By examining these we can further expose the shortcomings of state care in relation to the remaining victims. They can be traced to some extent to the poor health of the survivors. According to the Ministry of Public Welfare's survey (1987), in 1985 4.2 per cent of the survivors of Hiroshima and Nagasaki were hospitalized, and as many as 38.4 per cent regularly attended hospitals for treatment. As we have noted, under the A-bomb Victims Medical Care Law, those who have gained A-bomb Health Books enjoy free medical treatment. This entitlement eases the cost of living for the remaining victims, but it far from solves the financial difficulties stemming from the bombing. Many survivors and their families will have few savings and little capital on which to rely, as a result of which they can easily be propelled by the continuing health effects of the bombing into financial crises. What often makes matters worse is that it is common for households to contain more than one survivor: this applies to about 20 per cent of the 253 131 survivor households which existed in 1985 (Ministry of Public Welfare, 1987). In such households it is common to have a number of severely sick members. Often, the result is serious financial difficulties, which point to the gross inadequacy of the state's current welfare system.

Another important, indirect, effect of the atomic bombing is the way in which the loss of family members has led to suffering and hardship. For instance, many women lost their husbands, and reports have clearly shown how their widowhood has meant considerable personal, social and financial difficulties over the years. Furthermore, many children survived but with the loss of their parents, to some extent because the children had been previously evacuated from the bombed areas. It is estimated that between 3000 and 5000 children were orphaned by the bombing. Evidence suggests that the lives of those orphans who did not themselves sustain (at least long-term) physical injury have, nonetheless, been seriously marred by the bombing (Kodama, 1985; 1987). However, one of the major shortcomings of the current welfare system in relation to the Hiroshima and Nagasaki survivors is that unless people were directly affected, injured or damaged by the bombing, they do not qualify for any compensation or allowance. Hence, loss of family and perhaps parents, despite the resulting suffering and difficulties, is not by itself adequate grounds for making a successful claim for state assistance. In particular, the A-bomb orphans who happened to have been evacuees at the time of the bombing, are denied access to state care and financial aid, even though their lives may well have been and remain tragically affected (albeit indirectly) by the bombing.

This aspect of the aftermath of the 1945 events leads on to the issue of the psychological outcome. The colossal impact, devastation and trauma of the bombing has left a huge imprint in the memories and minds of the remaining victims. In interviews carried out with survivors of Hiroshima, I have been frequently surprised by the way people have retained vivid and detailed impressions of what happened all those years ago. This is apart from the way they also remain highly distressed and severely tortured by the event. One eminent psychologist, Robert Lifton (1967), has interpreted the psychological pain of the survivors using the expressions: 'taint of death' and 'death guilt'. By taint of death, Lifton is referring to how the deep and resilient psychological legacy endured by the survivors can be understood in terms of 'three aspects of their ordeal: the suddenness and totality of their death situation; the permanent taint of death associated with the radiation's after-effects; and their continuing group relationship to world fears about nuclear extermination'. According to Lifton, 'death guilt' entails the presence of a more or less insurmountable sense on the part of the remaining victims that their 'survival was made possible by others' death'.

In the process of trying to make sense of and evaluate the survivors' persistent psychological pain, it is important to view it as being linked to and an aspect of the damage caused by the bombing. It is important to realize that the full scope and detail of the damage inflicted by the atomic bombs is broad and complex. The suffering of the survivors is not only physical but also psychological. However, the extent and range of the survivors' pains are by no means addressed by the state through its current system of care.

TOWARDS THE A-BOMB VICTIMS RELIEF LAW

In order to overcome the shortcomings of the current welfare system in relation to the remaining victims of Hiroshima and Nagasaki, many survivors are firmly committed to the introduction of the A-bomb Victims Relief Law as demanded by the Confederation of A-bomb Sufferers as long ago as 1966. The purpose of this Law would be to compensate and assist all the survivors of the bombing as well as all the families of those who have not survived. It would also make allowances more substantial and realistic in recognition of the actual needs and the extent of the damage and suffering borne by survivors. Moreover, the Law would confirm the state's commitment to policies favouring the restricted rearmament of Japan along with the control and reduction of nuclear weapons throughout the world. Those who strongly urge the government to support the A-bomb Victims Relief Law argue that the suffering of, and so final peace for, the remaining victims of the Hiroshima and Nagasaki bombings will not be achieved until the threat of a nuclear holocaust is removed and the future of world peace is guaranteed.

The possibility of enacting the A-bomb Victims Relief Law has been discussed several times in the Japanese Diet. In 1989, it was even passed by the Upper House before being rejected by the Lower House. The ruling Liberal Democratic Party, which enjoyed an absolute majority of seats in the Lower House, is dismissive of the Law on the grounds that it stands in the way of Japan's rearmament. It seems that the issue of the Hiroshima and Nagasaki bombings and their aftermath has become entangled in debates over Japanese national security. However, I wish to conclude by subscribing to the view that the A-bomb Victims Relief Law would in practice contribute not only to the welfare of the Hiroshima and Nagasaki survivors, but also to the peace of Japan and thereby the rest of the world.

7 State Care and Control in Japan:
The Employment Guidance and Referral Process for Secondary School Leavers
Kaori Okano

This chapter explores the 'care', 'protection' and 'control' features of the process by which Japanese high school students make decisions about and obtain paid employment after school. The discussion is conducted around three main issues: (a) student-teacher interaction through consultation; (b) school collective interests compared and contrasted with student individual interests; and (c) the way the overall referral and guidance process contributes to the maintenance of current societal practices, arrangements and structures.

In order to generate original data concerning the transition of school students into paid employment, I conducted fieldwork in two Japanese inner-city high schools (one technical and one comprehensive) for a full academic year during 1989 to 1990. Towards the end of the fieldwork period, I presented the teachers at the technical high school with a chart (Figure 7.1) summarizing what I had discovered to be the main features of the routes and stages whereby senior students are given guidance and referral in the process of obtaining employment. The teachers tended to agree that the chart accurately represents the process while offering various views and assessments of the chart's implications. Some teachers responded approvingly that the process appears 'comprehensive' and 'protective'; while others responded more critically by making such comments as: 'It almost looks as if we are giving too detailed guidance – to the extent of controlling them!'. The accompanying discussion was far more elaborate and complex than these highly selected remarks indicate, but they conveniently set the scene for what emerge as prominent themes to be developed through this chapter.

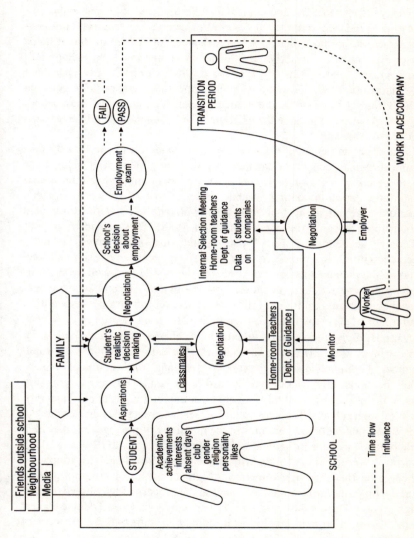

FIGURE 7.1   The process of choosing and obtaining a first job in Japan

The chart reflects how high school leavers in Japan make the transition into employment by way of a tightly supervised process involving close co-operation between three agencies: school; the state's Public Employment Security Office (PESO); and companies as employers. This particular employment guidance and referral system has received widespread commendation on the grounds that it is, for instance, 'effective' in that it helps ensure a 'smooth', 'orderly' and 'efficient' transition from school into employment (see Reubens, 1977; Horvath, 1986; United States Department of Education, 1987). Essentially, the co-operative relationships between school, the state (PESO) and employers means that the move from school into employment is notable for its absence of disjunction faced and experienced by students.

The chart and ensuing discussion will be made clearer by briefly outlining certain aspects of the Japanese high school system. High schools (or more precisely, 'senior high schools') are post-compulsory educational institutions, accommodating around 94 per cent of all fifteen to eighteen year olds, the remaining 6 per cent having already left school for the paid labour force (Japan, Ministry of Education, 1988). They provide two types of course: academic ('ordinary') courses and vocational courses. The latter include training in commerce, data-processing, mechanics, shipbuilding, automobile maintenance and construction, interior design, woodwork, agriculture, fishery and home economics among others. The students on vocational courses are required to follow specialist subjects for between a third and a half of their total study programme. There are two types of school, vocational high schools and academic high schools, which cater solely for one or other of the two types of course. At the same time, there is a small number of comprehensive high schools covering a cross-section of courses. The vocational high school type is further broken down into several sub-types, including technical high schools; commercial high schools and agricultural high schools. The vocational courses, wherever they are conducted, command relatively low rankings in the hierarchy of prestige at senior high school level, and accordingly are relatively easy to get into (Rohlen, 1983). During 1987, 36 per cent of the fifteen to eighteen years-old age group were undergoing the direct transition from high school into paid employment, and the majority of these students were in the process of leaving vocational high schools. During the same year, 71 per cent of vocational course leavers went directly into paid employment, compared with only 22 per cent of academic course leavers (Japan, Ministry of Education, 1988).

I collected data relating to the transition from school into paid employment by spending one complete academic year investigating what happened to the vocational course students on the third year in two senior high schools (my research schools). The first was a municipal technical high school offering courses in mechanics, shipbuilding, automobile maintenance and construction, and interior design. The second was a municipal comprehensive high school offering academic, commerce and data-processing courses. Both schools were ranked towards the bottom of the prestige hierarchy covering public (state) schools within the city, but higher than most of the private (fee paying) schools. This is indicative of how within Japan, in contrast with other capitalist societies, private schools in general attract lower status than public schools. During the year, I traced the progress of three class-groups of students: one in data-processing; one in interior design; and one in mechanics.

THE CALENDAR OF EMPLOYMENT GUIDANCE AND REFERRAL

The final, transitionary year of the Japanese high school students I investigated began in April and ended in the following March, allowing the students to take up paid employment in April. The year was strictly programmed around a calendar of well planned events and stages relating to employment guidance and referral; and the calendar for each of my research schools was broadly consistent with those outlined for other schools in previous studies (Evans, 1986; Horvath, 1986; Department of Education, United States, 1987; Taira and Levine, 1986; Umetani, 1985).

In each school, the Department of Guidance for Life-after-school (henceforth to be called simply the Department) along with the home-room teachers for third year students plays the leading role in the employment guidance and referral process. The Department's formal task is to provide information and guidance to help students make choices and plans with regard to life after school, further education, paid employment and careers. Around half a dozen highly experienced teachers perform duties on behalf of the Department, and accordingly are exempt from being responsible for home-room classes. These teachers operate from a special Departmental room, where they make themselves available for consultations with students who are not otherwise attending lessons. The Departmental room is where the school keeps its systematically stored records relating to employment and companies: records about those companies where students have gone in the past, along with information provided by companies on current recruitment cards, through which students can browse for guidance about job vacancies. Each student belongs to a home-room class, which like its counterparts elsewhere (such as in New Zealand), is the basic unit of school organization. In Japan, a home-room class group made up of a teacher-in-charge and about forty students has a strong sense of identity, cohesiveness and solidarity.

The employment guidance and referral process is arranged around a calendar consisting of nine distinguishable stages.

The first stage: during April, the in-coming third-year students inform the school of their preferences for 'life-after-school' by indicating one choice from (a) university (tertiary degree level courses over four years); (b) junior college (tertiary sub-degree level courses over two years); (c) private professional school (post-secondary courses of various durations – which count neither as nor preparation for tertiary education); (d) employment in either (i) public service or (ii) the private sector. The Department arranges meetings for the students and their parents principally to let them know about the school's employment guidance and referral procedure, as well as about the prevailing job market situation and prospects. The students are provided with details about the companies with which the previous year's students gained employment; and past students may come along to talk about their experience within paid employment and as employees of particular firms. Home-room teachers hold personal interviews with each student and his or her parents to discuss the student's employment possibilities in the light of, for instance, his or her scholastic progress and assessment.

The second stage: during March and April, employers formulate their hiring needs and plans in preparation for those students who will be leaving school during March of the following year. Companies may send representatives to attend seminars organized by PESO; to express their satisfaction and gratitude to those schools which supplied the previous round of recruits; as well as to seek out additional schools for future supplies. For each of its vacant posts, a company is required to complete a recruitment card, which covers such details as working hours and other conditions; pay and other remuneration; insurance schemes; holiday arrangements; and trade union agreements and policies. The completed recruitment cards are sent to PESO (by July) for checking and approval (indicated by a formal stamp). Following PESO's ratification, an employer is allowed to send copies of its recruitment cards to schools; and may do so accompanied by a representative, who will then make enquiries about the likelihood of the vacancies attracting applications from students. Companies and their representatives are at all times obliged to deal with schools and their Departments: under no circumstances are they permitted to approach students directly.

The third stage: at the beginning of July recruitment cards start to arrive at the schools. The cards are collected and filed by the Departments, and the information on the cards is computer processed to facilitate student access and use. The Departments have assigned to them small reception rooms where the schools can entertain visitors from companies and institutions of further education, as well as where the Departmental staff can consult with students and perhaps their parents. During the August vacation period, students examine the recruitment cards, choose those companies and vacancies which attract their interest, discuss with their families, and as a result attempt to arrive at a reasonable decision about which shortlist of vacancies they will try for. Students present their shortlists of vacancies in order of preference to the Departments. Usually, students will tend to opt for some posts with some companies rather than others, so that each year certain companies are confirmed as the popular ones.

The fourth stage: each school holds an internal selection meeting (the Meeting) in an attempt, essentially, to match students and vacancies. The Meeting sets itself the task of recommending, and perhaps urging, each student to apply for a particular vacancy, while at the same time 'selecting' from among all those students who have chosen a particular vacancy the one 'best' suited for that vacancy, and so the most likely applicant. The Meeting is attended by the Departmental staff, the home-room teachers of the third year students, and the third-year Dean. Due to the nature of its task and the composition of those in attendance, the Meeting tends to be a long, drawn-out and tedious event. Ostensibly, the principal concern of the Meeting is to ascertain the 'most appropriate' company for each student in accordance with such criteria as his or her academic performance, school attendance, fitness and health, personality, student council participation and sports club involvement; and to do so given the details of the job and the company involved. In other words, the Meeting assumes that its primary purpose is serving the 'interests' of the students, and certainly home-room teachers will represent their own particular students in a highly committed fashion. Often during the course of a Meeting, a home-room teacher will communicate by telephone with a student, especially when the Meeting raises the possibility of the student not getting his or her first choice, and so of the student altering his or her job preference. One session of the Meeting may not resolve all applications, and therefore may be followed by further sessions.

The fifth stage: during the August vacation, schools are allowed and perhaps encouraged by companies to arrange for parties of students to make visits. Such a visit will be an opportunity not only for interested students to view a company, but also for a company to gain an impression about the students. Accordingly, following a visit, a school Department may make an informal approach to the company in order to gain an insight into its opinions. A school will be especially concerned about what the company's views indicate with regard to the chance each student has of being success-ful at the imminent 'screening tests'. Quite simply, if the company ex-presses any kind of unfavourable judgement about a particular student, the Department will be in a position to come up with an alternative company for that student in time for the mid-September testing season. The process of finally deciding on which company a student should apply for is facilitated by the 'one-company-at-a-time' approach.

The sixth stage: still during the August vacation period, but towards the end of the month, a school puts on seminars and workshops in preparation for the all important, company 'screening tests'. These occasions are in-tended to help students with their curriculum vitae and job interviews, as well as to take written examinations on a wide range of topics. At the beginning of September, schools send application forms on behalf of stu-dents to companies in accordance with the students' eventual 'preferences'. Again, the one-company-at-a-time arrangement pertains in order to avoid the confusion that would arise out of one student being offered more than one job.

The seventh stage: in the middle of September, companies begin setting screening tests. A screening test often consists of two phases: examinations entailing a Japanese language essay, mathematics and general knowledge; followed by an interview. Smaller firms frequently conduct interviews only. The results of the tests are usually sent to schools within a week, and few students fail. For instance, at my two research schools under 10 per cent of all the students tested were deemed to have failed, a clear reflection of the way in which each school had beforehand thoroughly scrutinized and carefully guided the students in the direction of suitable vacancies. That the schools set themselves very high standards in this regard is indicated by a claim made by one Head of Department that 'we could have done more through guidance to prevent these failures'. The relatively small proportion of students who fail go on to attempt a second, and perhaps a third, screening test for any remaining job vacancies, which by this stage are likely to be with companies with relatively low prestige and appeal. Stu-dents are reconsidered at further internal sessions of the selection Meeting, that decide upon which jobs they will try for in the light of their applica-tions and failures so far.

The eighth stage: by the middle of October, a very large majority (around 95 per cent) of students seeking employment have received confirmation from a company that they have been accepted for a job. However, students continue to attend school in the usual way until the holding of the final school examinations in late January, even though their motivation to study declines considerably. Once vacancies have been filled, companies may arrange welcome meetings for the successful students, to whom also companies may dispatch introductory literature; company newsletters; company pamphlets and documents; essay writing exercises; and other preparatory items. Students view this kind of material as a 'welcome sign', and are encouraged to feel as though they are already part of their company.

The ninth and final stage: the Department continues with its job-search and placement activities until all students obtain paid employment, which may mean until the students formally leave school and even beyond. Although students finish school in March – by which time it has become extremely difficult to find employment vacancies – schools retain responsibility for helping students get jobs for a further two months.

STUDENT–HOME-ROOM TEACHER INTERACTION AND THE DECISION ABOUT APPROPRIATE EMPLOYMENT

Throughout the academic year, interaction between a student and his or her home-room teacher will take place over the issue of life-after-school, and such interaction represents the foundation of the process whereby a student arrives at a 'realistic' decision with regard to job and career. As we will see, the interaction takes place within the context of certain crucial conditions and constraints which mean firm limitations on what the teacher can advise and do. Nonetheless, it is abundantly clear that the teacher is very likely to have a genuinely strong commitment to the task of ensuring that the student will leave school into the 'best' possible employment; which is most suitable to his or her capabilities and 'needs'; and which is most conducive to his or her development and progress throughout life-after-school. It is common for a teacher to have both a strong emotional attachment to and practical investment in a student, so that a teacher will share the student's affective and instrumental orientations towards gaining appropriate employment.

To begin with, a student and teacher may not agree on what is appropriate employment, and as a result will have several consultations in order to resolve the difference. In the first instance, a student will decide on what type of employment he or she would like to go into after school, and will select several companies from those that have sent recruitment cards to the school. On occasions, a student will specify a company that has not sent a recruitment card, and this may lead a member of the Department's staff to visit the company to obtain a card. All students will end up with lists of choices in order of preference, lists which have received the approval of their home-room teachers. All students are required to have had their lists

endorsed by their home-room teachers before they are allowed to proceed
further with their applications for particular vacancies.

It will be instructive to have a look at some details of the kind of
consultations which take place between students and home-room teachers,
at least as I observed and recorded them in my research schools.

The case of Hiroaki (a male student)

Hiroaki entered the data-processing course at his high school because he
enjoyed playing with personal computer games and was interested in going
on to devise the programs for such games. At the beginning of his third year
he informed his mother about his preference to take a computer programming course at a private professional school, and his mother agreed. However, when Hiroaki's home-room teacher, Mr Kodama, learnt about this
arrangement, he advised against it. Hiroaki recalled:

> I had sort of expected what Mr Kodama was going to say about it, since
> he repeated in class that it's not worthwhile studying at private pro-
> fessional schools. Mr Kodama said to me in person . . . 'You will get a
> similar job in a better company through the school's referral channel
> rather than after spending an extra year at an obscure professional
> school. This school has a long history, and has contacts with several
> companies.' My mother then left the decision to me. I knew that I would
> have to help with the tuition fee. After all, I decided to get the employ-
> ment and looked through the list of companies for a programming
> position . . . In the end, I chose Ashi Software Company. Because I can
> learn programming further. Also, the company is located in a convenient
> place to commute. I hate commuting in a jammed train every morning.
> The second choice was Meiden Software Company. And up to the fifth
> choice I chose software companies.
>   When Mr Kodama saw this list of my choices, he said 'Ashi Com-
> pany is a small company. Small companies are fine as long as we know
> what it's like. We are not familiar with Ashi, and the school has never
> sent students to the company. I feel that you are taking a risk. I don't
> think it worthwhile to take a risk here since your second choice is good.
> Meiden Software Company is owned by a giant company. Working
> conditions are good. Why don't you go for Meiden instead of Ashi?'.
> I thought it over for a couple of days, and yet did not like the commut-
> ing involved. So I put Ashi Company as my first choice in the final
> submission paper to the school, against Mr Kodama's advice.

In response, Mr Kodama stuck to his original advice and pursued the Meiden Company on behalf of Hiroaki at the internal selection meeting, at which (as has been noted) no students were present. Helped by the fact that there were no other students contending for the position, Mr Kodama was successful in securing the Meiden vacancy for Hiroaki. Subsequently, Mr Kodama's actions were accepted and defended by Hiroaki, who argued that Mr Kodama must have had a good reason for his persistence in favour of Meiden as opposed to Ashi. Eventually, Hiroaki sat the screening test for the Meiden position and got the job.

The case of Mari (a female student)

At the time of entering senior high school, Mari (a Korean national) had sufficient achievement scores to enable her to get into a second rank academic school. However, she opted for the data-processing course of a vocational high school on the grounds that her family would not be able to afford to send her to university. The second rank academic high school she might have gone to, being primarily geared for university entrance, would not have provided the type and quality of employment guidance and referral she would receive in the vocational high school. Mari found the programming class on the course especially difficult, and she considered herself to be only a mediocre student. At the beginning of her third year, it occurred to her to aim for a clerical post after school. Mari's homeroom teacher, Mr Kodama, when giving his opinion and advice used the term '*gaiseki*', the most popular label among Japanese for Korean nationals living in Japan. The term is a modification of the word *gaikokuseki* meaning 'foreign nationality', but used to refer to Korean nationals only:

> I'm sorry to say this, but you realise that you're disadvantaged because you are *gaiseki*. You will be less disadvantaged if you go for a computer programming position rather than a clerical position. Why don't you study a little harder and apply for a programming position instead! In the long run, that's better for you. You will be a professional, right?

Although Mari was fully aware of the discrimination against *gaiseki* students when it comes to obtaining employment, she was dismayed about having to face the reality of it, especially in view of her own strong doubts about her competence for programming. Nevertheless, despite her misgivings, Mari eventually agreed to comply with Mr Kodama's recommendation.

Mari chose several companies from the Department's list and consulted Mr Kodama. He pointed out that some of Mari's companies did not take *gaiseki*, and referred her to several other companies that did. However, Mari decided that because companies do not necessarily publicize their policy towards *gaiseki*, she would make her own enquiries.

Mari eventually opted for a programming position with the Century Systems Company. She was attracted by the company's approach to promotion, which seemed to be awarded on the basis of current merit rather than past academic achievement and credentials. To begin with, Mr Kodama did not respond favourably to Mari's decision. He suggested alternative companies about which he was more familiar given that previous students had gone to them. In fact, because it was the very first time that the school had received recruitment cards from Century Systems, the school had next to no knowledge about the company. However, despite this, Mari insisted on trying for Century Systems, and Mr Kodama went along with her. After consulting the Department, Mr Kodama telephoned the company to enquire about its policy with regard to *gaiseki*. The company responded by making it clear that it did not judge applicants for posts in terms of whether they were *gaiseki*; it was only interested in a candidate's work capabilities and motivation. The Department made further inquiries and discovered that Century Systems had a close association with another company (a well known coffee company) with which the school also was well connected. This other company was complimentary about Century Systems, confirming the conclusion that Mari should apply. Mari did so, sat the screening test and got the job.

Mr Kodama, the home-room teacher in the cases of both Hiroaki and Mari, was keen to ensure as far as possible that the students in his charge were heading for sound, secure and predictable occupational careers after school. He wanted to try to reduce the risk to his students, and therefore he was very protective towards them. In Hiroaki's case, the teacher pursued his own inclination against the stated preference of the student; and in Mari's case, the teacher only very cautiously, after much background research, gave his final stamp of approval to the firmly stated wish of the student. What these instances reflect is the way, in general, teachers' guidance and decisions with regard to their students' occupational and career choices is based on *Bunan-shikou*: the principle that it is better to play safe and forgo excitement, than to take a risk with the chance of an improved outcome.

Teachers claim that they need to 'protect' students from making mistakes, which are likely given the students' immaturity and lack of experience in 'the real world'. They see their task and duty as that of more or less guaranteeing that their students' life-after-school will be the 'best' for them; will bring the least 'problems'; and will be the most secure. However, what this approach seems to ignore are the issues of whether students can be protected from making mistakes; whether, in any case, it is useful to students to be protected in this manner; and whether students really do need such protection at the age of eighteen. What the teachers may be doing inadvertently is helping prevent students from gaining useful social experience, and from realizing their human capacity and potential; they may be helping to regulate and restrict the process of individual and social development.

A further aspect of this interaction which has to be taken into account is the way the teachers, while attending to their students' instrumental and emotional needs, are guided by their own. The teachers will want to feel a sense of professional and personal satisfaction with what they do and achieve, and this will be facilitated through investigating and establishing good relationships with companies. Also, the teachers will be eager to demonstrate to their employers (the school and the local education board) that they are capable, efficient and effective employees. It is in the interests of home-room teachers to do well, and more specially to be seen to do well, in that as a result they may be promoted, such as into Departmental posts. Likewise, if the Departmental staff are seen to be doing a good job, they too will be promoted through the teaching and administrative grades. But, these instrumental attractions aside, the way teachers interact with and try to help students may well be strongly influenced by their emotional – almost parental – attachment to their students and their students' futures.

The resulting student-teacher interaction process will be variously and differentially experienced and perceived. That is, whereas the teachers will tend to see and emphasize the 'protection' they afford the students; the students will tend to feel that also they are being subjected to 'control'. Most students express the view that what teachers are doing is to give them well meaning and well informed, practical and useful advice and assistance. However, to an extent, students reported also that teachers tried to unduly influence and control their choices and decisions with regard to life-after-school.

THE MEETING: THE SCHOOL'S COLLECTIVE NEEDS VERSUS THE STUDENTS' INDIVIDUAL NEEDS

Of course, the student–teacher interaction which takes place, however important it may be, does not take place in isolation from the broader social context and conditions represented by the school. Apart from anything else, the progress and outcome of teacher–student interaction are closely monitored by the school through the internal selection meeting – the Meeting. The Meeting will check and decide on whether the choice of company arrived at by a student and approved by his or her home-room teacher should be sanctioned by the school and given the go-ahead. In other words, it is the Meeting which makes the final decision about which student will apply for what and where. In any case, more than one student may decide to apply for the same post, and this makes it necessary as far as the school is concerned to choose between them and thereby make a decision on their behalf.

The Meeting first all of looks at each student's first choice and in this way ends up with lists of students against a corresponding string of vacancies. When the number of potential applicants does not exceed the number of positions being offered by a company, then usually the students involved receive automatic approval. However, the Meeting's decision making process does not always run as simply and as smoothly as this. In certain situations, the Meeting after due deliberation, may decide to ask students to reconsider their choices. This may happen when the Meeting discovers that a student's academic record and school attendance are unsuited to the requirements of the post in question; or when the Meeting concludes that a student is too good for the post or company chosen. The case of Satoshi, a male student, illustrates this latter possibility. Satoshi was the best student on the ship-building course, but wanted to apply to be a bus driver with a small transport company.

Head of Department: Why on earth does he want this?

Mr Mori (Satoshi's home-room teacher):   Well, he says that his father has been a truck driver, and he has always wanted to be a driver of a big vehicle.

Another teacher: But he is so small and short.

Mr Mori: I know. I mentioned it to him. But he said that he had often been on the truck with his father and that he knows what's involved in the work.

Head of Department: It has to be OK if he likes the kind of job. But how about a bigger transport company, at least?

Mr Mori: I also said that to him. He prefers smaller companies. He is very determined about this, and I doubt that he will change his mind. I will talk to him again though.

There are further circumstances in which the Meeting may ask students to consider altering their choices. For instance, the Meeting may have doubts about a company (such as where there is a high staff turnover), or understands that a company has poor human relations, or learns (perhaps from past students) that a company is not very caring towards its employees. The Meeting may come to the view that a student is not a suitable candidate for a post on the grounds of personality or personal qualities, such as perseverence, fortitude or toughness.

On the other hand, the Meeting may recommend a reconsideration given that it, or the school, has very little or no experience and knowledge of a particular company to which a student wants to apply. In this situation, the student may be advised to try for a similar position with another, more familiar company. At the same time, however, while the Meeting may not have sufficient current knowledge, it may decide that a company is big or prestigious enough to warrant further investigation; or simply that the student has the kind of personal qualities which will stand him or her in good stead for facing the unknown.

The Meeting pays special attention to *gaiseki* students, or that is to what is known about the way such students are treated by the companies to which they wish to apply. If the Meeting either knows that a company is not favourably disposed towards *gaiseki* applicants or knows nothing at all about a company in this regard, it may suggest that a student alter his or her application to one which is known for its acceptable treatment. Occasionally, a home-room teacher may be asked by the Meeting to make inquiries with and about a particular company over its *gaiseki* policy. Essentially, the Meeting will want to be confident that a *gaiseki* student will be treated without prejudice before he or she is allowed to face a company's screening test.

Sometimes no students will apply for a position with a company when the Meeting feels that it would be preferable to send an applicant. This may be the case in recognition of the well-established relationship which the school has managed so far to build through students it has sent in the past, and has an interest in retaining for the sake of students in the future. Under these circumstances, home-room teachers may be directed to ask students to consider altering their choices to this company. For instance, on these grounds, even though two boys chose to apply for two positions with one company, the *Head of Department* suggested to the Meeting that one of the boys be asked to alter his choice in favour of another company.

Most frequently, however, the Meeting is faced with a situation where the number of prospective applicants outstrips the number of posts available with a company. Such cases are illustrated by the following record of a discussion which took place at a Meeting about which of three candidates to select for an especially popular vacancy.

The case of Shuu (a male student)

Three students, Shouji (mechanics B class), Susumu (shipbuilding class) and Shuu (mechanics A class) chose to apply for the same position with the Sharp Electric Company. At the previous session of the Departmental Meeting, held two weeks before, it emerged that no students had applied for the post. However, in the meantime, as a result of home-teacher persuasion, the situation had been dramatically reversed.

Head of Department: The three did not pick this position as their first choice. So, the starting point is the same for all. Is this OK? Now here are their marks:

	Position in course			Attendance	Average mark
	1st Year	*2nd Year*	*3rd Year*		
Shouji	3rd	17th	23rd	No absence	4.08
Susumu	1st	2nd	2nd	No absence	4.13
Shuu	14th	12th	5th	No absence	4.04

Head of Department: Could home-room teachers tell us about the students?

Mr Mori: Susumu was the Vice-Chairman of the students council and active in the bike race club. As you see, he is one of the top students in our class. He originally wanted to 'make something' with his hands at IBM. He selected IBM in the last survey. But, this year only the IBM manufacturing factory in Kakita prefecture sent recruitment cards to us. The local IBM company is only in charge of sales. He is from a solo-mother family, living with his sister and mother. Since both mother and sister are not healthy, they want him to work in a location close to them. So he searched for a good position in a good company nearby. His second choice is Naka Distribution Company, perhaps because his mother works for its subsidiary company.

Mr Ide: Shuu was the vice-captain of the handball club, and received respect from other members. From the beginning, he wanted to apply for this position at the Sharp Electric Company. But, because the company sent us recruitment cards very late, in the last survey Shuu picked the Nagami-city branch of the company for his first choice. The second choice was Honda in Soma-prefecture [a long way from the school]. He is a very reliable and articulate boy who gives a wonderful first impression. He is also from a solo-mother family. His father died in a traffic accident. His mother works in a cafeteria from 7.30 in the morning until 8.30 in the evening. He lives with his mother and his sister in Hinoki-ku. Shuu, being the only son . . . his mother wants him to be near her.

Mr Ikeda: Shouji has been active in the computer club. In the last survey he selected the Nagami-city branch of the Sharp Electric Company as his first choice. But another in the same class wanted the position and, as a result of negotiations between the two, Shouji decided to opt for this. His second choice is Toshiba Hayama branch. He has a second grade data processing certificate, a licence to handle a boiler, and is keen on acquiring these qualifications.

Mr Matsuhisa: The [recruitment] card says that they prefer mechanics course students.

Mr Sumi (seemingly pleased that someone has come up with a way of reducing the number of students):   Mr Mori, could you consider that comment?

Mr Mori (appearing very disappointed):   That is difficult.

Mr Sumi (to the HOD):   Are there similar positions . . . a technical position in electronics?

HOD: Sorry, there is no other technical position in electronics.

Mr Sumi: What shall we do then? No student has priority.

Mr Mori: I understand the difficulties here. But I don't want Susumu with such good marks to go to his second choice, the distribution company.

Mr Sumi: As far as academic marks are concerned, Shuu and Shouji are in the same boat.

Mr Mori (agitated):   I have no doubt about [Susumu], from club activities and student council work. If my appeal of this kind does not convince you, I don't mind leaving it to the majority vote.

HOD: Let's see . . . How about letting Shuu have a go for the Hankyuu Train Company?

Mr Ide: No. This is his choice.

Mr Okimoto (who runs the handball club):   Shuu decided on this position because of the kind of work, that is manufacturing. I don't think the Hankyuu Train Company will appeal to him, although the company is well known.

Mr Ikeda: Susumu also wants to manufacture something.

Mr Mori: What did Susumu and Shuu list as their second options?

Mr Ide: Shuu's second option is Honda. But his mother does not want him to be far away.

Mr Ikeda: Susumu's second option is Toshiba Hayama.

Mr Uno: It seems as though we teachers are running out of criteria to make a decision here. The three are very competitive. How about letting the three talk it over in the next few days?

Mr Sumi: Well, that should not make much difference. I really want to decide it today, so that we can do follow-up actions from here.

Head of Department: Even if one gets a technical position when being accepted into the company, he will be transferred if he is not assessed as suitable. So, how about sending one of them to Toshiba as a skilled worker trainee?

Mr Sumi: One of my ex-students got a technical position at Sharp Electric Company and quit in the end, saying that the kind of job was not something he had originally expected.

Mr Okimoto: We had a similar case for the Haru Sake Company last year involving one of my students. We let the two talk it over, but they still could not decide. After all, we decided it based on the latest mock exam result. Because we thought that the mock exam result would give some indication of how they would perform in the employment exam.

At this point, the home-room teachers left in order check on the three students' mock exam results, the outcome being that Shuu had the best marks. The meeting proceeded:

Mr Sumi: Is Shuu OK?

Mr Okimoto: The recruitment card says that the employment test consists of a basic achievement exam and interview. So I think it is appropriate.

Mr Sumi: Any disagreement on this?

Mr Mori: OK. I can't win with these marks. I will ask Shouji if he would like the trainee position at Mitsubishi.

A second case is instructive: that of Kenichi (a male student). In this instance, three boys applied for two vacancies with Ishino, a firm of stockbrokers. Two were Hiroshi and Kenichi, both from the data-processing class, and the third was Michihiro, from the academic class. Michihiro's home-room teacher was keen to point out that he was the captain of the baseball club, the most popular of all the clubs in the school. Mr Kodama, the home-room teacher for both Kenichi and Hiroshi, pointed out that Hiroshi was active in the handball club, and that Kenichi was a quiet boy. The positions of the three boys in the overall order of academic achievement were Kenichi at 74; Hiroshi at 95; and Michihiro at 160. On these grounds, Michihiro seemed to be at a distinct disadvantage. However, the

Meeting came to the conclusion that a job with a stockbroking firm required an energetic and outgoing personality along with physical health and fitness. On these grounds, the Meeting agreed that Hiroshi and Michihiro were more suitable than Kenichi for the two vacancies, and accordingly were selected.

When interviewed, Kenichi expressed not only his disappointment but also his anger about this decision because, after all, he had the highest academic placing. Moreover, he was very keen on a stockbroking job: he had received strong encouragement from a cousin already employed with a stockbroking firm. Kenichi said:

> It was totally unexpected that I did not get it. When I talked to Mr Kodama about Ishino stockbroker firm in the May consultation, he said 'there won't be any problems since I know of no one wanting that position.' That made me so optimistic that I did not even think seriously about my second choice. At that stage Mr Kodama had not expected that someone like Michihiro would apply for that. I was thinking that Hiroshi and I would get the positions. I could not think of my second choice for a month. Now I am going to a printing company as a computer operator.

Throughout the Meeting, home-room teachers provide unswerving support for their own students and offer relevant complimentary information. One of the home-room teachers commented: 'it's like marrying my daughter to someone else. I want to make sure her partner is OK'. The clear implication is that home-room teachers have a strong emotional commitment to and investment in the success and fulfilment of the students in their charge.

The Department will be conscious of what a particular company is seeking in its recruits, and with this in mind will pay attention not only to student academic achievement, but also student personality, leadership abilities, participation in sports clubs, and even voice quality. The Department acquires relevant information about companies through the way particular students have fared with previous applications; feedback from students who have been recruited in previous years; communications with company staff with regard to screening test results; and consultations with current company employees during school visits. The resulting information is methodically and systematically stored for Departmental use and convenience.

There is no doubt that teachers are very interested in promoting the welfare and interests of students. For instance, teachers advise students against applying to companies with questionable working conditions, and generally speaking will be keen to ensure a suitable match between the quality of the student and the quality of the company. Heads of Department eagerly stress how they see the role of Departments as enhancing the students' life-chances, increasing their opportunities, and even providing them with a challenge. In practice, however, a Department will in effect do the opposite, at least to some extent, by imposing decisions on students, and thereby placing limitations on their jobs, careers and futures.

An important consideration from the Department's point of view is its responsibility, not just to students, but to the school. The school needs to maintain good working relationships with companies, for no other reason than that this will facilitate the task of finding jobs for students in the future. Accordingly, the Department will want to ensure it supplies students that please companies; which means sending the 'best' students to the 'best companies', the 'not-so-good' students to matching companies, and so on. The Department, on behalf of the school, tries to build and maintain long-lasting and reliable relationships with certain companies, based on its provision of a regular supply of good students. On these grounds there is a major difference between a school's approach to employment guidance and its approach to university guidance. Schools simply do not have the kind of mutually supportive relationships with universities that they have with companies and employers.

Occasionally, the Meeting will sanction carefully selected students 'taking a risk' in applying for posts with companies which appear as though for most students they would be 'too difficult or demanding'. A student is selected for a challenge on the basis of such criteria as his or her confidence, fortitude, persistence, patience, dependability, and the like. In a sense, this particular aspect of student guidance and referral reflects the 'caring' side of the overall process, in that it entails 'protecting' the 'weaker' students from what are perceived as the hazards of certain jobs. It represents the double-edged character of the guidance and referral process in that the Department through 'protecting' weaker students not only 'cares for' and 'helps' them, but also in effect 'controls' them.

Through the deliberations and decisions of the Meeting, teachers allow 'stronger' students to take risks by applying for companies about which the school does not know very much. They may do this for one or more reasons: (a) they have confidence in the student; and (b) they want to discover more about the companies, perhaps because they recognize the prestige and importance of the companies. Here, it is clear that two distinct sets of interests are coming into play: those of individual students and those of the school. However, given this, the issues arise of the accuracy of the teachers' assessments of the students; the degree to which the students' interests are actually served; and the extent to which the teachers' assessments and decisions do in practice play a guiding role in the students' lives after school.

In this context, it is pertinent to note that teachers clearly regard students as highly immature 'beings', who are incapable of making sensible decisions by themselves on their own behalf. Teachers appear to regard certain students as more 'mature' and 'capable' than others, but the criteria by which such distinctions are made are not so much systematically arrived at and applied, as arbitrary and spontaneous, being affected to some extent by 'space and time'. That is, the conception of what constitutes 'maturity' varies between schools, not to mention between Meetings and cases. This may make the students' final applications for posts, and thereby their occupational careers along with their overall life-after-school, somewhat haphazard and precarious.

In effect, each student's individual decision becomes also his or her home-room teacher's decision, and in turn the school's decision. The school, like the home-room teacher, undoubtedly *cares* about the student's welfare, employment and life-after-school; and accordingly genuinely tries to ensure that the student has a secure and predictable future centred on job and career. At the same time, the school cares about not only current students, but also future students by way of the collective interests and needs of the school itself. In practice, as is amply demonstrated in the proceedings of the Meetings, the school's collective needs take priority. In pursuing its own needs, the school may make decisions on behalf of students which turn out to be inconsistent with the students' wishes, and even detrimental to their individual needs. At this point, in the interests of the collective needs and interests of the school, the students will be restricted and controlled.

AGENCIES AND THEIR INTERESTS IN THE GUIDANCE AND REFERRAL PROCESS

In effect, students will apply for the post which has been approved by their home-room teacher and school. They will sit the company's screening test, and if successful will begin to liaise with their forthcoming employer. However, even at this stage, students will remain closely supervised in accordance with the Japanese government's institutional arrangements and requirements. Figure 7.1 identifies the various agencies and their roles involved in the process of employment guidance and referral. The process is conducted under the auspices of three agencies: the school; the companies or employers; and the Public Employment Security Office (PESO). The system of guidance and referral which operates derives from the 1947 Employment Security Act (*Shokugyou antei hou*), which outlines the particular roles and responsibilities of each of the participating agencies. Essentially, the Law lays down certain broad parameters within which each agency has the right and authority to pursue its particular set of goals and interests. At the same time, over the years the agencies have considerably altered and adapted their activities and procedures in response to changing social circumstances and 'needs'. For instance, it is noticeable how the schools now offer much more detailed and systematic assistance to students in preparing for the screening tests; and how they now consider and pursue much more than they used to do the particular needs and interests of ethnic minority students.

Of paramount importance to the overall character of the guidance and referral process is that aspect of the Labour Law which specifically forbids adolescents from having any direct, independent contact with prospective employers. The Law stipulates that 'employment exchange services' on behalf of 'adolescents' may be provided by either PESO or by non-profit making organizations such as schools. The ostensible purpose behind this arrangement is to prevent direct negotiations between companies and adolescents, whose 'immaturity' would place them in a decisively disadvantaged position in finalising employment contracts and conditions (see Taira and Levine, 1986, p. 11). Companies wishing to take on new employees are required to provide recruitment cards spelling out its employment conditions for approval by PESO. Also, in order to avoid the problems and confusion which would arise out of upbridled competition between companies for new recruits, PESO sets the dates when companies can send their recruitment cards to schools; when schools are to send their students' applications forms to companies; and when companies can hold their screening tests.

The role of schools in the guidance and referral process is of crucial importance. They not only provide vocational instruction on such issues as 'the world of work', insurance schemes and tax arrangements; they also play (as we have seen) a vital role in the central activity of decision-making with regard to employment and careers. In fact, schools adopt and apply a policy of a 'guaranteed life-after-school', based on ensuring that every student will acquire appropriate employment on leaving school. This particular policy may be interpreted as very largely a response to the activities of various political movements and pressure groups which during the 1970s were concerned with protecting and promoting the civil rights of 'minorities' in Japanese society.

However, in practice, schools vary considerably in their commitment to such matters as minority rights; simply because each school's approach very much depends upon the commitment of individual teachers. There are some teachers who are deeply concerned about, and perhaps are actively involved pursuing, human rights issues, and such teachers may then lobby a Department to adopt a firm stance on behalf of minority students in their quest for employment.

The technical school which I researched had made appeals on behalf of two minority students (one in 1983 and the other in 1985) who had been turned down by companies in their applications for vacancies. In each case the student was *gaiseki*. The Department first of all asked each company the reason behind its decision, and received unsatisfactory answers. Then, after consulting with and receiving the support of the teaching staff (through the school's staff meeting), the Department went back to the company to ask it to alter its decision. The companies dismissed the appeals, but as a result the school would be strongly disinclined to allow its students to apply to them in future.

At the same time, as has been noted already, the school's paramount concern is that of pursuing its own 'collective interest', and this is served in various ways through its decision making on behalf of students. Thus, the school benefits from managing to get its students into the most prestigious companies – the school's own prestige is assured; consequently, the school attracts good students; and, in turn, the students are relatively easy to place in the better companies (Umetani, 1985, p. 21). Connectedly, schools have an interest in meeting the requirements and expectations of employers because this will result in the company allocating many vacancies to the school for consideration. Each of my research schools had compiled a list of those companies with which it had established good and reliable recruitment relationships, and to which it gave special attention. Here, the teachers knew personally company personnel, especially the recruitment officers. However, there has been concern expressed about such school–company ties, and the possibility that in trying hard to meet company requirements, schools are acting very much like company agents (Fujiwara, 1989).

The school-company tie can become so strong that a company will help a school out by taking on students when it does not really need them, such as during a period of economic downturn. In return, during periods of labour shortage, a school will make sure that the companies with which it has got special relationships have their recruitment needs catered for. Several studies have confirmed that most vocational schools have this sort of arrangement with companies (Amano et al., 1983), one spin-off being that new schools will have difficulty in establishing their place within the system and so in providing the help their students may require in getting suitable after-school employment.

Of course, companies have a common interest in maximizing profits, and therefore in securing and maintaining a labour force which is as productive as possible. This in turn means that companies are eager to enhance their reputation as employers, and connectedly in maintaining strong and reliable relationships with schools, especially the more respectable and popular ones. Like schools, companies compete among themselves to try to recruit the better students. This means that they have to engage in recruitment campaigns. Companies make decisions about the new employees they will require about a year in advance; complete the necessary recruitment cards; send the cards to PESO for approval; send the cards to schools; conduct screening tests; and so on. In effect, companies are under pressure from each other to engage in long term and continuous personnel planning.

PESO has the role of being formally responsible for mediating between employers and job-seekers of whatever age. However, due to the large number of senior high school students who in any year will be in the process of leaving school for gainful employment, in practice the schools assume this responsibility on behalf of most adolescents. Accordingly, PESO's main direct involvement as far as high school students are concerned turns out to be through the seminars it puts on for employers and school careers officers to clarify the employment guidance and referral process; through its monitoring of working conditions, hours, remuneration, and so on; and through its scrutiny and approval of employer recruitment cards. Apart from this, PESO acts as a source of information to schools about all matters to do with employment and recruitment. PESO regulates the competition that occurs among both schools and employers by making decisions and giving directives about their activities and relationships with regard to student applications and recruitment, such as by imposing the one-company-at-a-time policy.

PESO oversees the state's institutionalized arrangements and procedures by which students make the transition from school into employment and are, thereby, distributed within the paid labour force, among companies and between the various sectors of the economy. At the same time, the purpose is to ensure that this process of transition and distribution occurs as smoothly as possible, while taking into account the interests and needs of students especially given their assumed immaturity. In other words, through PESO, the system reflects the way in which the state tries to care for adolescents by protecting them during that crucial period in their lives when they are leaving school and starting jobs for the first time. But, in practice, what this

means is that the state, through PESO and the part it plays in the employment guidance and referral process, will to some extent be 'protecting'
students against not only their wishes, but also their actual needs and
interests as developing human beings and as individuals. The state's preferences, interests and needs in favour of social order, the prevailing social
system and the status quo, in effect if not by intention, take priority; and
so state protection becomes state control.

All this is not to ignore the point that the character and consequences of
the employment guidance and referral process in Japan are far more complex than being about social control and social order. Apart from anything
else, as we have noted, schools often and increasingly pursue the interests
of minority students in their dealings with employers, not to mention of
PESO. In this and other ways, the process exhibits a degree of opposition,
challenge and threat to current social practices. In effect, the process has
both positive and negative consequences in relation to the maintenance of
the prevailing social system. It is, in other words, contradictory in its
character and consequences.

In this chapter, I have examined the 'care', 'protection' and 'control'
aspects of the process by which senior high school students in Japan make
decisions about, apply for and obtain employment. The clear impression is
that within Japanese society, students are regarded as immature beings who
require care in the form of protection. Protection as it operates in the context
of the employment guidance and referral process means control. This point
has been observed in various and diverse instances; in overt and covert
ways; and at all levels of the process; when home-room teachers consult
with students; when the school vets the students' choices; and when the
school, employers and PESO conduct their activities and relations in accordance with state-run institutional arrangements.

8 Education and the Facade of Care:
An Australian Case Study
Elizabeth Hatton

This chapter concerns an attempt by the state to improve the educational process by introducing a fresh teaching mode into schools. It explores the implementation of team teaching in open-plan classrooms with the help of details from a case study undertaken in an urban primary school in Queensland, Australia. It reveals that the intentions of the state are filtered and to some extent undermined by the everyday, immediate social circumstances, contingencies and constraints which pervade and encompass schools. In particular, what emerges as crucial to the success or otherwise of the team teaching mode are the relationships, experiences and attitudes of those people at the forefront of its implementation, namely of the teachers involved.

It has been widely argued that the constraints associated with the traditional closed-classroom mode of school teaching tend to foster in teachers an individualistic, narrow and conservative orientation to work (Denscombe, 1982; Hargreaves, 1980; Hatton, 1985a; Hatton, 1985b; P. Jackson, 1968; Lortie, 1975). It is claimed that this orientation has disadvantageous consequences for teachers themselves and thereby for students. Essentially, arguments and evidence have been amply supplied in support of the conclusion that that traditional closed-classroom teaching has the effect of thinning the state's delivery of the goods and benefits which are the purported purpose of the educational system and process. The physical and social organization associated with team teaching in open-plan classrooms has been sharply contrasted with individual teaching in closed classrooms, and accordingly has been viewed as having the potential for improving the flow of educational goods and benefits (Cohen, 1976; Dale, 1973; Denscombe, 1982; Denscombe, 1982; Hamilton, 1973; La Prelle et al., 1976; Lortie, 1975; Marram et al., 1972; Richter, 1978; Shaplin and Olds, 1964; Zagami, 1971). The issue addressed in the following discussion is that of the validity of this view; and indeed of the background assumption that the organization of open-plan teaching is so distinctive. The discussion is not so much concerned with detailing and assessing the comparative virtues of each mode of teaching and classroom organization. Instead, it focuses on specifying the distinguishing features of the two approaches and on accounting for why the theoretical potential of the open-class approach has not been realized.

It will be useful to clarify a few central terms. The phrase 'team teaching' may be defined as 'a type of instructional organization involving teaching personnel and the students assigned to them, in which two or more teachers are given responsibility, working together, for all or a significant part of the instruction of the same group of students' (Shaplin, 1964, p. 15). The term 'team teaching' may be otherwise referred to as 'co-operative teaching'. The phrase 'open-plan classroom' has been defined by Galton et al. as 'one where space is provided for two or more classes to be taught in a single general area without dividing walls; although in some such areas withdrawal spaces are provided where a class may to some extent be separated from the rest' (Galton et al., 1980, p. 99). For instance, in Queensland schools, because of the size of the buildings provided, the teaching areas are often termed 'dual teaching spaces' or 'double teaching spaces',[1] denoting the fact that in this particular instance, the co-operative team is usually (but by no means always) made up of two teachers.

In Queensland during the early 1970s, the state through the Department of Education began providing open-plan classrooms (Zagami, 1971). This process continued into the 1980s, so that by 1983 about half of Queensland's primary teachers and students were accommodated in open-plan classrooms.[2] The subsequent school building programme entailed almost exclusively the construction of open-plan classrooms, so that by the start of the 1990s the bulk of primary teachers and students had been covered. The material input in open-plan classrooms has been immense. However, the issue arises as to whether such investment has been matched by a resulting improvement in outcomes in the form of an increase in the educational goods and benefits flowing through to students and thereby back into society. This may be judged by identifying and examining the principal educational mechanisms by which such an increase might be facilitated.

It has been assumed that the team-teaching approach to the organization of classrooms would bring with it a shared or joint work situation for teachers in which previously unaddressed pedagogic practices – including classroom management routines, discipline methods, and instructional and evaluational techniques – would be seriously debated, assessed and resolved to the benefit of the teachers and their students. It has been supposed that the teachers would have the opportunity to learn from each other through conversation and observation; to benefit from collegial comment, opinion and guidance; and to gain from collegial companionship and support. Moreover, it has been envisaged that the approach would facilitate the deployment of a greater variety of pedagogical and grouping routines. It has been argued that the physical and social conditions associated with the open-plan, team teaching mode has the potential to generate in teachers a corporate and progressive orientation to work, rather than the more individualistic and conservative orientation encouraged by the closed-classroom, single-teacher alternative. The expectation has been that the chief beneficiaries of the new approach would be the students, and that the benefits involved would largely derive from the sharing by their teachers of planning, implementation and evaluation in the educational process.

So far, there is a dearth of the kind of firm, systematic evidence on the open plan, team teaching venture in Queensland which would allow a confident assessment of its overall success or otherwise. However, informed impressions and judgements (Neate, 1983) tend to confirm the evidence derived from similar experiments in other locations (Denscombe, 1982) that there has been not just limited success but also some damage. Moreover, this conclusion is strongly supported by the findings of an indepth case study carried out in one particular Brisbane primary school which I will refer to as 'Suburbia'.[3] This example demonstrates that the state's apparent efforts to care for people through changes in the education system may be impeded by the social fabric and context of the school. But, in turn, what this possibility indicates is that the state's efforts are more apparent than real: are merely a facade.

THE SOCIAL SETTING OF 'SUBURBIA'

The social fabric and context associated with Suburbia can be examined along four dimensions: the community; the staff; the Parents and Citizens Committee (PCC); and the history of team teaching in open-plan classrooms.

Suburbia is a relatively new, medium sized, open-plan school with a staff of twenty-three teachers. It is located in a prestigious, outlying suburb of Brisbane,[4] so that the parental clientele is decidedly upper middle class.[5] In the short time that Suburbia has been operating, it has gained the reputation of being a 'good' school. However, this reputation does not prevent those parents who have just moved into the area from subjecting the school to considerable overt, critical scrutiny. The school Principal reports that parents have a tendency to 'shop around' in order to find what, as far as they are concerned, is the most suitable school for their children. This process entails parents telephoning and making visits to various schools; and in return Principals spending a considerable amount of time reassuring parents that their children will receive 'quality, caring education'. Since Suburbia's predominant form of classroom arrangements is open-plan, and because upper-middle-class parents frequently query or resist such an unconventional style (see Hatton, 1985c), some parents are prepared to accept the daily routine of transporting their children to the 'best' traditional school available. Other parents decide to enrol their children at Suburbia, but only on a trial basis. A few of these parents do remove their children from the school after the assigned period. However, a clear majority allow their children to stay, only to become (according to the Principal) highly attached and committed to the school. Parental commitment is played out through their financial support for the school, one result being that the shortfalls in materials and equipment which often afflict new schools have been avoided by Suburbia.

In that Suburbia is an open-plan school, we might expect to find practical evidence and teacher support for an 'invisible pedagogy' (Bernstein, 1977). However, instead, the emphasis remains squarely on a traditional pedagogy and a traditional curriculum. Such an apparent anomaly is a result of the Principal's concern – with Suburbia's community context in mind – to ensure that the school avoids the negative connotation according to which open-plan environment is interpreted as 'doing what you like'. Both new teachers and the parents of prospective students are carefully and categorically informed of the Principal's policy of adhering firmly to 'a programme of work based on Departmental syllabuses clearly defined in all areas as to scope and sequence in each Year Level'. Consistent with traditional pedagogy, the Principal claims that Suburbia's teachers are committed to the direct teaching style.

Suburbia's staff cover a wide range of teaching experience from relatively little (under five years) to a lot (over ten years), with the majority having been in teaching for at least five years. Because Suburbia is a growing school with an ever expanding number of students, it employs a new cohort of staff at the beginning of each school year. Nonetheless, Suburbia displays a relatively stable staff profile, with an absence of transfers during the school year and with only a few at the end. The Principal and the PCC lobbied the Regional Office of the State Education Department to allow the recruitment of one member of staff over the permitted figure for the number of students on the grounds that this would help facilitate pupil growth while reducing class disruption. Interestingly, the request to the Regional Office was backed by the threat of a PCC supported staff strike –

a tactic which proved successful for Suburbia when it is likely to have failed for schools in areas where the parents have less economic and cultural power (see Hatton, 1985c; Petrie, 1984).

All PCCs within Queensland provide the means through which local parents and community can have a forum for influencing school affairs. In many schools, PCCs are regarded as little more than useful fund raising bodies. However, at Suburbia and other schools with similarly upper middle class parental clientele, the PCCs cannot be treated so lightly (Hatton, 1985c).

The Principal at Suburbia emphasizes the importance of two aspects of his relationships and dealings with parents and the PCC. First, he is extremely careful to 'approach the parent[s] in the right way' and to keep the PCC fully in touch with school matters because, in his experience, the parents tend to be 'co-operative if they are informed about what the staff are doing for their kids', Second, he is conscious of the parents' power and wary of their potential for brushing aside his authority and autonomy. The Principal remarked that in dealing with parents of this kind 'you wouldn't want to be a fool'. The implication here is that a 'fool' would be overwhelmed by the PCC and have considerably reduced influence and independence in the running of the school. The Principal outlined a strategy he had devised for circumventing the possibility of the PCC interfering and upsetting 'professional decisions with regard to expenditure'. The strategy entails the staff submitting to the PCC a complete budget of all the expenditure they anticipate will be necessary for the year across the full range of curricula areas. Once approved, a budget sets the limits within which the staff can go ahead and purchase items as required without having to repeatedly and constantly return to the PCC. The Principal and his staff are relieved of having to approach the PCC on a case by case basis, and thereby are able to avoid giving the PCC greater scope for discussion, scrutiny, rejection and other delaying and complicating intervention. Thus, the Principal is keen to circumscribe the PCC's power with respect to what he labels professional decisions, even though on other occasions he may exploit this power – such as in order to achieve favourable staff-student ratios.

THE HISTORY OF TEAM TEACHING AT SUBURBIA

Suburbia had a troubled introduction to team teaching within double teaching spaces. For illustrative purposes, we will focus on the experiences of one particular teaching team composed of two teachers, Carol and Heather. Each of the teachers began working in the school during the second year of its operation: Carol as a class teacher; and Heather as a visiting Physical Education teacher for two days per week. Both teachers recall this period in the school's history as an especially unhappy time. Carol describes the team teaching situation she encountered in the Year One and Two block:

> For the first ten weeks there were three Year One teachers in a normal room [a double teaching space] with about eighty five kids. We were next door in Grade Two in the same situation. For two weeks of that time, each room had a [pre-service] student [teacher]. So there were four adults in each room. It was awful.

Problems arose because only the other teacher in Carol's team at the time had taught Year Two previously, and she 'monopolized' the activities. The team adopted a day-by-day approach to planning, whereby each day's teaching programme was decided the day before. Under such circumstances, the already experienced teacher was able to readily respond to calls along the lines of 'What shall we do for . . . ?'. At the same time, however, this teacher felt aggrieved because as far as she was concerned she was 'taking the load'. Her reaction was exacerbated by the fact that all the lessons except for two (Reading and Mathematics) were delivered to the full complement of eighty five children. On the other hand, Carol recalls feeling 'as though I could sit in a corner and not be missed'. Carol would return home at the end of the day depressed because of having had no opportunity to teach the children. Moreover, she felt disenfranchised within the teaching process in that she 'never knew what was coming next'.

The difficulties experienced by Carol during the introduction of team teaching at Suburbia were sorted out after about ten weeks. However, a number of teams failed to recover from the 'fights and tears' that occurred, and several teachers ended up rejecting team teaching on the grounds that 'it was easier to teach apart'. Nonetheless, even for these teachers problems remained 'because things were going on in one end of the room which would disturb the other half', when the teachers 'were not on speaking terms'. The difficulties and disruption which accompanied the introduction of team teaching at Suburbia meant that, in effect, team teaching had been operating fully for just two years. The Principal was committed to the mode, and he demonstrated his support by allowing staff to attend in-service training as well as to be responsible for the crucial matter of choosing their own team partners.

However, those teachers who preferred to teach on their own were given some opportunity to do so. That is, the school applied an exception to the general principle favouring team teaching. The physical layout of the school comprised almost exclusively double teaching spaces. At the same time, the school population of pupils and teachers permits three regular-sized class groups along with one 'left-over' group at each Year Level. These left-over groups are accommodated in a double teaching space, but are taught in accordance with the traditional closed classroom approach. Essentially, the Principal has adopted a rule against, say, Year Three and Year Four pupils being taught together on the grounds that such 'composite classes'[6] are viewed by parents as disadvantaging their children. It was therefore convenient to have the left-over groups taught separately by teachers who prefer to teach on their own.

If we examine more closely the way team teaching is conducted within one double teaching space through the everyday practices, experiences and views of Carol and Heather, it becomes clear that the state's modern, open-area schools fall far short of the promised and anticipated impact.

THE PROCESS OF TEAM TEACHING AT SUBURBIA

The conduct and complexities of team teaching in Suburbia can be unravelled by distinguishing and tracing four threads: the team; team planning; team implementation; and team evaluation. The two members of the team under investigation, Carol and Heather, were both within the age range twenty to thirty years; both had successfully completed a three-year Diploma of Teaching course at a local College of Advanced Education; and both were enrolled as part-time evening students on an in-service degree course, also at a local College of Advanced Education. Both were in the fifth year of their teaching careers. Carol had taught mainly in open-plan classroom settings, but had rarely been involved in sustained team teaching. Heather, whose Diploma included a Physical Education major, had spent the first three and a half years of her career as a Physical Education teacher and the next six months in a dual-teaching space partitioned by a curtain. The year under study constituted the first year of sustained team teaching for both Carol and Heather.

At Suburbia, the Principal allows the staff to sort themselves out into teaching teams. Towards the end of the previous school year, Carol and Heather had undertaken a careful and somewhat clandestine appraisal of their teaching colleagues with a view to choosing a compatible team partner: an activity which Carol described as 'a very tricky process of elimination, because you don't want to look obvious, but of course everybody's doing it'. Part of the strategy involves a teacher consulting those of her colleagues she regards as close friends in a confidential manner, the purpose being to obtain helpful impressions and opinions. Carol, the more experienced in the process of team partner selection, employed several guiding selection criteria. For instance, she eliminated any teacher who appeared more conscientious than herself, and explained:

> I think the priorities you put into school are important. I mean you've got to do things for the kids – that's your job. But some people put weekends in and they work at school until six o'clock. You have to put in the amount of time you can allocate without resenting it. Also, if I was doing college [pursuing a degree] and the other person wasn't . . . they wouldn't understand the time problem. It's really important not to go in with anyone more conscientious than yourself.

Carol considered Heather a good partner on the grounds that they had similar time constraints given their part-time study commitments. For Carol this consideration was important in that, she argued, 'we both knew we were not going to get much work done at school because we had major assignments to do.' Also for Carol, her partner's approach to classroom discipline was an important consideration:

> I've been in situations where small things happen and it's made out to be a big discipline problem. Or teachers go to kids through the conscience angle instead of getting straight into it. You know . . . instead of just saying 'don't do this', [they say] 'this is why you shouldn't' – this type of thing. It's impossible when you don't agree on something across the board like discipline.

The requirement was not so much that team partners had to operate with precisely the same approach to discipline, but more that they should agree on the discipline related issue and then be able to present a united front on the matter to the students. Heather remarked: 'We don't have the same discipline. I think I'm stronger. I'm more likely to give them a pat on the bottom than Carol is. We stipulated at the beginning that [the pupils] can't go to Carol and get away with it.'

Carol's previous observation of Heather had left her with a positive impression of Heather's teaching style and capacity to handle children:

> Before I started teaching with Heather . . . I had contact with Heather observing [her] Phys. Ed. [Physical Education] lessons.
> [These were] fairly structured – five minutes this, ten minutes that – and I liked that. Also, being Phys. Ed., she was pretty handy with the kids.

Carol, like Heather, emphasized the importance of teaching partners being similar in terms of age, personality, out-of-school interests and pattern of social life. Carol's dissatisfaction with an earlier teaching partner was the result to some extent of her being on a 'different wavelength'. She reported that there had been differences over the way the classroom was to be organized, and that neither she nor her partner had been prepared to compromise on the matter. Heather was especially anxious about avoiding a partner who was very different from herself. Referring to highly experienced teachers located in the lower school, she said:

> I mean, some of those women down there are very narrow minded, and their ways are old fashioned. I'd hate to be with them . . . the way they run their classrooms and their own thoughts about things. You couldn't have a joke with them or relax with them. I would hate to think I would always have to be on my toes all the time about my teaching performance.

For Heather, it was important for her and her partner to relate in a non-judgemental and non-self-conscious manner, conducive to a non-threatening, comfortable and relaxed work situation. She was concerned about 'getting on well and backing each other up' – which was helped by having 'talents on a par' with one another. The requirement was not for a completely identical outlook and approach to teaching. For instance, she occasionally smacked children (perhaps in a way which was somewhat more fierce than a mere 'pat on the bottom') contrary to Carol's practice and preference. However, such a difference did not cause any open dissension or major difficulties. Carol adopted a strategy of strenuously avoiding confrontation over any particular incident as well as over the general issue. She would allow and make it easier for Heather to withdraw from the violent situation: giving her time and space to 'cool down' and return refreshed. Carol's main concern – shared with Heather – was for a friendly partnership and untroubled work situation, even at the expense of putting to one side her considerable unease about Heather's support for and (even excessive) use of corporal punishment.

Securing a compatible and supportive partner was just as important for Carol as it was for Heather. Carol stated that if she were to have a judgemental partner, she would 'make sure that [she] was in the withdrawal room or in the spare room a lot of the time. [She would] use timetabling of specialist lessons to get away from the situation.

However, they still had to face and cope with the scrutiny and judgements of others, albeit outsiders. Both Carol and Heather experienced considerable discomfort if during their teaching activities other teachers or the Principal entered the room. Carol had devised a strategy for getting 'off the spotlight' when a visitor arrived. This entailed 'drawing the visitor into the lesson', thereby re-focusing everyone's attention on the visitor. Heather also had a strategy – she would simply stop teaching. In contrast with Carol, Heather was firmly against allowing others to participate in her teaching. In particular, she was concerned to ensure that her teaching was not 'taken over' by the Principal. But, Heather was conscious and sensitive about protecting her independence and autonomy as a teacher in general. She was not only wary about the prospect of the Principal interfering in her teaching activities, but also concerned about ensuring that her partner respected her teaching talents and her opinions and rights with regard to the affairs of the classroom. Thus, Carol was aware that in the process of finally choosing a partner, Heather had been 'worried because I hadn't taught a Year Four before, and I didn't know whether I'd always be following what you had to do'. Fortunately, this turned out not to be stumbling block. When Carol approached Heather in the staffroom and proposed a team partnership. Heather readily agreed. The Principal supported the choice, expressed the opinion that they would make a good team, and assigned them to teach a Fourth-Year class.

A notable feature of this particular team, and one which follows on from the careful assessment conducted during the selection process, is that Carol and Heather are so 'very much in line' that they rarely find difficulties in co-operating. When compromise is necessary, they adopt a conciliatory approach, as Carol explained:

> I think you've got to be willing to give the other person time to see whether their ideas will work or not. Heather believed that children should not have to turn their head to look at the blackboard. She wanted them sitting in rows facing the backboard. It is better if they can see the board [without having to turn], but it takes up more space. Because Heather was so strong on this we have them facing the board. I think you've got to weigh up the issue against a year-long relationship. Overall, you've got to end up friends if they face the board or not . . . so you've got to look at it that way.

Carol reported that participating in a team with Heather had had beneficial consequences for her teaching. She recognized that the 'easy atmosphere in class' resulting from her compatibility with Heather had valuable spin-offs. For Heather, on the other hand, there were adverse aspects to team teaching *per se*: 'I don't plan to the full extent that I want to teach at. I never have time for variations on the basic lessons. You can't do interesting lessons to big groups anyway.' In contrast, in 'a single class you are free to plan what you want to and to the depth you want to.' Interestingly, (as we will see) it emerges that the team had adopted a planning procedure which had the potential to allow Heather considerable freedom; but which in practice both Heather and Carol failed to make full use of.

Carol and Heather had already considered the possibility of teaching together again the following year, and had addressed the issue of 'what problems have we got that we should look at before we start again?' In conclusion, they had decided that 'we haven't come up with any [problems] really'. They had managed to avoid persistent problems, as becomes clear when looking in somewhat more detail at the way they had tackled the second thread of the team teaching process – that is, team planning.

Carol and Heather had begun the school year by working in a fully collaborative fashion on team planning. However, this approach did not last long because of the demands arising out of their part-time evening degree study: 'with college, we found that we didn't make the time each week. So, we split [the planning work load] up. We're actually doing separate subjects . . . like Social Studies and Science. That's basically how we work it.' Originally, they allocated one afternoon each week to cater for all collaborative planning; selecting a couple of hours immediately prior to their evening attendance at the College of Advanced Education. But, despite their good intentions and best efforts, they admitted that such a planning session 'doesn't happen very often'. Instead, the team tried to find alternative slots they could use during the daily round of teaching activities. One strategy was to build space into regular class times by having just one member teach the whole class, thereby freeing the other member for planning purposes. The method is outlined as follows: 'Well, it's pretty easy . . . we can say "gee, we need some more listening [lessons] this week". And I'll say "why don't you prepare something while I read this story?"' In addition, the team managed to squeeze planning into lunch breaks. The Principal at Suburbia operated with the somewhat unusual policy of timetabling both team members together on or off lunchtime playground duty, allowing the team some space 'to plan the afternoons'. Carol and Heather were not altogether happy with this arrangement given the proximity between the planning and the teaching itself. That is, 'it's too late to get full satisfaction'.

After the team planning comes the team implementation, and Carol and Heather organized this aspect of the team teaching process around three basic guidelines: each member was assigned to a specific set of ability groups; each member was responsible for a specific range of curriculum areas; and each member was responsible for specific lessons in mixed ability sessions. Mathematics was taught to two distinct ability groups: the 'top' forty pupils were taught as a class by Carol, and the 'bottom' ('below average') twenty pupils were taught as another class by Heather. However, this particular arrangement had become ruffled over the previous few weeks due to the intervention of a remedial teacher who had been removing various sections of the 'bottom group' for extra teaching. Heather dismissed the exercise as 'total confusion', and complained:

> I don't really know what [the remedial teacher is] doing with her kids. The kids are changing all the time because she says this one doesn't need this week's work . . . whereas before, I was settled with one group by myself.

Heather's experience of disruption and discomfort was uppermost in shaping her assessment of the remedial teacher's activities, so that she failed to recognize any benefits flowing to the pupils involved. The irony is that Heather's lack of appreciation of the remedial teacher's efforts stem from the latter's use of 'flexible groupings', something which has been specifically and strongly advocated by Queensland's Department of Education (1983).

Spelling was also taught to two ability groups, with about thirty pupils in each, and with Heather taking the slightly larger 'top' group. Reading was taught to three groups each of which was described as 'mixed ability' even though one of them contained all the 'bright' students. The rest of the curriculum (including Language Arts; Science; Social Studies, Art, Music and Health) was taught in a whole class mode by one teacher – the one who had undertaken the team planning. During whole class lessons, the non-teaching partner would often make use of the opportunity to catch up on planning, administration and marking – the result being that the teacher–pupil ratio would rise perhaps to double that found in a single classroom. However, sometimes both team members would participate, with the non-teaching partner taking a subordinate, supervisory role, while perhaps making inputs such as in the event of expository teaching. Language Arts was an exception to this general pattern in that occasionally both teachers would teach simultaneously, from opposite ends of the room.

The team provided an explanation for the predominance of whole class work. Dividing the class into two, each of which was given a separate lesson at one end of the room, had been tried and found to be unsatisfactory, largely because of insufficient space; timetabling problems; and noise and interference. Carol said: 'It worked well for a couple of weeks. Then one week, one group of children missed out on something. Then you had to use the next week to catch that up. And it threw out that week.' Consequently, the team adopted the whole class mode for the bulk of their teaching activities.

An alternative strategy had been attempted before being rejected in favour of whole class teaching. This entailed the simultaneous teaching of different aspects of Language Arts, with each teacher presenting a short lesson at one end before presenting the same lesson at the other end. However, the method failed because, as Carol put it, 'We ended up spending more time with one end, and the other end was getting less time when we swapped over. That was unfair. So we ended up having to do [a whole class] lesson'.

The teaching arrangement selected by the team gave the students little opportunity for independent work. The team rationalized the limitation in terms of the children's inappropriate behaviour and incapacity for independent activity. According to Carol: 'No matter what we do, they can't do anything. They are impossible to work by themselves'. The team claimed that their particular set of students was the 'most difficult class in the school', and that it had been 'a rotten class all through'. Carol and Heather were surprised that children from 'this area' – such a prestigious area – were naughty and undisciplined. They argued that the children were 'incapable of working productively without direction': without, that is, direct teaching. Heather offered a theory to explain why the class was unexpectedly 'scatty'. She argued that it is possible for children to be traumatized while in the womb during natural catastrophes, and estimated that the class had been affected in this way by a major Queensland flood. The children's traumatic experience in the womb accounted for their inability to work on their own, lack of discipline, talkativeness and general feeble-mindedness. Carol indicated her tacit support for this theory.

It became clear, however, that for Carol and Heather the major concern was not so much the children's inability to get down to work but more their talkative and disruptive behaviour. Heather mentioned: 'They can't stop talking while they do it'. She added: 'it's the better kids who are worst at independent work because they think they're the best . . . and they just chatter on.' In any case, Carol and Heather were reluctant about arranging independent work because of the amount of time and effort required for preparation purposes. Carol remarked:

> If we got them on doing independent work most of the day, so that they could feel they've achieved something at the end, they'd probably go all right. But, we'd never keep the work up to them. That's the thing. Once you've started, you'd have to keep it going.

Carol and Heather had differing views about the advantages or otherwise for teachers and students of the various aspects of team teaching implementation. In particular, Heather saw few practical benefits accruing to those students exposed to two teachers instead of just one. She acknowledged her own and Carol's distinct curriculum strengths – hers in Physical Education and Carol's in Music – but what mattered most was their overall teaching skills, and these were similar. On the other hand, Heather accepted that academic gains are possible in those cases where a teacher with, for instance, weak spelling is paired with another who is competent in this regard: 'Well, in Language, if the kids say to Carol "How do you spell that?". And Carol says "Oh Miss Jones, how do you spell that?". And I'll spell it out for them. And they learn that way I suppose.' Heather also accepted that there were some advantages flowing from team teaching in the area of administrative tasks, given that one partner could see to them while the other occupied the children. However, on the whole, Heather was more struck by the problems and difficulties of team teaching than the gains. Moreover, she regarded the problems involved as 'natural' and inevitable aspects of being required to teach in a dual teaching space. She had found direct teaching to be difficult in this situation, whether to half the class with the other half being taught in the remaining half of the room or to the whole class. Whole class teaching was difficult because, while she felt teaching all the pupils made her lessons more interesting, she found that 'My voice is going because you've got to speak to this end plus get to [be heard at] the other end of the room. I hate the way the room is because you have the class turned around and you've got children with jinked necks.' The room had been arranged to include a central gathering space, but Heather did not see this as suitable for teaching because 'the kids need to be structured . . . they need their desks.'

Carol, on the other hand, recognized a positive pastoral side to team teaching in that shy, diffident students had a choice of teachers to approach. Furthermore, the advantage to teachers is that team teaching makes it easier to cater for students with a range of abilities. Carol's first experience of team teaching had led her to favour the one teacher to one class style, but her subsequent experience resulted in a change of mind:

> I realized the bad things as well . . . like having three reading groups and the total range of ability to yourself. Even though you have half the number, you still have the full range. Whereas this way, you can cater for the full range without as much headache.

Carol mentioned another benefit to teachers: team teaching facilitated dealing with 'problem children'. When 'one teacher has had enough of that kid for the day', the other teacher can take over or remove the child. For Carol this was especially important given Heather's inclination towards corporal punishment. On those occasions when Heather was annoyed with a child,

Carol would be there to remove him or her from the situation by allowing time to go to the staffroom and calm down. Carol also acknowledged the benefits of having two teachers each with her own, distinctive subject specializations:

> We find teachers have different expertise like Heather with Phys. Ed. and me with Music. That works out well. And she loves Social Studies, which I hate. And I'll do the Science. She prefers the Language side of it, and I like Maths. So that way it's great.

The remaining strand to draw out of the team teaching process is that of 'evaluation'. In the Queensland primary school system, written reports on the students' progress are prepared twice a year for parents. In addition, in conjunction with the presentation of the first of these written reports, parents usually have the opportunity for a mid-year oral report, each teaching team being given a timetabled slot of two days to allow it to meet parents. The members of each teaching team at Suburbia are encouraged to take joint responsibility for student evaluation and report presentation, based on the assumption that the members are more or less equally familiar with all their students. Accordingly, as far as possible the various comments and gradings that go to make up the reports are preferably jointly composed. However, there are many instances where joint responsibility could not be carried through. This applied where each team member was attached to distinct ability groups, as in the teaching of Spelling, Reading and Mathematics; and where *turn teaching* was practised, as in Language, Arts, Science, Social Studies, Art and Music. Consequently, time spent on jointly writing reports was given not so much to trying to agree on accurate grades and comments, as to the problem of how to phrase the comments in the most tactful ways.

Carol and Heather were more content about operating as a team for the purpose of evaluation than for any of the other three strands which thread and tie together the team teaching process. This was because the team teaching approach meant that each teacher was able to rely on the support of her partner in dealing with a potentially critical parental clientele. Carol and Heather were wary of parental judgement and interference, so that neither encouraged parents to participate in any way in classroom activities. Carol's considerable antipathy towards parental participation was simply because of the way 'they criticize'. Heather felt a lack experience in how to deal with parents, and so her preference was to keep them at a distance as much as possible. She said 'I never had to do this with Phys. Ed., so I never had much parent contact. And I am not particularly up on how to handle parents.' Due to their nervousness, both teachers relied heavily on the reassurance given and the goodwill generated by the Principal in his meetings with parents: in effect exploiting the Principal's public relations activity to allay parental concerns and to keep parents at a distance.

DISCUSSION

Caution needs to be exercised in drawing conclusions from the case study examined in this chapter. However, it does raise the possibility that the apparent aspirations on the part of the Queensland government to improve its provision of 'care' through the education system by introducing a fresh teaching mode in primary schools have not been realized, and the further possibility that they cannot be satisfied because the conception or theory behind the innovation is seriously flawed. Between the intention and the implementation there is a gap due to the forceful influence of intervening physical, social, personal and psychological factors centred on those at the cutting edge of the process involved, namely the teachers. In the end, the success or otherwise of a teaching mode depends crucially on the way in which the theory is translated into practice by teachers who, as social agents, may not act simply and strictly in accordance with the theory.

The case study indicates that the team teaching in open-plan classrooms mode may be inefficient and ineffective in transforming massive educational investment into comparable and worthwhile educational outputs, 'goods' and benefits. Neither the teachers nor the students on whom the mode is imposed may benefit – in fact, on the contrary, those involved are likely to suffer relative disadvantages. Whereas the intention behind the development may have been to improve on the immediate teaching and learning environment, in practice the opposite may happen. In trying to do its best to implement the mode the teaching team may find it useful to adapt the mode so that, in effect, team teaching in the strict sense is not actually carried out. The team may adopt a division of time, labour and students whereby joint (if not co-operative) activity is restricted; and where, for instance, it reverts to the one teacher to one class mode. The upshot is that if one teacher is teaching and the other is not (because she is on the sidelines, planning, marking, recovering, or whatever), the student–teacher ratio rises to double that when each teacher has her own class. Already, on these grounds alone, we might expect the mode not only to be a failure but also to actually impede the implementation of state care judged in terms of student progress within the education system.

Team-teaching in an open-plan setting allows the teachers considerable scope for devising their own social arrangements, strategies and short cuts

for implementing the mode in a way which takes into account the various –
sometimes excessive – demands on their limited resources, space, time,
energy and enthusiasm; and connectedly which reduces as far as possible
problems, difficulties, stress and conflict within the work situation and
relationships. The mode permits teachers to devise means by which they
can resist extra and disruptive demands, such as those that arise out of
giving additional help to slow learners – precisely the kind of benefit
which the theory behind team teaching held would be forthcoming. Instead,
in practice, Carol and Heather treated such additional help as a nuisance
and as something which was highly and easily dispensable.

On the other hand, team teaching to the extent that it does occur may still
be to the relative disadvantage of students. Carol and Heather selected and
stressed one particular consideration for judging the success of team teaching from their point of view – and so from the crucial point of view. That
is, the team members need to get on with each other; they need to appreciate
and sympathize with one another; they need to compromise; they need to
co-operate; they need to support each other; and they need to present a
common front to the outside world – covering the Principal, other teachers,
parents and (most important) students. This extends as far as compromising
over – and even conspiring over – violence and corporal punishment.

Team teaching in open-plan classrooms brings with it several major
changes in the teachers' work situation, one of which is especially important to the success or otherwise of the mode. The one teacher to one class,
or individual, teaching mode allows teachers to make their own decisions
about when, where and how to plan their teaching activities. Planning and
decision-making can be accomplished speedily in that the teachers are not
obliged to consult with – to seek and accommodate the ideas and views – of
others. Thus, the individual teaching mode contrasts with the team teaching
mode in that – at least formally and ideally – the latter requires extensive
consultation. When the team teaching mode is imposed, teachers suffer a
loss of independence and freedom with regard to decision-making, along
with a loss of available time due to the lengthier planning sessions. The
outcome is a reduction in teacher and teaching flexibility, both at the
planning stage and (given that there will be some kind of agreed, joint plan)
at the implementation stage. In turn, the students may suffer. Whereas the
theory behind the team teaching mode contains the assumption that the
mode would be conducive to flexibility and variety, the practice of co-
operation during planning and implementation have, if anything, meant the
opposite. Strictly planning and rigidly implementing which teacher will do
what – such as take care of a distinct ability group or teach a particular
subject range – will be attractive to team teachers; but also, these things

may necessarily accompany the co-operative character of the team teaching mode as opposed to the individual teaching mode.

What emerges is a teaching mode that may still have enormous potential judged in terms of the possible benefits to teachers, students and society, but which in practice has been scuppered to the point that, if anything, it has resulted in teaching and learning practices and arrangements characterized by rigidity and closure beyond that found in traditional classrooms.

NOTES

1. See the kit provided by the Queensland Department of Education (1983).
2. See Department of Education, Queensland (1983).
3. Fictional names have been used for the school and the teachers.
4. Prestigious suburbs are those in which there is the most expensive housing and where most adults are employed in professional and managerial occupations.
5. A reasonable way of representing the class structure of Australian society is in terms of three analytically distinguishable but practically related social classes: an upper middle class, a white collar or lower middle class and a working class. The upper middle class is made up of owners, managers and professionals (and their families) – those who enjoy autonomy and power in their economic and social relationships. The parental clientele at Suburbia are upper middle class in this sense.
6. Interestingly, composite classes are commonly found in double teaching spaces. However, they are labelled 'multi-age groupings', and they are sold to parents on the grounds that they provide a 'natural' family-like setting in which children learn more effectively. In this way, many upper middle-class parents have been persuaded to accept multi-age groupings for their children, at least during the early years of schooling (see Hatton, 1985c).

9 Constructing Social Care:
The Australian Dilemma
Don Edgar

On the evidence of virtually all animal species, we have to believe that there is something instinctual about primal care. Call it maternal instinct or parental protectiveness, or take it further to the clear herd instinct which protects the group from external predators, the species can survive only if its young are properly cared for. At the other end of the scale, the elderly may or may not enjoy continued care, depending upon the adequacy of resources for their maintenance beyond the years of productive usefulness. There is an immediate dilemma: caring may have an instinctual component; but caring as manifested in actual behaviour depends upon social conditions and constraints. Care – like love, prejudice, hatred and jealousy – is socially constructed.

In this chapter, I will argue that Australia, like many other developed Western societies, is undergoing a dramatic shift in the social construction of caring. But, it is not yet certain whether we can succeed in altering social values in favour of public care as distinct from private care. Our sociological understanding of care within the family, the most intimate and basic social group, indicates that such a shift entails considerable contradictions and dangers with regard to care in general within Australian society.

Two perspectives on care underlie the following discussion. First, there is the view of care as an affective activity: as people 'caring about' other people. Second, there is the view of care as necessitated by 'dependency': by people's lack of those resources which would enable them to independently control their own well-being. Both aspects of care, however, are firmly linked by way of our sociological understanding of family life and its relations with the wider politics of modern society.

CARE AS 'CARING ABOUT'

The newborn child is totally dependent upon its parents and others for its basic survival. Without some affective bond – or at least some vested interest in its survival – a child's needs for food, warmth, care and protection would not be met. Fortunately, usually the act of breastfeeding and nurturing creates an emotional bond between a mother and her child. However, when a mother is not the principal carer, a child can instead forge close affective bonds of attachment with others who take on the role. Where an affective bond is absent, and thereby physical and perhaps psychological neglect occurs, a child learns to withdraw, to distrust others, and to view the world as a potentially indifferent or hostile environment. The main point is that in being – or not being – cared for by others, a child develops a socially constructed picture of the surrounding world which has important consequences for his or her own social relationships with and caring for others. For instance, in New Zealand, the social ecology of childhood for a Maori child is not confined to blood parents or relatives: it extends to the *iwi* (or tribe), any member of which may be called on to care for the child. In Australian society, the extended family group is less likely to play an active caring role. Moreover, many children grow up not only isolated from extended kin, but also with few siblings and perhaps absent fathers. Children's experience of their fathers' apparent lack of caring can then be linked with evidence which suggests that such children tend to exhibit low levels of self-esteem and confidence (Amato, 1987; Edgar, 1985).

In societies less advanced than Australia, the affective bond between a mother and her child may be attenuated by high infant mortality. Nonetheless, care will be motivated by the need for as many productive hands as possible to maintain the family and to support the parents when elderly (Shorter, 1976). Once children shift from being producers to being costly consumers of family resources, birth rates begin to fall. But, a parallel development is that the affective bond between parents and their smaller number of offspring increases. Potential investment in each child is greater, both financially and emotionally. Parents have a greater stake in ensuring that every child turns out satisfactorily: that the effort they put into caring is rewarded with the demonstrable success and social status of the following generation. Children in the advanced societies today are better cared for than ever before. Perhaps ironically however, as there has been an increase in the lavishness and effectiveness of parental care, parents are being more and more bombarded with advice from professionals and experts who themselves agonize over children's health, educational and psychological welfare.

A point sometimes missed during considerations of parental care is that the family setting represents a microcosm of the broader social universe into which children grow. The global lessons learned by children within the power relationships they have with parents and other family members set a pattern for their understanding of the world beyond the family. For most children, the key message is reciprocity: that their displays of need, good behaviour and love can be exchanged for, for instance, food, affection and care. Moreover, most important, children learn that the exchanges are not confined to the immediate situation: that they will carry over into long term reciprocal behaviour and relationships.

As the first and most emotionally intense social context of their lives, the family teaches children to know themselves; teaches them their obligations and rights in relation to intimate others; and teaches them their place within the pecking order of society. The powerplay of intimate relations is a universal obstacle to be dealt with and converted into general rules of behaviour for guiding relationships with less intimate others – with 'strangers' – beyond the family.

Yet the more private and idiosyncratic the ecology of family-based moral learning, the less generalizable the lessons, and thereby the fewer the agreed moral guidelines which help people meet their obligations to those strangers on whom they very much depend in modern society. A family's privacy and autonomy may obscure its actual dependence on, or rather its interdependence with, people and institutions beyond its immediate boundaries. Parental confusion along with public concern over the emphasis on individual rights to the neglect of social responsibility draws people into the grasp of a priesthood of *savants*. Society shifts towards, following Habermas (1986), a 'therapeutocracy' in which professional (usually psychological or psychiatric) expertise and intervention increasingly competes with and substitutes for independent family living and competence. In modern society, there is a crisis of care which has arisen out of not only the pressures on dual-career families to share their caring role with others, but also the cacophony of experts who are eager to advise on children's inner psyche, but with little attention being given to the impact on children's sense of moral obligations beyond the immediate affective environment of the family.

A crucial dilemma presents itself: when children learn how to care for others within the confines of the family, their sense of moral obligation to strangers may be thwarted and weakened, with the consequence that society may be undermined; but when the more powerful affective influence of the family is replaced by public care, children's sense of moral obligation may still be diluted.

In Australia today, this dilemma is abundantly clear. Over 56 per cent of married mothers contribute to family incomes through paid labour force participation. In particular, larger numbers of mothers of pre-school children are in paid employment. However, childcare options are limited – with a shortage of formal childcare places, most parents have to (not to mention prefer to) make use of informal assistance provided by relatives, neighbours and friends – simply because workplace practices are still based on the notion of a family unit in which mothers and children are occupied at home in a dependent fashion on husbands and fathers who therefore need paid employment. In fact, the 'traditional nuclear family', with its male bread-winner and housewife mother now represents only 28 per cent of all Australian families. Recent parliamentary elections have highlighted the childcare debate with promises of childcare rebates, more subsidized places and after-school care provision, concern for 'quality' care, and the establishment of national standards. Parental guilt is fostered by attacks on Yuppie selfishness, the neglect of children by their mothers, and inadequate discipline and direction-setting for children and adolescents by parents. Political parties are torn between a pragmatic concern about the need for extra-familial childcare and a fear about children being neglected and poorly socialized within the family by parents.

In my view, the debate over childcare has focused too much on the affective side of caring and too little on the issue of the part played by care in child development both morally and intellectually. Childcare is still seen as a 'soft' subject, dominated by women, poorly paid, and only on the political agenda in so far as women are required to participate in the paid labour force. In Australia, the history of childcare has been bedevilled by the old debate between the Froebelian 'garden of children' and the tougher approach of the 'educationalists', for whom social considerations and outcomes suggest a more structured approach to an investment in child-hood. The history of childcare has been guided especially by the philanthropic treatment of the poor; by paternalistic interference on the part of the wealthy in parental neglect; and by the assumption that childcare is a social mechanism for helping the deprived – a means of standing in for those parents who lack the resources required to provide private (and superior) childcare.

CARE AND DEPENDENCY

This last point leads on to the second, and closely connected, sense in which care is used within the public/private debate: care as a response to the unavoidable dependency of infants, the disabled, the handicapped and the aged. Because the human infant has a long maturation period, the task of care and nurture is prolonged. At the same time, this aspect of childcare is the result to an extent of prevailing social circumstances and values. In the past, young children in so far as they were capable of carrying and climbing were pushed into labouring in factories, just as previously they had been used to labour in fields and cottage industries. Only gradually did a combination of humanitarian concerns and the requirement for a literate and numerate labour force result in the introduction of child labour laws along with the conversion of 'child labour' into 'school work'. In turn, this development coincided with the separation of males (as paid labourers) from the home, along with the concomitant separation of females from the sphere of paid labour, resulting in the consolidation of the traditional nuclear family and the emergence of new psychological theory justifying the key role of mothers in childcare.

The outcome is a redefinition of children as 'dependent' beyond the period characterized by basic nurturing needs, alongside a redefinition of women as 'dependent' upon men for the financial resources they require to enable them to conduct their homemaking and caring roles. Other solutions were ignored in favour of a process whereby paid labour became 'masculinized' and caring was left in the hands of women as 'secondary dependents'.

This privatization of care within a family dependency context was accompanied by the presence of distinct political and economic ideologies vying to resolve the social problems associated with the emphasis on family autonomy. While the 'free market' approach appears consistent with the latter; the 'welfare state' approach appears to contradict it, encouraging the state to play the part of helping ensure social equity with regard to the distributions of financial resources and of care. However, the two approaches share a common tendency to remove from the process of moral decision making any sense that the individual has a personal stake in the fate of others. The market rests on individualistic moral codes; the state rests on collectivistic moral codes. Individuals are left to struggle with such thorny issues and dilemmas as: whether to contribute to collective well-being by paying taxes or to maximize self interest by cheating on the payment of taxes; whether to tackle the drug crisis by legalizing drugs and allowing market forces to prevail or by pursuing stricter laws and law enforcement; whether armed forces recruitment should resort to conscription or should rely on volunteers, even though the latter may be motivated not so much by a sense of moral obligation as by the attraction of the material benefits. Concerns about such matters as efficiency and costs lend themselves to market solutions. But, these lead to problems of inequality and injustice with the result that people turn to state solutions.

Neither the market approach nor the state approach encourages a strong sense of mutual obligation among people as people in the full sense. Each fails to properly recognize that people are cable of devising and forging their own moral codes – of turning to such assets as self-restraint, ties of solidarity, community norms and voluntary altruism whereby moral regulation is based on feelings of obligation to the well-being of others as people in civil society.

There has been a long period since the Second World War during which the breadwinner–housewife model of family life has prevailed. Essentially, the responsibility for the care of children, the disabled and the aged has been privatized in the hands of dependent women, with minor support from the state. Australia in contrast with Britain and the Scandinavian countries is not noted for having operated with welfare state principles. There has been a version of the social security 'safety net', with unemployment benefits; family and child allowances; sole parent support; aged pensions; and a national health insurance scheme. However, these measures do not amount to a 'welfare state' approach, even though it does appear more caring and supportive of family life than the far more 'free market' framework operating in the United States. Welfare benefits are fixed at a level below a very mean 'poverty line'. Some benefits, such as the Family Allowance, have been applied in a universal manner, but without being index linked to inflation, and this combined with taxation bracket creep has produced increasing deprivation for families with children. Recently, however, even these benefits have become income-tested, asset-tested – targeted on the grounds of 'expenditure blowout' at a time when monetary policy has reduced inflation but increased interest rates, thus driving many families out of housing purchase or full employment or both.

Dominant economic wisdom asserts that 'a little hardship' is necessary for the sake of long term Australian economic recovery, and contrary to repeated social justice rhetoric, there is no evidence of the caring society at either the national level as judged in terms of state policy or the community level as judged in terms of attitudes towards the needy. Indeed, just as Peter Townsend (1987) has argued in the case of the United Kingdom, a targeting, means-tested approach to welfare inevitably divides a society into 'the haves' and 'the have-nots'; with the better off resenting the tax spending on what are assumed to be 'welfare cheats' and 'dole bludgers', and distancing themselves from any sense of moral obligation to strangers within a highly interdependent economy.

It could be argued that the drive towards private responsibility for oneself and one's family has been evident in areas of state policy and practice other than that of social security. Thus, as far as family law is concerned, the consistent emphasis is on family autonomy even though there has been something of an alteration in specifics. Once this principle meant male control over wife and children as elements of matrimonial property. However, it has now shifted in favour of equality with respect to such matters as parental responsibility for the financial support of children, and a couple's rights over matrimonial property in the event of a divorce. However, there has been a much stronger and more resilient underlying principle at work: that of the state's and the law's neutrality in relation to the private and emotional sphere centred on family, marital and parental life. There remains an important sense in which the state treats family life as an autonomous arena of social relationships and decision-making. According to this view, how a person chooses to care for his or her spouse and children is a private affair: it is not the state's business. Accordingly, the introduction of 'no fault' divorce legislation – whereby a marriage can be dissolved on the sole grounds of 'irretrievable breakdown' judged on the basis of twelve months separation and one partner's decision to seek a divorce – has more or less brought an end to the state's scrutiny and possible condemnation of private marital behaviour.

Of course, in practice, the principle of equality has not been fully enforced. Although it is common in divorce settlements to use 'guardianship' to encourage joint involvement in major decisions concerning the care of children, the old terminology of 'custody' and 'access' implies a denial of equality and exacerbates the childcare problem. By 1985, ten years after the Family Law Act came into effect, it had become clear that over two-thirds of non-custodial fathers were failing to pay child support. Men were resentful of the way in which women gained custody; and frequently access orders were resisted by ex-wives and otherwise not enforced. Research by the Australian Institute of Family Studies generated evidence on the dramatic differences in post-separation incomes between men, on the one hand, and women and their children, on the other. The evidence clearly pointed to the feminization of poverty, and supported the conclusion that there was growing family poverty due to the combined effects of tax policy (through bracket creep), social security policy (through the absence of inflation indexed benefits), and family law policy (through the failure to adequately enforce the equality principle).

The response was a decision to realign social policy given that childcare was being jeopardized and that dependency on the state was reaching economically unacceptable levels. This perhaps best illustrates the state's dilemma over the issue of where the responsibility for care should lie. Under Australian law, both marital relationships and state–family relationships had become permanently negotiable. Each citizen had become free to negotiate his or her family, his or her law. But a crucial element had been neglected within the state's assertion of adult autonomy: the place of children and the obligations of parenthood. As Glendon (1977)

puts it, the state must intervene in the economic and child-related consequences of marriage breakdown as well as in the problem of dependency
more generally.

Accordingly, the state stepped back in, strongly. A new national Child
Support Scheme was introduced, to enforce court orders first via the tax
system, and then from 1989 via an administrative formula to boost the
level of child support paid by non-custodial parents. Yet even here, the
onus is very much on private care. All those eligible for the state's Supporting Parent Benefit, designed to provide a minimum income to help
parents survive outside marriage, now have child support payments included as part of the income test for benefit eligibility. So the state, while
acting forcefully rather than leaving matters to private choice, is fostering
the supportive role of parents to reduce reliance on the public purse (Cherlin
and Furstenberg, 1988). Some would see this as a further withdrawal from
the public 'caring' role of the state and consistent with further clear trends.

Space does not permit detailing the major shifts in Australian public
policy in favour of deinstitutionalization and integration in the case of the
physically and mentally disabled and handicapped. However, as in all
advanced societies, in Australia these processes have been presented as a
humanistic advance towards social justice for previously stigmatized sections of society, while at the same time being attacked as a cynical shedding
by the state of public cost and responsibility, adding burdens to families that
lack the resources and skills to adequately care for those with special needs.
Nor is it possible to detail the various laws affecting family care in relation
to adoption, child abuse, child welfare programmes and family support
services, which vary across Australia's separate territorial states; and which
without exception involve the same problematic with regard to family
autonomy and the role of the state. The important point is that Australia
seems to be determined to push the responsibility for caring back into
private hands while demonstrating a lack of appreciation of the support
required to ensure that the care given is adequate.

Support services tend to be focused on crisis intervention, rather than on
either prevention or community development. Marriage counselling, marriage education, pilot family-youth mediation schemes and some Family
Resource Centres are funded by the Australian federal government, and
block grants to the territorial states for other family support services are
provided. But the amounts of money entailed are miniscule in comparison
with other forms of governmental expenditure. Even though evaluation
studies point to the cost-benefits of prevention (see Wolcott and Glezer,
1990), short term policy perspectives prevail. The only sign of hope is the

current revisiting by some government ministers of the 'locational disadvantage' theme of the 1970s, with some attempt to examine unequal
regional access to services that can be seen as part of the 'social wage'.

What is missing is a policy perspective that links the two elements of
care with which I began: care as caring about and care as response to
dependency. The key to such a policy is the recognition of interdependency
within modern society. Long ago, Durkheim (1964) pointed out that an
increasingly complex social division of labour relies on interdependency
and free choice rather than repressive control. However, the implications of
this seem to have been missed by the state in modern society: the need to
avoid the anomie associated with atomization and to emphasize the mutuality and reciprocity of the various social spheres of care and responsibility.

I am convinced that the answer to the dilemma over care faced by the
state lies in 're-surrounding' the private family (Berger and Berger, 1983)
to enable children to have social experiences which link them with the
wider community along with older generations – experiences which in
many family settings are lacking at present. This approach will require
much greater attention being paid to the quality of childcare in the developmental sense, and an acceptance that children represent a social good
not just a private, parental concern. It will entail, in Alan Wolfe's terms
(1989), the rejuvenation of 'civil society': the regeneration of reciprocal
linkages in the home and neighbourhood, and the promotion of 'agency'
which lies at the heart of the sense of moral obligation to others.

The implication is that the underlying goal of family policy along with
the politics of care should be to encourage and extend those soladaristic ties
and those mutual moral obligations that make a society operate positively
for all citizens. The implication in the Australian case is that 'top down',
federal and territorial state policies and programmes will not be sufficient
in that the required sense of 'agency' will not develop properly if imposed
from above. Local effort, local networks, local neighbourhoods, local
schools, local decisionmaking, and local accountability are essential to
enable children to have those experiences through which they learn that
they and their families are tied inextricably to others to whom they owe and
from whom they deserve a sense of moral obligation. Yet, of course,
localism can be too narrow, fostering bigotry and divisiveness. The early
lessons learned by children, within the context of civil society and its
institutions such as the family, will carry over into a wider sense of moral
obligation to strangers, and thereby into a more 'caring' society.

In my view, family policy debate has omitted to seriously address the
central theme of moral obligation and social interdependence. If the goal
was the rejuvenation and sustenance of 'civil society', there would be a

greater possibility of cutting through the dilemmas of modern democracy with its confused approach to independence, family autonomy, and the role of the state in contrast to the 'free market' in caring. The debate would bring to the centre of family policy such topics as the social ecology of childhood (Popenoe, 1988); the importance of 'agency' in developing family support programmes; the efficacy of a 'public parent' as distinct from the emotionally and time-committed parent who is 'mad about the child' (Bronfenbrenner and Weiss, 1983); the damaging effects of both 'family autonomy' and public control, and how to bring about a suitable balance between them; and the moral as opposed to the merely political dimensions of social justice.

10 Against the Odds:
Community Based Care for Psychiatric Disabilities in Britain and New Zealand[1]
Julie Leibrich

This chapter describes the systematic failure of two countries to provide good care for people with psychiatric disabilities. For some years both Britain and New Zealand have been reducing the amount of care available within institutions. But this has been done without adequate provision of alternative sources of care. The process of 'deinstitutionalization' tends to be euphemistically referred to as 'community care'. Yet without a willingness to care and without resources with which to care, the community is unlikely to provide an environment in which people with psychiatric disabilities will have the chance of substantially better lives.

There are problems of under-funding, organization and resistance within the community. User groups, voluntary service groups and statutory agencies have all expressed grave concern about what is happening in the name of community care. Despite the steady tolling of warning bells from commissions and enquiries, neither Britain nor New Zealand has yet given community care a secure and adequate financial backing. In the meantime, the process of deinstitutionalization continues with sometimes devastating consequences for the individuals involved. The more insidious social consequence is that the failure to provide good community based care will almost inevitably lead to a return to the status quo – institutionalized care – a system which clearly causes fundamental problems for the people it is designed to help.

THE MOVE TO COMMUNITY CARE

Until the sixteenth century, insanity was seen as the work of demons and witches, whose victims were kept mainly in prisons and monasteries. The seventeenth and eighteenth centuries saw the building of 'mad-houses' in which:

the inmates were subjected to unspeakable hardships – chains, irons, collars, darkened cells, solitary confinement, filth and starvation [. . .] At Old Bedlam in England, a physician would visit once a year to prescribe treatment [. . .] At smaller private institutions, it was not unusual for a physician to visit once in ten years to prescribe treatment for the next decade'. (Goldenberg, 1973, p. 50)

However, in Britain towards the end of the eighteenth century, the care of people with psychiatric disabilities began to be influenced by the humanitarian reform movement. For instance, the Quaker, William Turk, established a retreat at York which offered 'moral treatment' – encouragement, kindness and participation in routine labour. Nonetheless, despite various attempts at social reform, most institutional treatment remained appalling in its character and quality.

During the nineteenth century there were renewed attempts at social reform stemming from the humanitarian reform movement, and inspired by a wish to prevent the ill-treatment of patients in madhouses. In 1808 legislation was passed which permitted the building of public asylums, financed through local government rates (property taxes); and in 1844 it became mandatory for such asylums to be provided by county authorities. As a result, whereas in 1844 about 5000 people were in asylums, by the end of the nineteenth century the number had risen to 68 000 (Busfield, 1985). Throughout the first half of the twentieth century, the asylum continued to be the principal source of treatment for people with psychiatric disabilities. Thus, in Britain, the number of people in long-stay institutions peaked in 1954. Subsequently, however, there was a move away from institutional care: a change helped by developments in both treatment philosophies and psychotropic drugs.

The trend in psychiatric care in Britain has been similar to that in New Zealand, which became colonized by the British during the first half of the nineteenth century. The 1840s and 1850s saw the building of asylums, which numbered eight in 1876 when the central government took them over. The provision and use of asylums continued to grow steadily throughout the nineteenth and twentieth centuries; and the administration of psychiatric hospitals was separated from that of other health services until 1972 (Abbott, 1988). However, today, like Britain, New Zealand is firmly on the path of deinstitutionalization. As a result, over the last forty years the number of people in psychiatric institutions has fallen steadily. Whereas in 1944 about one in two hundred people were in psychiatric and intellectual handicap hospitals, by 1986 the figure had fallen to about one in five hundred and thirty – with about two-thirds of this latter proportion being in psychiatric hospitals.[2] At the same time, the total number of places in such hospitals has dropped not so much through fewer admissions, but more through shorter stays. In other words, the clear trend in patient care over recent years has been firmly towards a faster rate of patient turnover and discharge back into the community. On the other hand, there has been a trend towards a higher rate of re-admission.

COMMUNITY CARE – THE MOTIVE FOR CHANGE

The burgeoning literature on institutionalization has shown beyond doubt that large psychiatric hospitals can and do produce their own sickness (Barton, 1959; Biklen, 1979; Braginsky et al, 1969; Goffman, 1961; Laing, 1969; Rapoport, 1977; Sommer and Osmond, 1961). At best, large mental hospitals provide asylum, protection and treatment; at worst, they are scandalous: measuring out punishment and abuse (Martin, 1984).

The ostensible motive for the move to community care has been the idea that people in institutions can live just as well, and probably better, outside them. Accordingly, the theoretical aims of community care cover seeking the least restrictive setting; a more ordinary life; personal support within a community environment; and the promotion of civil rights. However, people who make the move from the familiar hospital setting into an unknown future experience considerable problems of adjustment. Nonetheless, as studies have shown, people who have been hospitalized with mental illness tend to have a strong preference for community living (Cambridge and Thomason, 1988; Drake and Wallach, 1988; Gibbons and Butler, 1987; Okin et al., 1983; Sheerin and Gale, 1985; Weinstein, 1979).

While the primary motive behind the move from institutional care to community care may well have been therapeutic, a secondary incentive has been economic in character. As the Victorian monoliths began to decay and the cost of their maintenance become increasingly difficult, the prospect of closing institutions gained an added appeal. The savings anticipated as a result of closure were much needed in an increasingly costly health system. This prospect became a motive for change; a cause behind the provision of community care on the cheap.

THE BRITISH STORY

Over the last thirty years, an emphasis on policies of rehabilitation and deinstitutionalization has led to a large reduction in the occupancy of beds in mental illness hospitals (Towell and Kingsley, 1986). In that initially the people to leave institutions were the least dependent, so the first surge of entry into the community meant few visible problems. Perhaps this experience encouraged unreal expectations of community service needs, because the targets for these and associated funding arrangements turned out to be far too low. Thus, as the people to leave institutions became the more dependent, so the need for a different quality and a greater quantity of care provision became apparent.

At the same time, there has emerged considerable variation in the provision of community based services between different locations in Britain. For instance, a few places have developed comprehensive resettlement programmes for long-stay hospital patients being transferred into the community. However, it is more common to find merely isolated projects which fall short of anything like an integrated support network, even though by themselves they occasionally represent specially funded pockets of excellence. In many areas, services are far from fully developed and in some places, plans have not even appeared on the drawing-board. Overall, in other words, the picture is bleak. Community based services are severely under-funded. There are shortfalls in health funding generally, clamps on local authority spending, and inadequate transfers of funds from hospital services to community based services. Moreover, the way money has been distributed has not matched the spread of responsibilities for service development: the bulk of funding has gone directly to health authorities, even though a large part of the responsibility for community care lies with local authorities, volunteer groups and individuals, especially women.

In 1985, the House of Commons Social Services Committee published the results of its investigation of community based services 'with special reference to adult mentally ill and mentally handicapped people'. It reported that the service was under-financed and under-staffed, and that there was no consensus about what community care actually involved (Select Committee on Social Services, 1985). The Committee was struck by the appalling lack of day-care facilities for people with mental illness (ibid., p. xiv), and concluded by making a hundred and one policy recommendations, including a real increase in expenditure on services; the establishment of a central bridging fund while new services are being developed parallel to hospital care; the use of individual and closely monitored care plans for people leaving hospital; and the preparation by the Department of Health and Social Security of nationwide guidelines.

In 1986, the Audit Commission reported the results of its investigation of changes in the balance of care between institutional and community settings. The report, *Making a Reality of Community Care* (Audit Commission, 1986), considered how well the targets set out in a 1975 White Paper (Department of Health and Social Security, 1975) were being met. There were, for instance, proposals for day care services: that there should be sixty social service day care places for every 100 000 of the general population. However, by 1984, only one-sixth of the target for England as a whole had been achieved, and there was a nationwide shortfall of between 25 000 and 30 000 places. Moreover, the 5361 local authority places actually available were very unevenly spread: twenty social service departments provided a hundred or more places – with East Sussex providing 215 and Nottinghamshire providing 212; and thirty two social service departments providing no places at all (Audit Commission, 1986).

The Commission found that, in general, progress in meeting targets was slow and uneven, and that community care policies were being adopted in a limited manner. It warned that the prospects for the future were 'unattractive'. Thus, while the number of hospital beds had been reduced by 25 000, community places – covering day-hospitals and day-centres – had shown an increase of only 9000. Not only were the targets not being met, but they were being outpaced by strategic advances, the result being that the targets had become too low. Also, the Commission found that there was not enough bridging finance available to cater for the size of the problem:

> In 1984–5 on average there were 10 200 fewer patients in mental handicap hospitals, and 16 800 fewer patients in mental illness hospitals than in 1976–77. Local authorities are having to meet the cost of services to replace these reductions; and the [National Health Service] must cover the extra £95 million [rising costs] for hospitals. It is these costs that must be bridged while the two services run in parallel. (Audit Commission, 1986, p. 39)

The Commission suggested several strategic options, including that local authorities be made responsible for the long-term care of all but the most severely disabled people; that, accordingly, resources be transferred to local authorities from health authorities; that funding policies be rationalized so that local authorities would not be hindered when setting up facilities; that adequate short-term funding be provided; that social security policies be co-ordinated with community care policies; and that more rational organizational structures be established. The Commission proposed a high level investigation of its list of options, and warned that the one untenable option was to do nothing.

A National Consumer Council survey carried out during 1987 found that the lack of day care services topped the concerns listed by health authorities and community health councils. One of the least well-provided services was crisis care: only nine of the district health authorities had a 24-hour crisis intervention team, and only thirty seven of them provided (that is, support for carers). The survey also found that the standard of accommodation for the disabled was often inappropriate, and that the level of support for both them and their carers was patchy and frequently inadequate (NCC/CHC, 1987). In almost half of ninety three district health authorities studied, the major part of the accommodation provided was in purpose-built units or converted hospital stock rather than in ordinary housing. This was despite the fact that the policy of community care was inspired by, at least in part, the belief that community settings are more desirable precisely because accommodation would be in ordinary housing and closer to community services.

In 1988, Sir Roy Griffiths and a team of specialist advisers published the findings of the review they had undertaken in response to the 1986 Audit Commission report (Griffiths, 1988). The report had requested a review of the way public funds were being used to support community care policy, and consequently for advice on the options for action to improve the use of the funds in contributing to more effective community based services. The review team's basic premise was that the role of the public sector is to ensure that care is provided as well as to encourage location innovation with regard to care. As required, the team limited itself to considering options within current funding levels.

The resulting Griffiths report recommended that (a) there be a Minister of State in the Department of Health and Social Security – 'seen by the public as being clearly responsible for community care' – who would publish a statement of the Government's community care objectives and priorities, allocate resources, and stipulate and monitor standards of service delivery; (b) local authorities assess community needs, arrange for services to meet such needs, and have transferred to them the resources for these tasks; (c) health authorities continue to be responsible for community medical services. Echoing the 1985 Select Committee's view, the Griffiths report warned: 'No person should be discharged without a clear package of care devised and without being the responsibility of a named care worker' (Griffiths, 1988, p. v).

The Government's detailed response to the Griffiths report arrived almost two years later in the form of a White Paper with the title *Caring for People* (1989). The Secretary of State accepted the central piece of advice from the Griffiths team that local authority social service departments should become the 'lead agencies' within the provision of community care.

A year or so later, however, there was still no sign of any additional public money being used to help implement the plans for better community care (Office of Health Economics, 1989).

THE NEW ZEALAND STORY

In New Zealand, as in Britain, the last thirty years has witnessed a substantial reduction in the number of beds in psychiatric hospitals alongside the inadequate provision of community based services. Recent reviews of the provision of health services in New Zealand have documented the urgent need for service development – especially in the area of community care (Department of Health, 1986; Mental Health Foundation, 1986 and 1988; Wellington Community Mental Health Services Group, 1986). The 1986 review of psychiatric hospitals along with hospitals for people with intellectual disabilities found that many patients remained in hospital who might have been receiving care within the community. Many of these patients either had been or were being considered for community care, even though the evidence suggests that many of those already in community care were failing to receive adequate care (Department of Health, 1986). The National Health Foundation's survey of community mental health services for people with severe psychiatric disabilities carried out in 1987 found that, despite progress with deinstitutionalization, the services were severely under-resourced. Most acutely, there was a lack of sheltered housing, recreational facilities, employment opportunities, patient and family support, and educational services (Mental Health Foundation, 1988).

The plight of people who fall in between the justice system and the health system has received special attention in recent years, mainly in view of the resulting deprivation (Department of Justice, 1981; Gallen Inquiry, 1983; Mason Report, 1988; Roper Report, 1987; Te Ara Hou, 1989). The Mason Report in 1988 was deeply critical of service provision: 'Nowhere in New Zealand has the development of community services kept pace with the growing need that has resulted from deinstitutionalization' (Mason Report, 1988, p. 147). Moreover, the need for community health services will continue to increase if a proposed Mental Health Bill (No. 18–1) is approved and becomes law. The Bill, first presented to Parliament during December 1987, includes a major review of the 1969 Mental Health Act, and it introduces the concept of compulsory psychiatric treatment into the community.

Another major factor behind the criticisms of health care provisions in New Zealand has been that, until recently, Maori people have not been invited to participate in the planning of the health services. As a result, the services have been developed within a non-Maori framework, even though Maori people have a high profile in the service provision statistics (Durie, 1984; Dyall, 1988; Pomare and de Boer, 1988).

Maori people's cultural identity has been eroded as a result of their socio-economic circumstances combined with the effect of past and present social policies. For many Maori people the stress and alienation associated with this particular process has brought about health problems, and especially mental health problems. Over the thirteen year period from 1974 to 1986, the average rate of first admissions for twenty- to twenty-nine year olds among Maori people was 1.7 times higher than the rate among non-Maori people (381 per 100 000 and 222 per 100 000 respectively). Moreover, at the end of this period, in 1986, the Maori rate had reached a figure which was 2.3 times higher (533 per 100 000 compared with 228 per 100 000). Also in 1986, the overall rate of first admissions (that is, independent of age) was 219.7 per 100 000 Maori in contrast with 128.7 per 100 000 non-Maori. The differential of 1.7 for 1986 was slightly lower than the figure for 1985, but nonetheless remains more or less consistent with a firm trend whereby the Maori rate of first admissions continues to rise while the non-Maori rate has levelled off[3]. In 1986, the proportion of first-time admissions who had been referred for treatment by law enforcement agencies was 21.4 per cent for Maoris compared with 8.3 per cent for non-Maoris[4].

During the 1980s, Maori began strongly advocating their own design and delivery of mental health services, and their views regarding health have been richly described (Durie, 1984; Murchie 1984; Potaka-Dewes, 1986). The government Departments of Social Welfare and of Health have expressed a commitment to the process of incorporating the values and beliefs of Maori people into all their policies (Department of Health, 1984; Department of Social Welfare, 1986; New Zealand Board of Health, 1988). However, although the general thrust of mental health policy supports the process of deinstitutionalization, it is no where near as far reaching as Maori development plans. Maori proposals include the rebuilding of various social institutions, such as the *whanau* (family), *whenua* (land), *hapu* (sub-tribe), *iwi* (tribe) and *te reo* (language), the intention being to restore power, prestige and identity to the Maori, and to establish a level of well-being which would allow improved support and care for Maori people with psychiatric disabilities.

As in Britain, in New Zealand there has been a complex funding situation for psychiatric care. The Departments of Health, Social Welfare, Housing, Labour and Justice – along with the area health boards – all provide funding for community care either directly or indirectly. However, none of them has been given or has assumed (through legislation or convention) the overall responsibility for organizing the services involved. Mechanisms for the co-ordination of policy formulation and operational activity have been absent. Therefore, the degree of integration of roles which does occur takes place in an *ad hoc* manner or by chance.

One of the greatest difficulties facing the process of co-ordination has been the way in which the funding through area health boards and government departments is organized. There are several aspects to this. Historically, funding has been institutionally based, and boards have funded hospital based services at the expense of community based services. Services have had to compete for funding, and there has been no national agreement on the proportion of funding for mental health services. The result has been that mental health services have been low on the list of priorities, with funding being too easily diverted to alternative uses. There has been no clear demarcation of responsibility for the funding of services, and this has led to a lack of funds for some, overlaps for others, and inadequate co-ordination of the use of funds for most. Funding transportablity has been poor, so that funds have not followed individuals during the process of deinstitutionalization. There has been a lack of equity: mental health services being under-resourced compared with other sectors. There have been many gaps in funding, including in the areas of service development; day activities and employment programmes; consumer networks; self-help groups; crisis care; and daily living support for privately housed people.

In 1988, the New Zealand Government established the National Mental Health Consortium for the purpose of setting policy objectives and priorities for the development of community health services within the statutory sector. The Consortium limited itself to 'a priority population', defined as those people severely disabled by an enduring or life-long psychiatric illness. It is argued that this group not only has the greatest service needs, but is the least able to voice its needs, the result being that it is the one most often excluded from community care developments (Audit Commission, 1986; Kay and Legg, 1986; Leibrich, 1988).

The Audit Commission has listed several principles for service development (National Mental Health Consortium Report, 1989): community care should be holistic and comprehensive; it should offer a continuum of care, and be accessible, responsive, effective and cost efficient; consumers should be empowered to participate at all levels of service development and delivery, and they should enjoy services which protect and promote their rights; services should be located and integrated within the community; needs assessment should precede planning, and planning should involve partnerships among the many groups involved in community care; the Treaty of Waitangi (the agreement signed in 1840 establishing the future relationship between Maori and non-Maori) should be honoured, and services should be sensitive to cultural and other variations between different sections within society.

The Consortium recommended that responsibility for the development and delivery of community care should rest at the national level with the Department of Health, and at the regional level with area health boards; that a National Community Care Policy Group, established by the Department of Health for an initial period of three years, should monitor the implementation of the Consortium's recommendations and develop policy as required; that a regional mental health consortium, established by each area health board, should be the key group for developing and delivering community care; that each consortium should undertake the assessment of regional needs, identify funding sources, develop joint funding packages, prepare a strategic plan, advise the board on priorities and service contracts, and allocate service development funding; that each regional consortium's membership should include representatives of the area health board, of other funding agencies, including *iwi* (tribal) authorities, and of community agencies, families and consumers.

Although area health boards and other statutory groups would directly provide some services, the Consortium envisaged many other service providers (consumer groups, family support groups, community agencies and Maori groups), and recommended that these be given appropriate support, encouragement and funding. The Consortium proposed the co-ordination of the delivery of community care through local resource centres, funded and operated by area health boards. Such centres, it was suggested, should organize needs assessment along with the process of referrals to services, involving the provision of individual care plans and the identification of a primary therapist and a community liaison worker. The Consortium recommended that community care be accompanied by strategies to improve the image and status of people with psychiatric disabilities; that services be well advertised and accessible; that staff employed by an area health board or contracted to provide services be given adequate ongoing training; and that special training be provided for various other groups concerned with the provision of care.

The Consortium proposed that the Department of Health provide a comprehensive review of progress with regard to the delivery and quality of care over the following three years; that it develop a national community care database; and that it establish service standards for area health boards;

that area health boards establish regional recording systems for collecting and assessing information about service use; and that there be evaluations by consumers and Maori groups as well as by service providers. The Consortium recommended that the Department of Social Welfare pay a community care subsidy to meet the operational costs of residential care and daily living support; and that a personal allowance be paid for each client along with an activities subsidy to cover day activities. It proposed that area health boards should fund all clinical services, including institutional care, crisis care, professional back-up support, and the operation and staffing of local resource centres; and that the boards should make available service development funding for the non-statutory sector. The recommendations suggested that the Department of Health be accountable to the Minister of Health for the provision of policy advice, as well as the development of standards and performance measures against which area health boards would be evaluated.

The development of contracts between the Minister of Health and the area health boards were viewed as the mechanism through which the accountability of the area health boards would be improved. The Consortium proposed contracts which detail the participation of the various non-statutory agencies in community care: contracts which would specify the responsibilities of the agencies, and the resources – including funding – to be made available to help agencies meet their responsibilities. Finally, the recommendation was made that, if service providers are to be properly accountable to consumers, it is essential to improve the representation of consumers on advisory bodies and within the evaluation procedure.

In June 1989, the Consortium reported back to the Government, but so far – about a year later – there has been no public announcement that its recommendations have been accepted for implementation. At the end of 1989, the decision was made that one particular state agency – the Department of Health – will be responsible from July 1990 for the funding of services for the psychiatrically disabled. But so far, there have been no published plans spelling out the way in which this decision will be implemented. As yet, no new funds have been released for the provision of community care.

THE KEY ELEMENTS OF CARE IN THE COMMUNITY

There are certain key elements which combine to ensure the provision of good community care. In both Britain and New Zealand, major reviews have advised that the success of any move from institutional to community care is dependent upon the provision of adequate and reliable funding. Such financial support would entail an immediate boost of transitional funding; a real increase in secure long term funding; and an improvement in the matching of responsibility with funding.

One problem to be tackled is that during the stage when any hospital is transferring patients into the community, two parallel systems of care will require funding – the hospital and the community services. Hospital costs will remain high despite the reduction in the number of patients. At the same time, new services will have to be set up within the community, and existing services will have to be expanded. Therefore, during the transitional period there will be a need for extra funding in the form of bridging finance. In the longer term, it is probable also that the costs of community care will be higher than that of institutional care if, that is, a high quality comprehensive network of services is intended. The cost of care can remain the same or allowed to fall only if patients are discharged into the community without adequate support services (Ennals, 1987; Griffiths, 1988; Heginbotham, 1988).

Even though funding is an essential requirement for good care, it is not the only requirement. Also, there is a need for (a) improved co-ordination of systems which build on collaborative partnerships between consumers, statutory agencies and non-statutory groups, and (b) clear delineation of responsibility and accountability. Basic service requirements for people with psychiatric disabilities include a needs assessment procedure and an arrangement for resource referral in conjunction with individual care plans, covering advocacy, therapy, crisis care, accommodation, financial security, daily living support, respite care, employment, education, and social and leisure activities. All the services should be flexible, catering for changes in people's health status, life situation, place of residence, and so on. Good community care requires, therefore, a planned and co-ordinated process of care management, along with appropriate education, information and training programmes, as well as continuous monitoring and evaluation. Consumers should be empowered to participate at all stages of community care planning, delivery and provision.

A LACK OF COMMITMENT

One of the most frustrating features of the move to community care is that there has been much talk, but little action. Successive reports have spotlighted the human suffering that results when community care policies are under-funded and badly implemented. Various strategic planning groups have offered detailed recommendations about how to rectify the situation. Moreover, in New Zealand, the recommendations reflect the views of representatives of consumers, Maori, families, voluntary groups and government departments. Obviously, there is a lack of commitment to community care on the part of politicians.

Despite many analyses of the community care problems to be tackled, and despite considerable agreement on the basic requirements of good community care, there seems to be little chance that very much improvement will be carried out in either Britain or New Zealand. It is likely that one of the main factors behind the low priority given to people with psychiatric disabilities lies in the widespread negative attitudes towards mental illness and disability.

A QUESTION OF ATTITUDES

Some years ago, lunatics were socially transformed into the mentally ill. Later still, they were socially reconstructed as the psychiatrically disturbed. Next, they became – and to some extent remain– 'clients', people with 'special needs' or the 'vulnerable'. But today, they tend to be labelled as 'consumers' or 'recipients of care'. As the formal adjectives and nouns are changed in an attempt to soften the negative connotations of the labels used, perhaps the newer notions with their coy neutrality do indicate some improvement. However, any change in labels by itself does not necessarily mean a change in attitudes. Perhaps instead, the underlying attitudes remain the same, merely becoming more slippery and difficult to grasp. Recipients of care continue to be derogatively labelled as 'loonies', 'crazies' and 'weirdos', both in private and on the streets.

People tend to be ignorant about mental illness, with most believing the mentally ill to be unpredictable and dangerous, the result being distrust and fear. There is a widespread assumption which attributes the causes of mental illness to a lack of moral strength or low intelligence or insincerity and worthlessness (Lehman et al., 1976; Nunnally, 1961; Rabkin, 1972; Seagal, 1978). New Zealand research among students has indicated that negative attitudes have declined very little over the years (Green et al., 1987).

Even though, in fact, much has been happening with regard to the move to community care which is good, beneficial and promising, it nonetheless appears to be easy for the media to spotlight and reinforce the bad and negative (Matas et al., 1985; Matas et al., 1986). Following the move to community based care, there has been a steady diet of scare stories in the media in both Britain and New Zealand, encouraging negative attitudes. It appears to take just one salient case of a mentally ill person to become, in the absence of adequate community based support, aggressive to offset and perhaps erase the hundreds of cases where this does not happen.

Recently, it has been argued that it is merely a highly vocal minority who transform their strongly negative attitudes into discriminatory action (Dear and Taylor, 1982; Rabkin et al., 1984). However, it still has to be recognized that the resulting actions can be appalling. For instance, resettled patients in the United States have been not only branded with spray paint but also shot at (Lewis, 1986). In England, a drug rehabilitation centre was fire-bombed (Laurance, 1986).

At the same time, it has been shown that the view of psychiatrically disturbed people as dangerous weakens as contact with such people increases (Link and Cullen, 1986; Sellick and Goodyear, 1985). Moreover, it has been revealed that the degree to which resettled patients are accepted within the community is strongly influenced by the carers involved (Sherman et al., 1984). In conjunction with these findings, the possibility arises of making use of the mass media in order to improve the image and reception of patients – although in practice the mass media has hardly ever been used in this regard (Lamontagne and Verreault, 1986). It has been argued that, in fact, the most effective educators about mental illness are – or would be – the mentally ill themselves (Parker, 1986). But, in the absence of alternatives, perhaps the most effective approach is to educate those with mental illness about 'the public' (Angermeyer et al., 1987).

Of course, attitudes are firmly rooted in and reinforced by patterns of belief, knowledge, emotions and behaviour. So that once established, they become highly resistant to modification. Nonetheless, change is possible, dependent upon a strong commitment to and clear strategies for change. One of the factors which would help remove negative attitudes to mental illness would be to allow people with psychiatric disabilities to be actively involved in the planning and delivery of services. At present, the psychiatrically disabled themselves are an under-used and under-valued resource, no doubt due in part to the way in which there are few expectations about their becoming fully functioning members of society. They tend to be excluded from service development despite the richness of their relevant experience and valuable social networks, probably as a reflection of the greater value placed on expertise instead of experience in modern society (Sang and O'Brien, 1984; Drucker, 1987; O'Hagan, 1989).

THE CONSEQUENCES OF CARE ON THE CHEAP

The immediate result of inadequate funding, combined with haphazard service development and prejudice against mental illness, is that a disadvantaged section of society is put under greater pressure. The image of a warm, secure and caring society is myth as judged in terms of what happens to most people with psychiatric disabilities. Many of these disabled have experienced society as unfriendly, inhospitable and unaccommodating. Within the health and social services there remain strong patterns of paternalism, monoculturalism, insensitivity, and resistance to power sharing. Advocacy schemes are under-developed, and therefore the protection of the rights of the mentally ill and disabled is a major concern.

People with disabilities suffer many losses. As part of the illness itself, they are likely to experience reduced self-esteem, competence and independence. In addition, the more severely disabled will suffer a loss of choice with regard to accommodation, employment, recreation and social relationships. There is a very good chance of the disabled becoming poor and losing social status and credibility. Moreover, the longer the experience of psychiatric illness, the greater the associated social disability and the deeper the downward spiral. Patients in mental illness hospitals have often lived previously in poverty (Bradshaw and Davis, 1986): but also, they are perhaps even more likely after leaving hospital to end up in poverty (Patmore, 1987). An apt way of summing up what happens is that the disabled have enough money to survive, but not enough money to live on.

Housing is a major problem (Braisby et al., 1988; Housing Corporation, 1989; Kay and Legg, 1986; National Federation of Housing Associates, 1987), so that fresh ghettos are constantly being created as the disabled come to rely on impoverished accommodation solutions. Similarly, being provided with a home on one of the older municipal housing developments can inflate the odds against success. At the same time, many disabled are even worse off: that is, the number of people with mental illness who are homeless is on the increase. In Britain, there are growing numbers of homeless people, many of whom have once lived in psychiatric hospitals. A survey by the Salvation Army of those who use its hostels in Britain discovered that one in three had a serious mental illness, and an estimate from a survey of housing agencies indicates an increase from ten to fifty per cent of residents with serious mental health problems (Leibrich, 1988).

Even though psychiatric disability may not mean the complete loss of a person's natural and acquired abilities, it may mean that the usual demands of paid employment are too great. The employment opportunities for those with psychiatric disabilities are limited by the type of work available, by fixed expectations about hours and output of work, as well as by social discrimination. Such restrictive factors, especially in the context of a society in which unemployment is a major social problem, mean that the chances of the disabled having regular paid work are negligible. The alternative is sheltered workshops, but although these may provide opportunities for a degree of activity and social contact, they usually offer work which is highly repetitive and boring, as well as payment which is extremely low.

Most of those who are discharged from long stays in mental illness hospitals tend to be unemployed within the community. In a survey in London, almost half of those who had entered the community reported having wanted a paid job, but

> many had been trying unsuccessfully to get a job and said that having a record of mental illness was a definite stigma: many thought that the kinds of jobs they would get would bring in less than living on social security . . . they were caught in the poverty trap. (Kay and Legg, 1986, p. 30)

As the number of people in psychiatric hospitals declines, so the number of those in prisons rises. In Britain in 1977, the average daily prison population was 41 570; but ten years later, the figure had increased by 17 per cent to an average daily population of 41 570[5]. Similarly in New Zealand there has been a rise in prison figures by almost a fifth over the last ten years: in 1977, 4597 distinct prisoners were received; in 1988, the figure was 5386[6].

While the correlation by itself between the reduction in the number in people in psychiatric hospitals and the rise in the number in prisons between the late 1970s and the late 1980s does not mean that the former caused the latter, there is separate support of such a connection (Rabkin, 1979). Thus, the Audit Commission has warned:

> If the recent US experience is any guide, it is likely that a significant proportion of those discharged from [National Health Service] hospitals will have been before the courts and will now be imprisoned; others will have become wanderers, left to their own devices with no support from community based services. (Audit Commission, 1986, p. 17)

The Select Committee on Social Services commented:

> Hardly a month now passes without a judge being obliged to pass a custodial sentence explicitly against his [or her] better judgement on someone who all agree needs secure psychiatric care. (Select Committee on Social Services, 1985, p. lxxxii)

The plight of 'difficult people' – those with severe behavioural problems, dementia or substance abuse problems – is especially regrettable. But, perhaps the most disadvantaged of all are those who are not only mentally ill, but also elderly, for whom the old mental asylums have become dumping grounds. Moreover, as the hospital services are reduced, so those people who are left to the end within institutions will receive ever worsening care – unless a strategy for dealing with the transitional period is thoroughly worked out and applied.

There is the danger of the transition to community based services involving a decline in hospital services and thereby, among the mentally ill and disabled, leading to a sense of distinction and discrimination between the 'ones chosen' and the 'ones that stayed'. Long-stay patients are already required to tolerate second best because hospitals provide the better facilities to those who are identified as having the best chance of an early recovery linked to a relative early release (Dowland and McKinlay, 1985). In Britain, my own research has uncovered several instances of mental patients being shifted summarily, without preparation, between wards in accordance with hospital closure plans (Leibrich, 1988).

It is not only the psychiatrically disabled themselves, but also their families and various informal carers who experience the pressures, demands and burdens which attend inadequate resourcing. In New Zealand, a recent study conducted by the Schizophrenia Fellowship indicates that the families of the disabled are extremely under-supported. The Fellowship's survey of about two hundred families detected a widespread sense of being over-burdened and powerless.[7]

A PROBLEM UNRESOLVED

The problems occurring for individuals as a result of the process by which hospitals are being emptied in the absence of adequate provision of suitable community services are abundantly clear. However, a more insidious prospect is that the move to community based care will be so badly done that the search for an alternative to institutional care will be abandoned: that there will be a reversion to traditional institutional care with all its unacceptable features. A sign of this occurred when the 1989 British Medical Association Conference voted in favour of a halting the hospital closure programme. But, undoubtedly the resulting stalemate would be a tragedy for people with psychiatric disabilities because the history of institutional care has produced a system which is a failure. A better system has to be found.

Perhaps the greatest impediment to improving the state's provision of effective care for people with psychiatric disabilities is that of the attempt to find the 'correct solution' instead of the 'best fit'. In other words, the search for better care is unlikely to be successful by adopting the 'either-or' approach which often accompanies the current debate on community care versus deinstitutionalization.

In 1987 at the annual conference of MIND, Su Kingsley (representing the London borough of Haringey's Area Health Authority) argued that in dealing with mental illness there are two types of problem: 'tame problems' and 'wicked problems' (Kingsley, 1987). Tame problems are unidimensional in that there is one target factor which needs to be identified and tackled in order to arrive at a solution. But, wicked problems are multidimensional in that they entail a complexity of factors, issues and interests. Tame problems are relatively limited in scope in terms of the information required to deal with them; but wicked problems are wide-ranging, and even unlimited, with regard to the kind of information required to tackle them. In effect, tame problems are technical matters requiring the acquisition and application of the appropriate technical expertise; but wicked problems are not amenable to 'right' or 'final' decisions, only to preferences in accordance with opinions, values and ideals. Tame problems have an endpoint which can be envisaged, worked towards and achieved; in contrast, wicked problems will not lie down. Wicked problems are never ending; they do not get solved, only resolved. One wicked problem is community care.

NOTES

1. This chapter is substantially based on two previous publications: Leibrich, 1988; National Mental Health Consortium Report, 1989.
2. National Health Statistics Centre, *Mental Health Data 1986*, Table 4, p. 22. At the end of 1986, 4599 residents (71 per cent) were in psychiatric hospitals; and 1841 (29 per cent) were in intellectual handicap hospitals.
3. Analysis of ethnic differentials for first admission rates provided by Yvonne Underhill-Sem, Strategic Planning Unit, Auckland Area Health Board. Source: *Mental Health Data 1986*, p. 13. Plus supplementary data by National Mental Health Statistics Centre. Source: *Mental Health Data 1986*, p. 46.
4. *Mental Health Data 1986*, p. 46.
5. These figures come from the National Association for the Care and Resettlement of Offenders.
6. *Justice Statistics 1988*, Table 1, p. 28.
7. These figures come from an unpublished survey by Schizonphrenia Fellowship (NZ). The survey was based on 218 respondents – the response rate being forty per cent.

Bibliography

Abbott, M. (1988) 'Community Directions in Mental Health Delivery in New Zealand', *XXIV International Congress of Psychology*.

Allan, G. (1985) *Family Life* (Oxford: Blackwell).

Amano, I. et al. (1983) 'Koutougakkou no Shuushoku Shidou to Seito Shinro Keisei', *Bulletin of Tokyo University Faculty of Education*, 23, pp. 45–76.

Amato, P. (1987) *Children in Australian Families: the Growth of Competence* (Sydney: Prentice-Hall).

Andrews, K. and J. Jacobs (1990) *Punishing the Poor: Poverty Under Thatcher* (London: Macmillan).

Angermeyer, M. et al. (1987) 'Stigma Perceived by Patients Attending Modern Treatment Settings', *Journal of Mental and Nervous Disease*, 175, pp. 4–11.

Anyon, J. (1980) 'Social Class and the Hidden Curriculum at Work', *Journal of Education*, 162, pp. 67–92.

Apple, M. (ed.) (1982a) *Cultural and Economic Production in Education: Essays on Class, Ideology and the State*, (London: Routledge and Kegan Paul).

Apple M. (1982b) 'Reproduction and Contradiction in Education: an Introduction', in M. Apple (ed.), *Cultural and Economic Production in Education: Essays on Class, Ideology and the State*, (London: Routledge and Kegan Paul).

Ariès, P. (1973) *Centuries of Childhood* (Harmondsworth: Penguin).

Arnott, M. and C. Whitty (1982) 'From Reproduction to Transformation: Recent Radical Perspectives on the Curriculum from the USA', *British Journal of Sociology of Education*, 3, pp. 93–103.

Arnstein, S. (1971) 'A Ladder of Citizen Participation', *Journal of the Royal Town Planning Institute*, 57, pp. 176–182.

Audit Commission (1986) *Making a Reality of Community Care: a Report by the Audit Commission for Local Authorities in England and Wales* (London: HMSO).

Australian Bureau of Statistics (1987) *The Labour Force, Australia* (Canberra: AGPS).

Backett, K. (1982) *Mothers and Fathers: a Study of the Development and Negotiation of Parental Behaviour* (New York: Macmillan).

Barton, R. (1959) *Institutional Neurosis* (Bristol: John Wright).

Bates, S. (1991) 'More Teachers Quit for Health', *Guardian*, 25 January.

Beavis, S. (1989) 'Whitehall Boosts Child Care for Working Mothers', *Guardian*, 17 February.

Bebbington, A. and J. Miles (1989) 'The Background of Children Who Enter Local Authority Care', *British Journal of Social Work*, 19, pp. 349–68.

Bell, C. and L. McKee (1984) 'His Unemployment, Her Problem. The Domestic and Marital Consequences of Male Unemployment', *British Sociological Association Annual Conference*.

Bell, D. (1970) 'The Cultural Contradictions of Capitalism', *Public Interest*, 21.

Bell, S. (1988) *When Salem Came to Boro: the True Story of the Cleveland Child Abuse Crisis* (London: Pan 1988).

Berger, B. and P. Berger (1983) *The War Over the Family* (London: Hutchinson).

Bernstein, B. (1977) 'Class and Pedagogies: Visible and Invisible', in J. Karabel and H. Halsey (eds), *Power and Ideology in Education* (New York: Oxford University Press).

Biklen, D. (1979) 'The Case for Deinstitutionalisation', *Social Policy*, 10, pp. 48–53.

Bilton, T. et al. (1987) *Introductory Sociology* (London: Macmillan, 2nd edn).

Boulding, K. (1973) 'The Boundaries of Social Policy', in W. Birell et al, (eds), *Social Administration: Readings in Applied Social Science* (Harmondsworth: Penguin).

Bourdieu, P. (1973) 'Cultural Reproduction and Social Reproduction', in R. Brown (ed.), *Knowledge, Education and Cultural Change* (London: Tavistock).

Bourdieu, P. and J. Passeron (1977) *Reproduction in Education, Society and Culture* (London: Sage).

Bowlby, J. (1951) *Maternal Care and Mental Health* (Geneva: World Health Organization).

Bowles, S. and H. Gintis (1976) *Schooling in Capitalist America* (London: Routledge and Kegan Paul).

Box, S. (1971) Deviance, *Reality and Society* (London: Holt, Reinhart and Winston).

Bradshaw, M. and A. Davis (1986) *Not a Penny to Call My Own: Poverty Amongst Residents in Mental Illness and Mental Handicap Hospitals* (London: Kings Fund Centre).

Bradshaw, J. and J. Morgan (1987) *Budgeting on Benefit: the Consumption of Families on Social Security* (London: Family Policy Studies Centre).

Braginsky, B., et al. (1969) *Methods of Madness: the Mental Hospital as a Last Resort* (New York: Holt, Rinehart and Winston).

Braisby, D., et al. (1988) *Changing Futures: Housing and Support Services for People Discharged from Psychiatric Hospitals* (London: Kings Fund Centre).

Brake, M. (1985) *Comparative Youth Culture* (London: Routledge and Kegan Paul).

Bremner, C. (1990) 'Exam Fails to Quell US Row', *The Weekend Australian*, 3 November.

Brofenbrenner, U. and H. Weiss (1983) 'Beyond Policies Without People: an Ecological Perspective on Child and Family Policy', in E. Zigler, S. Kagan and E. Klugman (eds), *Children, Families and Government* (New York: Cambridge University Press).

Brownlee, H. (1990) 'Tax and Social Security Changes Affecting Family Life', *Family Matters*, 26, pp. 28–31.

Bryson, L. (1985) 'Gender Divisions and Power Relationships in the Australian Family', in P. Close and R. Collins (ed), *Family and Economy in Modern Society* (London: Macmillan).

Burghes, L. (1990) 'Self Sufficiency for Lone Parents in the US', *Family Policy Bulletin*, 8, p. 3.

Burton, C., (1985) *Subordination: Feminism and Social Theory* (Sydney: Allen and Unwin).

Busfield, J. (1985) *Managing Madness: Changing Ideas and Practice* (London: Hutchinson).

Byrne, E. (1978) *Women and Education* (London: Tavistock).

Byrne, D. (1987) 'Rich and Poor: the Growing Divide', in A. Walker and C. Walker (eds), *The Growing Divide: a Social Audit 1979–1987* (London: Child Poverty Action Group).

Cambridge, P. and C. Thomason (1988) 'Care in the Community', *Personal and Social Services Research Unit Regional Seminar*, London.

Carnoy, M. (1982) 'Education, Economy and the State', in M. Apple (ed.), *Cultural and Economic Production in Education: Essays on Class, Ideology and the State* (London: Routledge and Kegan Paul).

Carnoy, M. and H. Levin (1985a) 'Contradiction in Education', in M. Carnoy and H. Levin, *Schooling and Work in the Democratic State* (Stanford, California: Stanford University Press).

Carnoy M. and H Levin (1985b) *Schooling and Work in the Democratic State* (Stanford, California: Stanford University Press).

Cashmore, E. (1985) *Having To: the World of One Parent Families* (London: Allen and Unwin).

Casimir, J. (1990) 'In Trouble at 11. He's Against the Trend', *Sydney Morning Herald*, 29 September.

Centre for Policy Studies (1989) *Who Cares? Children at Risk and Social Services* (London: Centre for Policy Studies).

Cherlin, A. and F. Furstenberg (1988) 'The Changing European Family: Lessons for the American Reader', *Journal of Family Issues*, 9, pp. 291–7.

Clarke, J. (1979) 'Capital and Culture: the Post-War Working Class Revisited', in J. Clarke, C. Critcher and R. Johnson (eds), *Working Class Culture* (London: Hutchinson).

Clarke, J. and P. Willis (1984) 'Introduction' in I. Bates et al., (eds), *Schooling for the Dole*? (London: Macmillan).

Close, P. (1985) 'Family Form and Economic Production', in P. Close and R. Collins (eds), *Family and Economy in Modern Society* (London: Macmillan).

—— (ed.) (1989a) *Family Divisions and Inequalities in Modern Society* (London: Macmillan).

—— (1989b) 'Family Theory and Economic Structure', in M. Sussman (ed.), *Cross Cultural Perspectives on Families, Work and Change* (New York: Haworth Press).

—— (1989c) 'Toward a Framework for the Analysis of Family Divisions and Inequalities', in P. Close (ed.), *Family Divisions and Inequalities in Modern Society* (London: Macmillan).

Close, P. and R. Collins (1983) 'Domestic Labour and Patriarchy', *International Journal of Sociology and Social Policy*, December.

Close, P. and R. Collins (eds) (1985) *Family and Economy in Modern Society* (London: Macmillan).

Coates, K. and R. Silburn (1970) *Poverty: the Forgotten Englishmen* (Harmondsworth: Penguin).

Cohen, B. (1988) *Caring for Children: Services and Policies for Childcare and Equal Opportunities in the United Kingdom. Report for the European Commission's Childcare Network* (London: Family Policy Studies Centre).

Cohen, E. (1976) *Problems and Prospects of Teaming* (Stanford, California: Stanford Centre for Research and Development in Teaching).

Cohen, S. (1985) *Visions of Social Control* (Cambridge: Polity Press, 1985).

Cohen, S. and A. Scull (eds) (1983) *Social Control and the State* (New York: St Martin's Press).

Collins, R. (1985) '"Horses for Courses": Ideology and the Division of Domestic

Labour', in P. Close and R. Collins (eds), *Family and Economy in Modern Society* (London: Macmillan).

—— (1989) 'Illegitimacy, Inequality and the Law in England and Wales', in P. Close (ed.), *Family Divisions and Inequalities in Modern Society* (London: Macmillan).

—— (1991) 'Upholding the Nuclear Family: a Study of Unmarried Parents and Domestic Courts', in C. Marsh and S. Arber (eds), *Households and Families: Divisions and Change* (London: Macmillan).

Collins, R. and A. Macleod (1990) *The End of Illegitimacy* (London: ESRC).

Connell, R. (1979) 'A Critique of the Althusserian Approach to Class', *Theory and Society*, VIII (1979) pp. 303–45.

Connell, R. (1985) *Teachers Work* (Sydney: Allen and Unwin).

Connell, R. et al. (1982) *Making the Difference: Schools, Families and Social Divisions* (Sydney: Allen and Unwin).

Corrigan, P. and P. Leonard (1978) *Social Work Practice Under Capitalism: a Marxist Approach* (London: Macmillan).

Craib, I. (1984) *Modern Social Theory* (Brighton: Wheatsheaf).

Crompton, R. and J. Gubbay (1975) *Economy and Class Structure* (London: Macmillan).

Crow, G. and M. Hardey (1990) 'Categorisation of Social Groups and Social Policy: the Case of Lone-Parent Households', in C. Marsh and S. Arber (ed), *Household and Family: Divisions and Change* (London: Macmillan).

Dale, R. (1973) 'Co-operative Teaching and the Multiple-Area School', *Quest*, 12, pp. 25–29.

—— (1982) 'Education and the Capitalist State: Contributions and Contradictions', in M. Apple (ed.), *Cultural and Economic Production in Education: Essays on Class, Ideology and the State* (London: Routledge and Kegan Paul).

Dale, R., et al. (eds) (1981) *Schooling and the National Interest* (Lewes: Falmer Press).

Dalley, G. (1988) *Ideologies of Caring* (London: Macmillan).

Davies, M. (1983) *The Essential Social Worker* (Aldershot: Gower).

Dawson, C. (1990) 'Productivity: the Key Factor', *The Australian*, 3 October.

Deakin, N. and Wicks, M. (1988) *Families and the State* (London: Family Policy Studies Centre).

Dear, M. J. and S. M. Taylor (1982) *Not On Our Street: Community Attitudes in Mental Health Care* (London: Pion, 1982).

Deem, R. (1978) *Women and Schooling* (London: Routledge and Kegan Paul).

Denscombe, M. (1982) 'The Hidden Pedagogy and its Implications for Teacher Training', *British Journal of Sociology of Education*, 3, pp. 249–65.

Department of Education, Queensland (1983) *Co-operative Teaching in Double Teaching Spaces* (Brisbane, Queensland: Department of Education).

Department of Education, United States (1987) *Japanese Education Today* (Washington DC: United States Department of Education).

Department of Health, New Zealand (1984) *Hui Whakaoranga/Maori Health Planning Workshop* (Wellington: Department of Health).

Department of Health, New Zealand (1986) *Review of Psychiatric Hospitals and Hospitals for the Mentally Handicapped* (Wellington: Department of Health).

Department of Health, United Kingdom (1989) *An Introduction to the Children Act*

1989: a New Framework for the Care and Upbringing of Children (London: HMSO).

Department of Health and Social Security, United Kingdom (1975) *Better Services for the Mentally Ill* (London: HMSO).

Department of Justice, New Zealand (1981) *Report of the Working Party on Psychiatrically Disturbed Prisoners and Remandees* (Wellington: Department of Justice).

Department of Social Security [United Kingdom] (1990) *Which Benefit? A Guide to the Social Security and NHS Benefits You Can Claim* (London: HMSO).

Department of Social Welfare, New Zealand (1986) *Puao-Te-Ata-Tu/Daybreak* (Wellington: Department of Social Welfare).

Dickenson, J. and B. Russell (1986) *Family, Economy and the State* (London: Routledge).

Dornbusch, S. and K. Gray (1988) 'Single Parent Families', in S. Dornbusch and M. Strober (eds), *Feminism, Children and the New Families* (New York: the Guildford Press).

Dowland, J. and R. McKinlay (1985) *Caring, Curing and Controlling: an Outsider's Look at Life and Work in New Zealand Psychiatric Hospitals* (Wellington: Department of Health).

Drake, R. and M. Wallach (1988) 'Mental Patients' Attitudes Towards Hospitalization: a Neglected Aspect of Tenure', *American Journal of Psychiatry*, 145, pp. 29–34.

Drucker, N. (1987) 'Introduction', in N. Drucker (ed.), *Creating Community Health Services in Scotland* (Edinburgh: Scottish Association of Mental Health).

Dunleavy, P. and B. O'Leary (1987) *Theories of the State: the Politics of Liberal Democracy* (London: Macmillan).

Durie, M. (1984) 'Te Taha Hinengaro: an Integrated Approach to Mental Health', *Community Mental Health in New Zealand*, 1, pp. 4–11.

Durkheim, E. (1964) *The Division of Labour in Society* (New York: Free Press).

Dyall, L. (1988) 'Oranga Maori: Maori Health', *New Zealand Health Review*, 8, pp. 13–21.

Edgar, D. (1985) 'Getting the Family Act Together – Children, Competence and Family Progress', *Australian Journal of Family Research*, (November 1985).

Edgell, S. (1980) *Middle-Class Couples* (London: Allen and Unwin).

Egan, C. (1990a) 'Schools Learn to Fight Crime', *The Weekend Australian*, 15 September.

Egan, C. (1990b) 'Teachers Mobilise to End Student Attacks', *The Weekend Australian*, 15 September.

Elliot, F. Robertson (1986) *The Family: Change or Continuity?* (London: Macmillan).

Ennals, D. (1987) 'Opening Address', MIND Annual Conference, Blackpool.

Evans, R. (1986) *Vocational and Occupational Training of Non-College Bound Youth* (Washington DC: United States Department of Education, Office of Educational Research and Improvement).

Family Policy Bulletin 5 (1988) (London: FPSC, Summer).

Family Policy Bulletin 8 (1990) (London: FPSC, Spring).

Ferrari, J. (1990) 'System is "Killing Love of Learning"', *The Australian*, 3 October.

Field, F. (1989) *Losing Out: The Emergence of Britain's Underclass* (Oxford: Basil Blackwell).

Finch, J. (1987) 'Whose Responsibility? Women and the Future of Family Care', in I. Allen, et al., *Informal Care Tomorrow* (London: Policy Studies Institute).

Finch, J. (1989) *Family Obligations and Social Change* (Cambridge: Polity Press).

Finch, J. and D. Groves (eds) (1983) *A Labour of Love: Women, Work and Caring* (London: Routledge and Kegan Paul).

Finer, M. (1974) *Report of the Committee on One-Parent Families* (London: HMSO).

Finn, D. (1984) 'Leaving School and Growing Up: Work Experience in the Juvenile Labour Market', in I. Bates et al., (eds), *Schooling for the Dole?* (London: Macmillan).

Fletcher, R. (1988) *The Shaking of the Foundations* (London: Routledge and Kegan Paul).

Foucault, M. (1977) *Discipline and Punishment* (London: Allen and Unwin).

Foucault, M. (1982) 'The Subject and Power', *Critical Inquiry* 8, pp. 777–95.

Foyster, N. (1990) 'A Vignette from Britain', *Education. Journal of the New South Wales Teachers' Federation*, August.

Francis, R. (1990) 'NZ Students "Privileged"', *The Australian*, 3 October.

Fujiwara (1989) 'Koukou Kara Shokuan Dairi Gyoumu o Nakuse', *Asahi* (newspaper), 27 July.

Gallen Inquiry (1983) *Report of the Committee of Inquiry into Procedures at Oakley Hospital and Related Matters* (Wellington: Government Print).

Galton, M., et al. (1980) *Inside the Primary Classroom* (London: Routledge and Kegan Paul).

Garfinkel, I. (1988) 'The Evolution of Child Support Policy', *Focus* (Spring) pp. 11–16.

Garland, D. (1985) Punishment and Welfare (Aldershot: Gower).

General Household Survey 1983 (1985) (London: HMSO).

George, V. and P. Wilding (1984) *The Impact of Social Policy* (London: Routledge).

Gibbons, J. and J. Butler (1987) 'Quality of Life for "New" Long-Stay Psychiatric In-Patients: the Effects of Moving to a Hostel', *British Journal of Psychiatry*, 151, pp. 347–354.

Giddens, A. (1979) *Central Problems in Social Theory: Action, Structure and Contradiction* (London: Macmillan).

Giddens, A. (1980) *The Class Structure of the Advanced Societies* (London: Hutchinson, Second Edition).

Gintis, H. and S. Bowles (1981) 'Contradictions and Reproduction in Educational Theory', in R. Dale et al., (eds), *Schooling and the National Interest* (Lewes: Falmer Press).

Glendinning, C. (1987) 'Impoverishing Women', in A. Walker and C. Walker (eds), *The Growing Divide: a Social Audit* (London: Child Poverty Action Group).

Glendon, M. (1977) *State, Law and Family: Family Law in Transition in the United States and Western Europe* (New York: North Holland Publishing Company).

Goffman, E. (1961) *Asylums: Essays on the Social Situation of Mental Patients and Other Inmates* (New York: Doubleday).

Goldenberg, H. (1973) *Contemporary Clinical Psychology* (Monterey: Brooks/Cole).

Goldstein, J., et al. (1973) *Beyond the Best Interests of the Child* (New York: Free Press).

Gough, I. (1979) *The Political Economy of the Welfare State* (London: Macmillan).

Graham, H. (1984) *Women, Health and the Family* (Brighton: Wheatsheaf).

Graham-Hall, J. (1968) *Report of the Committee on Statutory Maintenance Limits* (London: HMSO).

Green D., et al. (1987) 'Community Attitudes to Mental Health in New Zealand Twenty Years On', *Social Science and Medicine*, 24, pp. 417–22.

Griffiths, R. (1988) *Community Care: Agenda for Action. A Report to the Secretary of State for Social Services* (London: HMSO).

Habermas, J. (1976) *Legitimation Crisis* (London: Heinemann).

Habermas, J. (1977) 'Law as Medium and Law as Institution', in G. Teubner (ed.), *Dilemmas of Law in the Welfare State* (Berlin: de Gruyter).

Hamilton, W. (1973) 'The Multi-Area Primary School', *Quest*, 12, pp. 25–9.

Handler, J. (1973) *The Coercive Social Worker: British Lessons for American Social Services* (Chicago: Rand McNally).

Haralambos, M. (1985) *Sociology: Themes and Perspectives* (Slough: University Tutorial Press).

Hardill, I. and A. Green (1990) *An Examination of Women Returners in Newcastle* (Newcastle upon Tyne: The University).

Hargreaves, A. (1982) 'Resistance and Relative Autonomy Theories: Problems of Distortion and Incoherence in Recent Marxist Analysis of Education', *British Journal of Sociology of Education*, 3, pp. 107–26.

Hargreaves, D. (1980) 'The Occupational Culture of Teachers', in P. Woods (ed.), *Teacher Strategies* (London: Croom Helm).

Harris, C. (1983) *The Family and Industrial Society* (London: Allen and Unwin).

Harrison, M. (1989) 'Child Support Scheme Stage Two', *Family Matters*, 25, p. 38.

Haskey, J. (1989) 'Cohabitation in Great Britain: Characteristics and Estimated Numbers of Cohabiting Parents', *Population Trends*, 58.

Hatton, E. (1985a) 'Team Teaching in Open-Plan Classrooms: Innovation or Regression?', *School Organisation*, 5, pp. 203–9.

Hatton, E. (1985b) 'Team Teaching and Teacher Orientation to Work: Implications for the Pre-Service and In-Service Preparation of Teachers', *Journal of Education for Teaching*, 11.

Hatton, E. (1985c) 'Equality, Class and Power: a Case Study', *British Journal of Sociology of Education*, 6, pp. 255–72.

Heginbotham, C. (1988) 'Shelter from the Storm', *Health Service Journal*, 98, pp. 644–55.

Higgins, J. (1980) 'Social Control Theories of Social Policy', *Journal of Social Policy*, 9, pp. 1–23.

Hiroshima Prefectural Office (1976) *Genbaku Sanjunen* (Hiroshima: Prefectural Office).

Hiroshima-Nagasaki Testimony Association (1976) *Hiroshima-Nagasaki Sanjunen no Shogen* (Tokyo: Miraisha).

Hochschild, A. (1990) *The Second Shift: Working Parents and the Revolution at Home* (London: Piatkus).

Holman, R. (1980) *Inequality in Child Love* (London: Child Poverty Action Group).

Holmwood, J. and A. Stewart (1983) 'The Roles of Contradiction in Modern Theories of Stratification ', *Sociology*, (May).

Horvath, P. (1986) *Career Counselling for Non-College Bound High School Seniors In Japan* (Washington DC: OERI).

Housing Corporation of New Zealand (1989) *Manakau Housing Corporation, Re-*

search Strategy Unit. Psychiatric Disability and Housing Need in South Auckland (Wellington: Housing Corporation of New Zealand).

Ignatieff, M. (1978) *A Just Measure of Pain* (New York: Columbia Press).

Ignatieff, M. (1983) 'State, Civil Society and Total Institutions', in S. Cohen and A. Scull (eds), *Social Control and the State* (Oxford: Basil Blackwell).

Illich, I. (1973) *Deschooling Society* (Harmondsworth: Penguin).

Institute of Personnel Management (1990) *Work and the Family: Carer-Friendly Employment Practices* (London: IPM).

Iwadare, H. (1982) *Kakuheiki Haizetsu no Uneri* (Tokyo: Rengo Shuppan).

Jackson, B. (1984) *Fatherhood* (London: Allen and Unwin).

Jackson, B. and S. Jackson (1981) *Childminder: A Study in Action Research* (Harmondsworth: Penguin).

Jackson, P. (1968) *Life in Classrooms* (New York: Holt, Rinehart and Winston).

Jackson, S. (1987) 'Fathers in Great Britain', in M. Lamb (ed.), *The Father's Role: Cross Cultural Perspectives* (New Jersey: Lawrence Erlbaum).

Jackson, S. (1989) 'The State as Parent: Assessing Outcomes in Child Care', in J. Hudson and B. Galaway (eds), *The State as Parent: International Research Perspectives on Interventions With Young Persons* (Dordrecht: Kluwer).

Janowitz, M. (1976) *Social Control of the Welfare State* (New York: Elsevier).

Johnson, N. (1987) *The Welfare State in Transition* (Brighton: Wheatsheaf).

Johnson, R. (1979) 'Histories of Culture/Theories of Ideology: Notes on an Impasse', in M. Barrett et al. (eds), *Ideology and Cultural Reproduction* (New York: St Martin's Press).

Judicial Statistics (1989) *Annual Report* (London: HMSO).

Kay, A. and C. Legg (1986) *Discharged From the Community: a Review of Housing and Support in London for People Leaving Psychiatric Care* (London: Good Practices in Mental Health).

Kennedy, F. (1990) 'The Good, the Bad and Education', *The Weekend Australian*, 10 November.

King, R. and R. Young (1986) *A Systematic Sociology of Australian Education* (Sydney: Allen and Unwin).

Kingsley, S. (1987) Address to the MIND Annual Conference, Blackpool.

Knapp, P. (1990) 'Curriculum Development Post Carrick/Scott', *Education. Journal of the New South Wales Teachers' Federation*, November.

Kodama, K. (1987) *Genbakukoji-Ruten no Hibi* (Tokyo: Chobunsha).

Kodama, K. (1985) 'A Study of the Hibakusha Peace Movements', in *Soka University Peace Research* (Tokyo: Soka Institute of Peace Studies).

Kodama, K. and V. Vesa (eds) (1990) *Towards a Comparative Analysis of Peace Movements* (Dartmouth: Dartmouth Press).

La Prelle, M., et al. (1976) *Alternative Building Design: a Study of Self-Contained and Open Space Class Area* (Boulder Valley, Colorado: Northern Colarado Education Board of Co-operative Services).

Laing, R. D. (1969) *The Divided Self: an Existential Study in Sanity and Madness* (London: Tavistock).

Lamb, M. (ed.) (1976) *The Role of the Father in Child Development* (New York: Wiley).

Lamontagne, Y. and R. Verreault (1986) 'The Use of Mass Media in Mental Health', *Canadian Journal of Psychiatry*, 31, pp. 617–20.

Laurance, J. (1986) *Birmingham's Mad Samaritans'*, *New Society*, 76, pp. 5–6.

Leder, G. and S. Sampson, (1989), *Educating Girls* (Sydney: Allen and Unwin).

Lehman, S., et al. (1976) 'Responses to Viewing Symptomatic Behaviours and Labelling Prior to Mental Illness', *Journal of Community Psychology*, 4 (1976) pp. 327–34.

Leibrich, J. (1988) *An Outside Chance: Community Care for People Discharged from Psychiatric Hospitals in Britain* (Wellington: Department of Health).

Levine, J. (1980) *Who Will Raise the Children? New Options for Mothers and Fathers* (Philadelphia: Lipincott).

Lewis, C. (1986) *Becoming a Father* (Milton Keynes: Open University).

Lewis, C., E. Newson and J. Newson (1982) 'Father Participation Through Childhood in Relation to Career Aspirations and Delinquency', in N. Beail and J. McGuire (eds), *Fathers – Psychological Perspectives* (London: Junction Books).

Lewis, J. and B. Meredith (1988) *Daughters Who Care* (London: Routledge).

Lewis, R. (1986) 'Undesirable Neighbours', *American Journal of Nursing*, 86, pp. 535–6.

Lifton, R. (1967) *Death in Life – Survivors of Hiroshima* (New York: Random House).

Lindberg, L., et al. (eds) (1975) *Stress and Contradiction in Modern Capitalism* (Lexington Mass.: Lexington Books).

Link, B. and F. Cullen (1986) 'Contact with the Mentally Ill and Perceptions of How Dangerous They Are', *Journal of Health and Social Behaviour*, 27, pp. 289–302.

Local Housing Statistics in England and Wales 39 (1990) (London: HMSO, April).

Lockwood, D. (1958) *The Blackcoated Worker* (London: Allen and Unwin).

Lortie, D. (1975) *Schoolteacher* (Chicago: University of Chicago Press).

Lukes, S. (1974) *Power: a Radical View* (London: Macmillan).

McCrae, S. (1986) *Cross-Class Families: a Study of Wives' Occupational Superiority* (Oxford: Clarendon Press).

McDonald, J. and Z. Spindler (1988) 'Benefit Induced Sole Parenthood in Australia, 1973–1985', *Australian Economic Papers* (June) pp. 1–19.

McGregor, O., et al. (1970) *Separated Spouses: a Study of the Matrimonial Jurisdiction of Magistrates' Courts* (London: Gerald Duckworth).

McGuire, J. (1982) 'Gender Specific Differences in Early Childhood – the Impact of the Father', in N. Beail and J. McGuire (eds), *Fathers – Psychological Perspectives* (London: Junction Books).

McRobbie, A. (1990) *Feminism and Youth Culture* (Methuen).

Mann, M. (ed.) (1983) *The Macmillan Student Encyclopedia of Sociology* (London: Macmillan).

Mao Tse-Tung (1958) *On Contradiction* (Pekin: Foreign Language Press).

Marram, G., et al. (1972) *The Impact of Teaming and the Visibility of Teaching on the Professionalism of Elementary School Teachers* (Stanford, California: Centre for Research and Development in Teaching).

Martin, J. (1984) *Hospitals in Trouble* (Oxford: Basil Blackwell).

Martin, J. and C. Roberts (1984) *Women and Employment: a Lifetime Perspective* (London: HMSO).

Mason Report (1988) *Report of the Committee of Inquiry Into Procedures Used in Certain Psychiatric Hospitals in Relation to Admission, Discharge and Release on Leave of Certain Classes of Patients* (Wellington: Department of Health).

Matas, M., et al. (1985) 'Mental Illness and the Media: an Assessment of Attitudes and Communication', *Canadian Journal of Psychiatry*, 30, pp. 12–17.

Matas, M., et al. (1986) 'Mental Illness and the Media: Content Analysis of Press Coverage of Mental Health Topics', *Canadian Journal of Psychiatry*, 31, pp. 431–3.

Mattinson, J. (1988) *Work, Love and Marriage: the Impact of Unemployment* (London: Duckworth).

Mayall, B. and P. Petrie (1983) *Childminding and Day Nurseries: What Kind of Care?* (London: Heinemann).

Melhuish, E. and P. Moss (1990) *Day Care for Young Children: International Perspectives* (London: Routledge).

Mental Health Foundation (1986) *Deinstitutionalization: Volume 2 of the Future of the Mental Health Services in New Zealand* (Auckland: Mental Health Foundation).

Mental Health Foundation (1988) *Community Health Services in New Zealand and the Role of the Voluntary Sector* (Auckland: Mental Health Foundation).

Merton, R. (1968) *Social Theory and Social Structure* (New York: Free Press).

Meyer, J. (1983) 'Notes Towards a Working Definition of Social Control', in S. Cohen and A. Scull (eds), *Social Control and the State* (New York: St Martin's Press).

Millar, J. (1987) 'Lone Mothers', in C. Glendinning and J. Millar (eds), *Women and Poverty in Britain* (Brighton: Wheatsheaf).

Millar, J. (1989) *Poverty and the Lone-parent Family: the Challenge of Social Policy* (Aldershot: Gower).

Ministry of Education, Japan (1988) *Statistical Abstract of Education, Science and Culture* (Tokyo: Ministry of Education, Science and Culture).

Ministry of Public Welfare, Japan (1987) *Report of the 1985 Survey of the Survivors of Hiroshima and Nagasaki* (Tokyo: Ministry of Public Welfare).

Mishra, R. (1977) *Society and Social Policy: Theories and Practice of Welfare* (London: Macmillan).

Mitchell, J. (1971) *Women's Estate* (Harmondsworth: Penguin).

Morgan, D. (1975) *Social Theory and the Family* (London: Routledge and Kegan Paul).

Morris, L. (1990) *The Workings of the Household: a US-UK Comparision* (Cambridge, Polity Press).

Morton, J. (1990) 'The Development of Event Memory', *Psychologist*, 3, pp. 3–10.

Murchie, E. (1984) *Rapuora: Health and Maori Women/Na te Wahine Maori Toko Ite Ora* (Wellington: The Maori Women's Welfare League).

Murgatroyd, L. (1985) 'The Production of People and Domestic Labour Revisited', in P. Close and R. Collins (eds), *Family and Economy in Modern Society* (London: Macmillan).

Musgrave, P. (1987) *Socialising Contexts* (Sydney: Allen and Unwin).

National Audit Office (1990) *Department of Social Security: Support for Lone Parent Families* (London: HMSO).

National Consumer Council (1987) *Care in the Community* (London: National Consumer Council).

National Economic Development Office (1989), *Defusing the Demographic Timebomb* (London: NEDO).

National Federation of Housing Associations (1987) *Housing, the Foundation of Community Care* (London: NFHA).

National Health Statistics Centre (1986) *Mental Health Data 1986* (Wellington: NHSC).

National Mental Health Consortium (1989) *Report of* (Wellington: Department of Health and Department of Social Welfare).

Neales, S. (1990a) 'Great Strides in Eighties, but Injustices Still Remain', *Financial Review*, 19 December.

Neales, S. (1990b) 'Schools Planning to Nip Stereotyping in the Bud', *Financial Review*, 23 January.

Neate, E. (1983) 'Teacher Autonomy and Team Teaching in Open-Plan Classrooms: Unmasking Hidden Aspects of Pedagogy', unpublished honours thesis (Brisbane: University of Queensland).

New C., and M. David (1985) *For the Children's Sake* (Harmondsworth: Penguin).

New Earnings Survey (1986) (London: HMSO, April).

New Zealand Board of Health's Maori Health Advisory Committee (1988) *Standing Committee on Maori Health: Submission to the Minister of Health* (Wellington: New Zealand Board of Health).

New Zealand Planning Council (1987) *Care and Control: the Role of Institutions in New Zealand* (Wellington: New Zealand Planning Council).

Newson, J. and E. Newson (1963) *Infant Care in an Urban Community* (London: Allen and Unwin).

Newson, J. and E. Newson (1968) *Four Years Old in an Urban Community* (London: Allen and Unwin).

Newson, J. and E. Newson (1976) *Seven Years Old in an Urban Community* (London: Allen and Unwin).

Nichols, M. (1990) 'I Owe it to My Students to Strike', *The Telegraph* (NSW, Australia), May.

Nunnally, J. (1961) *Popular Conceptions of Mental Health: Their Development and Change* (New York: Holt, Reinhart and Winston).

Ochiltree, G., (1990) 'The Place of Children in Society', *Family Matters. Journal of the Australian Institute of Family Studies*. April.

O'Connor, J. (1973) *The Fiscal Crisis of the Welfare State* (New York: St. Martin's Press).

Offe, C. (1982) 'Some Contradictions of the Welfare State', *Critical Social Policy*, 2.

Offe, C. (1984) *Contradictions of the Welfare State* (London: Hutchinson).

Office of Health Economics (1989) *Mental Health in the 1990s: From Custody to Care?* (London: Office of Health Economics).

Office of Population Censuses and Surveys (1989) *OPCS Monitor* SS 89/1 (London: Governmental Statistical Service).

——— (1990a) *Birth Statistics 1988* (London: HMSO).

——— (1990b) *Population Trends* 60 (London: HMSO).

——— (1990c) *Population Trends* 61 (London: HMSO).

——— (1990d) *Population Trends* 62 (London: HMSO).

O'Hagan, M. (1989) *The Consumer Perspective* (Wellington: Department of Health).

Okin, R., J. Dolnick and D. Pearsall (1983) 'Patients' Perspectives on Community Alternatives to Hospitalization: a Follow-up Study', *American Journal of Psychiatry*, 140, pp. 1460–4.

Open University (1988) *Social Problems and Social Welfare* (Milton Keynes: Open University).

OECD (1989) 'OECD in Figures: Statistics on the Member Countries'. *Supplement to the OECD Observer*, 158.

OECD (1985) *Social Expenditure 1960–1990: Problems of Growth and Control* (Paris: OECD).

Osborn, A., et al., (1984) *The Social Life of Britain's Five Year Olds* (London: Routledge and Kegan Paul).

Packman, J. (1986) *Who Needs Care? Social Work Decisions About Children* (Oxford: Basil Blackwell).

Palmer, J. and I. Sawhill (eds) (1984) *The Reagan Record* (Cambridge, Mass.: Balinger).

Parker, Z. (1986) 'The Chronically Mentally Ill. Will the Community Accept Them?', *Hygiene, V*, pp. 13–17.

Parkin, F. (1972) *Class Inequality and Political Order* (St Albans: Paladin).

Parsons, T. and R. Bales (1955) *Family, Socialization and Interaction Process* (New York: Free Press).

Parton, N. (1985) *The Politics of Child Abuse* (London: Macmillan).

Patmore, C. (1987) 'Strategies to Counter Poverty', in C. Patmore (ed.), *Living After Mental Illness – Innovations in Services* (London: Croom Helm).

Petrie, S. (1984) 'Delinquency in the School', unpublished Ph.D. thesis (Brisbane: University of Queensland, 1984).

Piachaud, D. (1987) 'The Growth of Poverty' in A. Walker and C. Walker (eds), *The Growing Divide: a Social Audit 1979–1987* (London: Child Poverty Action Group).

Piven, F. and R. Cloward (1972) *Regulating the Poor: the Functions of Public Welfare* (London: Tavistock).

Promare, E. and G. de Boer (1988) *Hauora: Maori Standards of Health* (Wellington: Department of Health).

Poole, M. (1986) 'Choices and Constraints: the Education of Girls', in N. Grieve and A. Burns (eds), *Australian Women: New Feminist Perspectives* (Melbourne: Oxford University Press).

Popenoe, D. (1988) *Disturbing the Nest: Family Change and Decline in Modern Societies* (New York: Aldine de Gruyter).

Poster, M. (1975) *Critical Theory of the Family* (London: Pluto).

Potaka-Dewes, E. (1986) *Maori Illness and Healing* (Auckland: Legal Research Foundation).

Pugh, G. and E. De'Ath (1984) *The Needs of Parents* (London: Macmillan).

Qvortrup, J. (1985) 'Placing Children in the Division of Labour', in P. Close and R. Collins (eds), *Family and Economy in Modern Society* (London: Macmillan).

Qvortrup, J. (1990) *Childhood as a Social Phenomenon. An Introduction to a Series of National Reports* (Vienna: European Centre).

Rabkin, J. (1979) 'Criminal Behaviour of Discharged Mental Patients: a Critical Appraisal of the Research', *Psychological Bulletin*, 86, pp. 1–27.

Rabkin, J., et al. (1984) 'What the Neighbours Think: Community Attitudes Toward Local Psychiatric Facilities', *Community Health Journal*, 21, pp. 304–12.

Rabkin, J. (1972) 'Opinions About Mental Illness: a Review of the Literature', *Psychological Bulletin* 77, pp. 153–71.

Ramazanoglu, C. (1989) *Feminism and the Contradictions of Oppression* (London: Routledge and Kegan Paul).

Rapoport, J. (1977) *Community Psychology: Values, Research and Action* (New York: Holt, Rinehart and Winston).

Rapoport, R. and R. Rapoport (1976) *Dual Career Families Reassessed* (New York: Harper and Row).

Regional Trends 23 (1988) (London: HMSO).

Renshaw, J. and M. Knapp (1987) *Mental Health Care: Costing the Alternatives* (Canterbury: University of Kent).

Reubens, B. (1977) *Bridges to Work: International Comparisons of Transition Services* (New Jersey: Allanheld, Osmun and Company).

Richter, M. (1978) 'Open Spaces Can Open Minds', *Teacher*, (April) pp. 29–30.

Rock, P. (1983) 'Social Control', in M. Mann (ed.) *The Macmillan Student Encyclopedia of Sociology* (London: Macmillan).

Rodger, J. (1988) 'Social Work as Social Control Re-Examined: Beyond the Dispersal of Discipline Thesis', *Sociology* 22, pp. 563–81.

Rohlen, T. (1983) *Japan's High Schools* (Berkeley: University of California Press).

Roper Report (1987) *Report of the Ministerial Committee of Inquiry Into Violence* (Wellington: Government Print).

Runciman, W. (1969) *Relative Deprivation and Social Justice* (Harmondsworth: Penguin).

Russell, G. (1987) 'Fatherhood in Australia', in M. Lamb (ed.), *The Father's Role – Cross-Cultural Perspectives* (New Jersey: Lawrence Erlbaum).

Rutter, M., et al. (1979) *Fifteen Thousand Hours: Secondary Schools and their Effects on Children* (Shepton Mallet: Open Books).

Saha, L. and J. Keeves (eds) (1990) *Schooling and Society in Australia* (Canberra: Australian National University Press).

Sang, B. and J. O'Brien (1984) *Advocacy: the United Kingdom and American Experiences* (London: Kings Fund Centre).

Saunders, P. (1990) 'To Market, to Market . . . ', *Social Policy Research Centre Newsletter* (Sydney) December.

Saville-Smith, K. (1987) 'Women and the State', in S. Cox (ed.), *Public and Private Worlds* (Wellington: Allen and Unwin).

Sayers, J. (1986) *Sexual Contradictions* (London: Routledge and Kegan Paul).

Sayers, J. (1990) *Mothering Psychoanalysis* (London: Hamish Hamilton).

Scott, J. (1982) *The Upper Classes* (London: Macmillan).

Scott, J. (1986) *Capitalist Property and Financial Power* (Brighton: Wheatsheaf).

Seagal, S. (1978) 'Attitudes Towards the Mentally Ill: a Review', *Social Work*, 23, pp. 211–17.

Select Committee on Social Services (1985) *Second Report: Community Care With Special Reference to the Adult Mentally Ill and Mentally Handicapped People* (London: HMSO).

Sellick, K. and J. Goodyear (1985) 'Community Attitudes Towards Mental Illness: the Influence of Contact and Demographic Variables', *Australian and New Zealand Journal of Psychiatry*, 19, pp. 293–8.

Shaplin, J. (1964) 'Descriptions and Definitions of Team Teaching', in J. Shaplin and H. Olds (eds), *Team Teaching* (New York: Harper and Row).

Shaplin, J. and Olds, H. (eds) (1964) *Team Teaching* (New York: Harper and Row).

Sharp, S. (1976) *Just Like a Girl* (London: Pelican).

Shaver, S. (1988) 'Class and Gender in Australian Income Security', *Australian and New Zealand Journal of Sociology*, 24, pp. 377–97.

Sheerin, I. and R. Gale (1985) 'Quality of Community Care for the Long-Term Mentally Disabled', *Community Mental Health in New Zealand*, 1, pp. 2–14.

Sherman, S., et al. (1984) 'Community Acceptance of the Mentally Ill in Foster Family Care', *Health and Social Work*, 9, pp. 188–99.

Shorter, E. (1977) *The Making of the Modern Family* (London: Fontana).

Showstack Sasson, A. (ed.) (1987a) *Women and the State* (London: Hutchinson).

Showstack Sasson, A. (1987b) 'Women's New Social Roles: Contradictions of the Welfare State', in A. Showstack Sassoon (ed.), *Women and the State* (London: Hutchinson).

Simms, M. and C. Smith (1982) 'Young Fathers: Attitudes to Marriage and Family Life', in L. McKee and M. O'Brien (eds), *The Father Figure* (London: Tavistock).

Simms, M. and C. Smith (1986) *Teenage Mothers and Their Partners* (London: HMSO).

Simpson, P. (1990) 'So You Want to form a School Council?', *Education. Journal of the New South Wales Teachers' Federation*, December.

Smart, C. (1984a) 'Marriage, Divorce and Women's Economic Dependency: a Discussion of the Politics of Private Maintenance', in M. Freeman (ed.), *State, Law and the Family* (London: Tavistock).

—— (1984b) *The Ties that Bind* (London: Routledge and Kegan Paul).

—— (1987) 'Securing the Family? Rhetoric and Policy in the Field of Social Security', in M. Loney et al. (eds), *The State Of the Market: Politics and Welfare in Contemporary Britain* (London: Sage).

Snider, G. (1989) 'The Maintenance Process', *Family Matters*, 24, pp. 32–3.

Social Trends 20 (1990) (London: HMSO).

Sommer, R. and H. Osmond (1961) 'Symptoms of Institutional Care', *Social Problems*, 8, pp. 254–63.

Spender, D. and E. Sarah (1980) *Learning to Lose* (London: The Women's Press).

Spicker, P. (1988) *Principles of Welfare* (London: Routledge and Kegan Paul).

Stanworth, M. (1983) *Gender and Schooling: a Study of Sexual Divisions in the Classroom* (London: Hutchinson, 3rd edn).

Steadman Jones, G. (1983) 'Class Expression Versus Social Control', in S. Cohen and A. Scull (eds), *Social Control and the State* (New York: St. Martin's Press).

Steinmetz, S. (1988) *Duty Bound: Elder Abuse and Family Care* (New York: Sage).

Sunday Telegraph (1990) (NSW, Australia), 21 October.

Swann, P. and M. Bernstam (1987) 'Brides of the State', *Institute of Public Affairs Review*, 41, pp. 22–5.

Taira, K. and S. Levine (1986) *Education for Labour Force Skills in Postwar Japan: Final Report* (Washington DC: OERI).

Taylor, S. (1984) 'Reproduction and Contradictions in Schooling: the Case of Commercial Studies', *British Journal of Sociology of Education*, 5, pp. 3–18.

Taylor-Gooby, P. (1985) *Public Opinion, Ideology and State Welfare* (London: Routledge and Kegan Paul).

Te Ara Hou (1989) *Prison Review: te Ara Hou/the New Way* (Wellington: Government Print).

Thomas, C. (1980) 'Girls and Counter-School Culture', in D. McCullum and U. Ozolins (eds), *Melbourne Working Papers 1980* (Parkville: University of Melbourne).

Thompson, E. P. (1978) *The Poverty of Theory* (London: Merlin Press).

Thorogood, N. (1987) 'Race, Class and Gender: the Politics of Housework', in J. Brannen and G. Wilson (eds), *Give and Take in Families* (London: Allen and Unwin).

Totaro, P. (1990) 'Teachers to Act Over Playground Violence', *Sydney Morning Herald*, 4 August.

Towell, D. and Kingsley, S. (1986) *Developing Psychiatric Services in the Welfare State* (London: Kings Fund College).

Townsend, P. (1979) *Poverty in the United Kingdom* (Harmondsworth: Penguin).

Townsend, P. (1987) 'Deprivation', *Journal of Social Policy* (April).

Umetani, S. (1985) *Occupational Information, Placement and Choices for Japanese Youths* (Washington DC: OERI).

Ungerson, C. (1985) 'Paid Work and Unpaid Caring: a Problem for Women or the State?', in P. Close and R. Collins (eds), *Family and Economy in Modern Society* (London: Macmillan).

Ungerson, C. (1989) *Policy is Personal: Sex, Gender and Informal Care* (London: Tavistock).

Upton, S. (1988) 'The Caring Society in Ruins', *The Dominion* (Wellington, New Zealand), March.

US Bureau of the Census (1989) *Statistical Abstract of the United States 1989* (Washington DC: US Department of Commerce).

Walker A. and C. Walker (1987) *The Growing Divide: a Social Audit 1979–1987* (London: Child Poverty Action Group).

Walker, J. (1988) *Louts and Legends* (Sydney: Allen and Unwin).

Walsh, K-A (1990) 'Compo Plans for Housework' *The Telegraph* (NSW, Australia), 7 October.

Waters, M. and R. Crook (1990) *Sociology One: Principles of Sociological Analysis for Australians* (Melbourne: Longman Cheshire).

Weinstein, R. (1979) 'Patient Attitudes Toward Mental Hospitalization: a Review of Quantitative Research', *Journal of Health and Social Behaviour*, 20, pp. 237–58.

Weitzman, L. (1985) *The Divorce Revolution: the Unexpected Social and Economic Consequences of Divorce for Women and Children in America* (New York: Free Press).

Wellington Community Mental Health Services Group (1986) *Mental Health Care in the Community* (Wellington: Inner City Ministry).

Wicks, M. (1987) 'Family Policy: Rights and Responsibilities', *Family Policy Bulletin*, 3.

Wicks, M. (1990) 'Child Maintenance – Lone Parent Lessons from Australia', *Family Policy Bulletin*, 8, p. 6.

Willis, P. (1977) *Learning to Labour: How Working Class Kids Get Working Class Jobs* (Farnborough: Saxon House).

Wolcott, I. and H. Glezer (1990) *Marriage Counselling in Australia: an Evaluation* (Melbourne: Australian Institute of Family Studies).

Wolfe, A. (1977) *The Limits of Legitimacy* (New York: Free Press).

Wolfe, A. (1989) *Whose Keeper?: Social Science and Moral Obligation* (Berkeley, California: University of California Press).

Woods, P. (1983) *Sociology and the School: an Interactionist Perspective* (London: Routledge and Kegan Paul).

Woolett, A., et al. (1982) 'Observations of Fathers at Birth', in N. Beail and J. McGuire (eds), *Fathers – Psychological Perspectives* (London: Junction Books).

Zagami, U. (1971) 'Multi-Area Teaching Spaces Come to Queensland', *Queensland Teachers' Journal*, 76, pp. 54–5.

Index